The State, the Law, and the Family

The State, the Law, and the Family
Critical Perspectives

Edited by Michael D. A. Freeman

Tavistock Publications
Sweet and Maxwell

London and New York

First published in 1984 by
Tavistock Publications Ltd
in association with Sweet and Maxwell Ltd
11 New Fetter Lane, London EC4P 4EE

Published in the USA by
Tavistock Publications
in association with Methuen, Inc.
733 Third Avenue, New York, NY 10017

Printed in Great Britain at the University Press,
Cambridge

British Library Cataloguing in Publication Data
The State, the law and the family.——(Social
  science paperbacks)
  1. Domestic relations
I. Freeman, M.D.A. II. Series
342.61'5   K670

  ISBN 0-422-79080-X

Library of Congress Cataloging in Publication Data
Main entry under title:

The State, the law, and the family.

  Bibliography: p.
  Includes index.
  1. Domestic relations—Great Britain—Addresses,
essays, lectures. 2. Family policy—Great Britain—
Addresses, essays, lectures. I. Freeman, Michael D. A.
KD750.A75S73 1984   364.4101'5   84-16183
ISBN 0-422-79080-X (pbk.)   344.10615

Contents

Notes on contributors

ANNE BOTTOMLEY is a senior lecturer at the North East London Polytechnic. She lectures on family law, property, and the English legal system. Her research interests are in the history of family law, cohabitation, and the development of informal mechanisms of dispute resolution. She is a feminist and is a member of Rights of Women, a feminist legal collective. A co-author of *The Cohabitation Handbook* (new edition in 1984) she has worked with the ROW Family Law Group in organizing conferences on current legal issues and in submitting evidence to government bodies.

ERIC CLIVE was Professor of Scots Law at Edinburgh University until 1981. Since then he has been a full-time member of the Scottish Law Commission. He has a special interest in family law and is the author of *The Law of Husband and Wife in Scotland* (2nd edn, 1982).

MADELEINE COLVIN was admitted to the Bar in 1970. She practised for ten years specializing in family and children's law. In 1980 she joined the newly established Children's Legal Centre.

RUTH DEECH is a Fellow and Tutor in Law at St Anne's College and CUF Lecturer in Law at Oxford University, and barrister-at-law of the Inner Temple. A former member of the family law team of the Law Commission, she is presently working on reviews of current developments and policies in English divorce law and maintenance laws.

ROBERT DINGWALL is a Senior Research Officer at the ESRC Centre for Socio-Legal Studies, Wolfson College, Oxford. He has worked on decision-making in child abuse and neglect and is now studying conciliation in divorce.

The State, the Law, and the Family

JOHN EEKELAAR is a Fellow of Pembroke College, Oxford, Lecturer in Jurisprudence and a part-time Research Fellow at the ESRC Centre for Socio-Legal Studies. He has written extensively on topics in family law and is the author of *Family Law and Social Policy* (2nd edn, 1984). His current work relates to the financial consequences of divorce.

MICHAEL FREEMAN is Professor of English Law at University College London and the author of a number of books including *Violence in the Home – a Socio-Legal Study* (Saxon House, 1979), *The Rights and Wrongs of Children* (Frances Pinter, 1983) and co-author (with Tina Lym) of *Cohabitation Without Marriage – an Essay in Law and Social Policy* (Gower, 1983).

ANTONIA GERARD specialized in family law as a practitioner (at the Bar), as an academic (as Senior Lecturer, later Visiting Fellow, in the University of Southampton) and as a judge (Assistant Recorder). Since 1982 she has been a conciliator attached to the Family Conciliation Bureau in Bromley, Kent. She continues her regular sessions there. Her law teaching included comparative law, while conflict of laws has always been of special interest to her. In November 1983 she was appointed full-time Legal Officer to the Foreign Compensation Commission.

MICHAEL KING lectures at the Law School, Warwick University. He also practises as a solicitor. He has written extensively on the administration of justice and is the author of *The Framework of Criminal Justice* and editor of *Childhood, Welfare and Justice*. His current work includes research into the role of the *juge des enfants* in France and into the selection and appointment of black magistrates in England and Wales.

HILARY LAND is a Reader in Social Administration at the University of Bristol. One of her main interests is the impact of state social policies on the family and her publications include *Large Families in London* (Bell, 1969), *Change, Choice and Conflict in Social Policy* (with P. Hall, R. Parker, and A. Webb) (Heinemann, 1975), 'Who Cares for the Family?', *Journal of Social Policy* (1978), and 'The Family Wage', Eleanor Rathbone Memorial Lecture 1979.

JENNIFER LEVIN (Solicitor) was previously Senior Lecturer in

Law at Queen Mary College, University of London and co-director of the Legal Action Group. At present she is Head of Law and Government at the Polytechnic of the South Bank, London and Vice Chair of the National Council for One Parent Families.

MAVIS MACLEAN is a Senior Research Officer at the SSRC Centre for Socio-Legal Studies. Her research interests centre around the social and economic consequences of major life events. These have included accidents and illness and she is now studying family breakdown and reconstitution.

SUSAN MAIDMENT has been a Senior Lecturer in Law at the University of Keele since 1976. She has written extensively in the field of family law with a special interest in children. She conducted the first empirical study into custody decisions, and is the author of a new book, *Child Custody and Divorce: The Law in Social Context* (Croom Helm, 1984). She has been the General Secretary of the International Society on Family Law since 1979.

JUDITH MASSON is a Lecturer in Law at Leicester University, specializing in family and child welfare law. Between 1978 and 1981 she undertook research on the Children Act 1975 for DHSS with Daphne Norbury from British Agencies for Adoption and Fostering. In 1981 she was awarded a Harkness Fellowship to study making decisions about children at the National Institute of Child Welfare, Ann Arbor, Michigan. She is currently working on a study of provision for dependants in pension schemes.

KATHERINE O'DONOVAN teaches family law at the University of Kent. Born in Dublin, she has also taught at universities in Belfast, Addis Ababa, and Kuala Lumpur. At present she is completing a book on sexual divisions in law.

JAN PAHL is a Research Fellow at the University of Kent at Canterbury. She is attached to the Health Services Research Unit and teaches for the Board of Studies in Social Policy and Administration. Her publications include *Managers and Their Wives* (1971) and *Private Violence and Public Policy* (1984). Currently she is writing up her research on the control and allocation of money within the family and is working on an evaluative study of community services for mentally handicapped children.

MADZY ROOD-DE BOER is Professor at the Catholic University of Tilburg and the State University of Utrecht. Her chair is in the Law Faculty at both universities. She specializes in family law, youth law, and youth protection law. She is a Vice-President of the International Society in Family Law and has published widely, mainly in the Dutch language.

CAROL SMART is the Director of the National Council for One Parent Families. Until March 1984 she was doing research on social policy and drug addiction at the Institute of Psychiatry, London. She was formerly SSRC Research Fellow in the Centre for Criminological and Socio-Legal Studies at the University of Sheffield and prior to that Lecturer in Sociology at Trent Polytechnic. She is author of *Women, Crime and Criminology* (Routledge and Kegan Paul, 1976), *The Ties that Bind* (Routledge and Kegan Paul, 1984) and several articles on women and law.

ELIZABETH SZWED is the Secretary of Justice for Children and the co-author of *Justice for Children* (1980) and *Providing Civil Justice for Children* (1983). She is a practising barrister.

Foreword

A workshop for law teachers has been held each year at the Institute of Advanced Legal Studies since 1966. The workshop is now supported by the Senate of the University of London under the terms of the W. G. Hart Bequest.

In 1983 Michael Freeman of University College London agreed to act as academic director of a workshop on aspects of family law. Mrs Dawn Oliver, also of UCL, acted as assistant director. The papers in this volume resulted from the workshop.

The contributors cover a wide span of interests and experience – judicial, legal practice, law reform, administration, academic lawyers, and social scientists. In most fields lawyers lose much if their study is confined to the legal, but of no topic is this as true as family law. These papers on *The State, the Law, and the Family: Critical Perspectives* will be invaluable to law teachers, but will also be of interest to all concerned with the law and the family who wish to see the topic from different perspectives.

The Institute of Advanced Legal Studies wishes to acknowledge its indebtedness to all those who contributed to and participated in the W. G. Hart Workshop in July, 1983, and in particular to Michael Freeman as editor of this volume.

Institute of Advanced Legal Studies   AUBREY L. DIAMOND
Charles Clore House   Director
17 Russell Square
London WC1B 5DR

New Year's Day 1984

Introduction: Rethinking family law

Michael D.A. Freeman

The family is rarely out of today's headlines. Variously described as 'anti-social' (Barrett and McIntosh 1982) and 'subversive' (Mount 1982), said to be 'in the firing line' (Coussins and Coote 1981) and 'here to stay' (Bane 1976), fought over by each political party at each successive general election, the family has figured in some of today's most bitter controversies. The family was once described as a 'haven in a heartless world' (Lasch 1977). For too many the reality is that the family is a site of oppression and inequality.

Much of today's debate focuses on the limits of state intervention into the family (Dingwall, Eekelaar, and Murray 1983; Freeman 1983; Goldstein, Freud, and Solnit 1979). To what extent is domestic violence or cohabitation a private matter? How much autonomy in child rearing practices should parents be accorded? Is the relationship of a divorcing couple any business of the state? What support duties should the state impose on ex-spouses? Is the welfare state replacing the state (Bane 1983)? These questions are controversial and are likely to remain so for the foreseeable future.

The debate is often conceptualized in terms of a public/private paradigm (Elshtain 1981). It is, however, by no means clear that the dichotomy stands up to rigorous examination.[1] The 'private' does not exist outside the 'state', since each contains the other at the level of social practices and power strategies. 'The private' denotes a constructed space. To say that a domain is private is not to argue that it is thereby free. The current controversies about the respective realms of public and private and about the limits of state intervention into the family thus distort and perpetuate a mystifying discourse which sees 'the family' as separate from and in opposition to the state. The relation of the public to the private is itself a political issue (Gamarnikow *et al.* 1983; Jaggar 1983; Siltanen and Stanworth 1984). This issue is usually raised in the context of contemporary debates about the

1

participation of women in the economy and in the political arena. But the issues are more pervasive than this, as this volume illustrates.

The essays collected here do a number of other things as well. They remind us of the need for theory in family law. For too long policies and concepts have been taken for granted. Much that is problematic has not been recognized as such. Family law studies have matured considerably in the last twenty years. They have become contextual (Eekelaar 1971, 1978, 1984; Hoggett and Pearl 1983): now they need also to become critical in orientation. The essays in this collection demonstrate how concepts like protection, welfare, and rights must be critically re-examined; how techniques, practices, and institutions (conciliation and the family court ideal, two current sacred cows, are but examples) must be seriously questioned; how conventional wisdoms, official versions of the truth, for example that there are a large number of 'alimony drones', undeserving women milking ex-husbands, need to be scrutinized to demonstrate not only that they are myths but what the function of such mystification is. Further, the inclusion of some comparative material enables the reader to see that other jurisdictions come to different conclusions when tackling similar problems. The examples drawn from Scotland, The Netherlands, and France are intended to be just that, but each does throw interesting light upon current English debate and may help us to question our approach.

It is difficult to resist returning to the aspect of myth in family law. It emerges strongly from many of the papers in this collection just how entrenched myths are in the law and politics of the family. It is not new for debates about the family to be governed by myth. Thus, Beveridge ignored the evidence and concentrated instead in his report on what he thought the family *ought* to be doing. Or, to take a second example, consider the extent to which family policy (the existence of which is questionable but which I assume for present purposes exists) has been predicated on the basis of a husband wage-earner, a wife homemaker and a little over two children in each household unit: the concept of the 'family wage' for example (Land 1980). The current debate about the financial support of ex-wives, now crystallized in legislation engineered by a middle-class lobby and brusquely piloted by a 'stand-no-nonsense' Lord Chancellor, who was also instrumental in cutting back on the protection that women can expect from ouster injunctions (see *Richards* v. *Richards* [1984]), has largely ignored the available empirical evidence. This evidence shows that it is ex-wives and the children who usually remain with their mothers who suffer the greater economic hardships on divorce, and not ex-husbands and their second wives or cohabitants (see Smart, Chapter 1 and Eekelaar and Maclean, Chapter 13); see also for strikingly similar American evidence Weitzman 1981). Many of these women will have to fall back on social security provision. But, yet again, as Land (Chapter 2) points out, many of the recent changes in welfare state legislation that purport to be, and seem, favourable to women in practice achieve less than most think they do.

I have contrasted myth and social reality. But the dichotomy can be a false one. There may be, for example, areas where doubt exists as to what the 'facts' actually are. Facts depend upon interpretation and interpretation upon values. We have witnessed recently practitioners working within the same psycho-analytical framework examining the same 'facts' and coming to diametrically opposed conclusions (cf. Goldstein, Freud, and Solnit 1973; Wallerstein and Kelly 1980). Within this volume there is a lively confrontation between Dingwall and Eekelaar, on the one hand, and Colvin and King, on the other. The Dingwall and Eekelaar essay (Chapter 6) challenges the new orthodoxy represented in this volume by Colvin and King (Chapters 7 and 9) and elsewhere by the authors of *Justice For Children* (Morris *et al.* 1980) and by organizations like the Family Rights Group. In part what divided the disputants is their analysis of the facts, though there is clearly an ideological chasm as well. The essays raise the question: how best can children be protected and from what and whom do they need protection? The limits of effective state intervention, the difficulties and the dangers of doing so are brought out in each of these contributions. At root the debate is one about children's rights (Freeman 1983), about the ambiguity of this concept and about its links with other equally problematic concepts like justice and welfare (Dingwall, Eekelaar, and Murray 1983; King 1981).

Another theme that emerges from this collection of essays is the recognition that family law is not some 'brooding omnipresence in the sky', not a neutral arbiter, and that it does not have functions outside of itself (Eekelaar 1978, 1984). It is rather a cultural underpinning and in part is constitutive of the social order of which the family is a part. There are biases in the law. O'Donovan (Chapter 5) describes the way in which the law is constructed with adult men in mind and exceptions are grafted on for children, women, and defectives. The law often reflects, Elizabeth Wilson said at the workshop, a biologism. Women are often seen as property and so, of course, are children. The fiscal and social security systems of this country also express a patriarchal bias (Freeman, Chapter 4). How then can the state intervene to 'protect' when part of what victims and potential victims need protection from are rules and practices legitimated by the state itself? The irony of removing children from parents who abuse them to put them in homes that practise an institutional form of abuse known as corporal punishment is too obvious to need spelling out further.

There are biases also in the administration of the law. Welfare rules in practice hit women more than men (Land, Chapter 2). The provision in the Matrimonial Causes Act (s.41) providing minimal surveillance of custody arrangements in uncontested cases operates differentially with lower-class families (Maidment, Chapter 10). Child-protective legislation is class-oriented, as is its management and administration. Many more examples could be given of the ways in which laws contain ideological messages. The resuscitation of the one-third rule in *Wachtel* v. *Wachtel* [1973] on the ground that men need home makers and thus have greater calls on their income. The extension of grounds upon which a local authority may assume parental rights to include three years in care has important messages for parental responsibility. Language itself may be significant, as for example with 'alimony drones'.

It is noticeable and highly significant how in current debates the state often remains invisible, just as social class does. There is a strong case for arguing, however, that the invisible hand may be more lethal than the one that comes out into the open. It is important, many of the contributors to this volume stress, for those who see issues in these ways to recapture the ground, to redefine the issues, and to spell out the implications of particular policies. Even a reformulation of questions, a change of language, may produce more positive responses, as Smart (Chapter 1) notes. She found the attitudes of magistrates changed when the discussion shifted from talking about wives to talking about mothers. Many examples could be given of their need for a re-adjustment of focus and many are in the essays in this volume.

In pursuing the themes of public and private, the state and the family, the essays in this volume are divided into four sections, though there are necessarily overlaps between different sections. The essays in the first part examine from feminist perspectives issues concerning women and the state. The second part focuses on questions relating to children, in particular to issues centred on the protection of children. The third part investigates a number of problems that arise on or after divorce, both those concerned with economic assets (property and support) and those which can be regarded as some of the psychological consequences of marital breakdown. The final section looks at the institutional framework within which the state attempts to resolve family conflicts, in particular at conciliation and the prospects of a family court.

Note
1 I owe this point to Ann Gainsford of the Institute of Criminology, Cambridge and gratefully acknowledge her assistance.

References

Bane, M.J. (1976) *American Families in the Twentieth Century.* New York: Basic Books.
—— (1983) Is the welfare state replacing the family? *The Public Interest* 70: 91–101.
Barrett, M. and McIntosh, M. (1982) *The Anti-Social Family.* London: Verso Books.
Coussins, J. and Coote, A. (1981) *The Family in The Firing Line.* London: NCCL/CPAG.
Dingwall, R., Eekelaar, J., and Murray, T. (1983) *The Protection of Children.* Oxford: Basil Blackwell.
Eekelaar, J. (1971) *Family Security and Family Breakdown.* Harmondsworth: Penguin.
—— (1978) *Family Law and Social Policy.* 1st edn. London: Weidenfeld and Nicolson.
—— (1984) *Family Law and Social Policy.* 2nd edn. London: Weidenfeld and Nicolson.
Elshtain, J. B. (1981) *Public Man, Private Woman.* Princeton, NJ: Princeton University Press.
Freeman, M. D. A. (1983) *The Rights and Wrongs of Children.* London: Frances Pinter.
Gamarnikow, E., Morgan, D., Purvis, J., and Taylorson, D. (1983) *The Public and the Private.* London: Heinemann.
Goldstein, J., Freud, A., and Solnit, A. (1973) *Beyond the Best Interests of the Child.* New York: Free Press.
——(1979) *Before the Best Interests of the Child.* New York: Free Press.
Hoggett, B. and Pearl, D. (1983) *The Family, Law and Society.* London: Butterworths.

Jaggar, A. M. (1983) *Feminist Politics and Human Nature*. Totowa, NJ: Rowman and Allanheld.

King, M. (1981) *Childhood, Welfare and Justice*. London: Batsford.

Land, H. (1980) The Family Wage. *Feminist Review* 6: 55–77.

Lasch, C. (1977) *Haven in a Heartless World*. New York: Basic Books.

Morris, A., Giller, H., Geach, H., and Szwed, E. (1980) *Justice for Children*. London: Macmillan.

Mount, F. (1982) *The Subversive Family*. London: Jonathan Cape.

Siltanen, J. and Stanworth, M. (1984) *Women and the Public Sphere*. London: Hutchinson.

Wallerstein, J. and Kelly, J. B. (1980) *Surviving the Break-up*. New York: Basic Books.

Weitzman, L. (1981) The Economics of Divorce: Social and Economic Consequences of Property, Alimony and Child Support Awards. *UCLA Law Review* 28: 1181.

Cases

Richards v. *Richards* [1984] All ER
Wachtel v. *Wachtel* [1973] Fam 72

PART ONE
WOMEN, THE STATE, AND THE LAW

CHAPTER 1

Marriage, divorce, and women's economic dependency: a discussion of the politics of private maintenance

Carol Smart

Marriage and the family have recently become the focus of much political attention. In 1979 both major political parties were discussing the possibility of creating a Minister for the Family and in the first few months of 1983 the Conservative Government's thoughts on the role of family were revealed. These not only reflected the admiration which that party has for Victorian values, but indicated plans to further reduce the welfare state and to further 'privatize' the family.[1] At the same time there has been a growing concern over the rising divorce rate which is seen as both hugely expensive in terms of the public funds that pay for legal aid costs and enforcement procedures, and generally undesirable in terms of the social costs of breaking up families. Some of these concerns have become specifically linked with a belief that whilst divorce has political, social, and economic consequences, it is essentially a personal hardship for husbands rather than for wives. This belief has been fostered by such groups as Campaign for Justice on Divorce and Families Need Fathers, and has apparently been embraced by the English Law Commission and the Lord Chancellor's Department. It is increasingly argued that the pendulum of law reform has swung too far to the advantage of women and that in ameliorating the wrongs done to wives in the past we have created a system which now wrongs husbands.

This tide of opinion brought forth, in November, 1983, the Matrimonial and Family Proceedings Bill which became law in 1984. This legislation introduces a number of changes to the divorce law, including giving greater priority to children (in theory at least) and giving more emphasis once again to the conduct of the parties during their marriage. However, the most popular, or at least the most widely publicized, aspect of the legislation has been its promise to reduce husbands' financial liabilities towards their ex-wives. The following newspaper headlines are not untypical:

'Clean-break divorce Bill to end "meal ticket"'
(Sunday Telegraph, 30 October, 1983)

'Divorcees "to lose meal ticket"'
(*The Guardian*, 3 November, 1983)

'New Charter for children and husbands'
(*Daily Express*, 21 September, 1983)

The popular support for a change in legislation is based on a view of ex-wives as drones and parasites content to live off their poor, hard-working husbands who are probably struggling to keep a new family whilst paying out large sums to their work-shy former wives. This outrage against such women is further fuelled by the belief that, in these days of supposed sex equality and equal pay, women cannot demand the advantages of liberation and independence without accepting the disadvantages of self-sufficiency. The fact that the overwhelming majority of women have not achieved financial independence or the same level of earnings as men[2] does not seem to detract at all from the force of these arguments. Basically it is popularly felt to be unfair that women should enjoy all the advantages under our modern matrimonial law.

Whilst this interpretation of events has no doubt caught the public imagination and has already produced changes to legislation, it is nonetheless still important to deconstruct the argument that the law has come to favour women. In the first place this is not a new fallacy. Consider, for example, the following statements:

'Even the disabilities, which the wife lies under, are for the most part intended for her protection and benefit. So great a favourite is the female sex of the laws of England.'
(Blackstone's comment on eighteenth-century law, quoted in Blom-Cooper and Drewry 1976: 155)

'The fact that women [have] gained equality with men [has] tremendous potentialities for civilisation, but whether it [is] for

good or bad has yet to be seen . . . [the wife] is now the spoilt darling of the law, and [the husband] the patient pack horse.'
(Lord Denning, *The Times*, 13 May, 1950)

If we bear in mind that in the eighteenth and nineteenth centuries married women had virtually no legal rights at all (Reiss 1934) and that in the 1950s husbands could more or less evict their wives and children at will, could only be made to pay maintenance if they were guilty of a matrimonial fault, and could inflict violence on their wives and children without any real concern over legal redress, it is hard to imagine how wives could have been perceived as favourites and spoilt darlings. These historical statements bore no relationship at all to the material position of women in marriage. But equally, more contemporary statements about how the law favours women in the 1980s ·bear no direct relation to the material position of the majority of married women. Although there have been important legal changes that have improved the status of married women *vis-à-vis* their husbands many of these reforms have benefited women only indirectly, through their role as the carers of children. In other words the law has attempted to improve the lot of children and has done so by extending protection to their primary carers (Brophy and Smart 1981). These legal changes, welcome as they might be, have not touched upon the fundamental structure of marriage and the family which is premised upon women's economic dependency on men. Although the conditions of women's dependency have been ameliorated it remains the case that the law (e.g. social security, taxation, pensions), as well as other social and economic policies (for example, the failure to provide nurseries or equal pay and work opportunities to women), obliges women to look to men for economic security once they are married or have children. Women with children who live without men are amongst the poorest groups in contemporary society and it is extremely difficult, if not impossible, for them to lift themselves out of the poverty trap without the help of an extra income in the household (Finer 1974; Maclean and Eekelaar 1983). Although this economically inferior position occupied by women frequently remains invisible for the duration of a marriage, it becomes immediately visible on marriage breakdown, at which point the poverty of women becomes a public problem. It is this structural economic inequality in marriage the law has failed to address and that has now become popularly reinterpreted as an indication of the parasitical nature of divorced or separated women. It is absolutely essential therefore that the concept of the 'alimony drone' should be recognized as a process of blaming women for their economic inferiority, and not as a new category of women created by an unduly biased family law.

The current backlash against benefits achieved by women in family law is based not solely on a belief that ex-wives are parasitic upon their husbands, but also upon certain misconceptions about how private law actually operates. For example there appears to be a belief that the courts require a second wife to work in order to provide maintenance to a first wife. Although the courts have no powers to do this, it may well be the experience of some second wives that their earnings do indirectly benefit the first family and the resentment felt may be attributed mistakenly to the law. A feeling that the law is unjust may therefore be rooted in experience but is in fact based on a misunderstanding of the law. It is not possible to deconstruct all the myths surrounding contemporary family law here, but I nonetheless wish to concentrate on two basic assumptions that appear to fuel debates in this field. These are that (1) private maintenance is a major source of income to divorced and separated wives, and that there are consequently numerous husbands supporting two families, and (2) the hardship inflicted on husbands by the courts is directly beneficial to separated and divorced wives.

Private maintenance

Unfortunately there is not a great deal of empirical evidence available on the financial consequences of divorce or separation. Marsden's early study (1969) revealed the extent to which working-class women were reliant on national assistance rather than private maintenance, and Graham Hall (1968) also produced figures to show the extensiveness of women's reliance on state benefits. More recently Mavis Maclean (1982, 1983) at Wolfson College and Davis, MacLeod and Murch (1983) at Bristol University have shown that private mainten-ance is not the major source of income for the majority of divorced women. In fact Maclean (1982) argued that there was no evidence of the 'drones' that have become almost a modern folk devil. My own research in Sheffield in the magistrates' domestic courts (Smart 1984) would also support the idea that women do not live on the mainten-ance provided by their ex- or separated husbands. In fact many of their children could not be expected to live on it either.

Just over half (56 per cent) of the children in the Sheffield magistrates' courts sample were awarded under £6.50 per week. This

Table 1   **Maintenance for children, Sheffield Magistrates' Court,
1 October to 31 December, 1980**

amount per week (£s)			no. of children	percentage of children
less than	£1.00		42	13
between	£1.00 and	£2.50	35	11
	£3.00	£4.50	28	9
	£5.00	£6.50	71	23
	£7.00	£8.50	58	18
	£9.00	£10.50	49	16
	£11.00	£12.50	11	3
	£13.00	£14.50	4	1
	£15.00	£16.50	9	3
	£17.00	£18.50	7	2
	£19.00	£20.50	1	1
total			315	100

figure compares with the 1980 DHSS supplementary benefit rates for children between five and ten years which was £6.25 per week. Hardly any children (in fact only 10 per cent) were awarded more than £11 per week. The fact that these amounts coincide roughly with DHSS figures is not surprising as the Sheffield magistrates tended to use the DHSS rates as a guideline. However, unless these amounts should appear adequate to the cost of child rearing, it is instructive to compare with the National Foster Care Association's figures which give the average cost of boarding out a child in 1979/80 as £20 per week. The cost of residential care was put at £132 per week.[3] Although few fathers could afford the latter figures these comparisons show how unrealistically low both the courts and the DHSS set the cost of child care.

If we turn to maintenance for wives, the Sheffield Magistrates' Court's sample lends more support to the growing evidence that private maintenance is a minor source of income to separated and divorced women. Just over one-fifth (21 per cent) of the wives were awarded less than £1 per week and just over half (56 per cent) were awarded less than £5 per week. In 1980 the basic supplementary benefit rate for a single householder was £18.30 per week (this did not include rent). It can be seen therefore that the vast majority of wives in the Sheffield sample were not being awarded an amount of maintenance on which they could be expected to live. Only 12 per

Table 2 **Maintenance for wives, Sheffield Magistrates' Court
1 October to 31 December, 1980**

amount per week (£s)			no. of wives	percentage of wives
less than	£1.00		13	21
between	£1.00 and	£4.50	21	35
	£5.00	£8.50	5	8
	£9.00	£12.50	2	3
	£13.00	£16.50	6	10
	£17.00	£20.50	7	11
	£21.00	£24.50	3	5
	£25.00	£28.50	1	2
	£29.00	£32.50	2	3
	£33.00	£36.00	1	2
total			61	100

cent were awarded amounts of £12 or over, and although this sum is higher than DHSS rates, the fact that they had a court order for these amounts was no guarantee that they received their maintenance regularly and in full.

Hardships to husbands

These figures can give no support to the myth of alimony drones and certainly render the notion that marriage is a 'meal ticket for life' for women quite nonsensical. However, the belief that the law is biased is not derived simply from the actual amounts awarded to women, which are extremely low in real terms, but also from the hardship caused to men who are ordered to pay maintenance. This hardship, which is undoubtedly very real in some cases, is believed to be inflicted on men in *direct* relationship to the degree of indolence enjoyed by the former wife. There is, however, no *direct* relationship between these two states. The courts, especially the magistrates' courts, which deal consistently with the poorest groups in society, can depress a man's income to subsistence level (or below) with a very small maintenance order that will do nothing to lift his wife and children out of poverty. Indeed, if a woman has 'signed her book over' to the DHSS so that they pay her direct and recoup payment from her husband, she will not benefit at all from her husband's sacrifice since any extra money he pays is retained by the DHSS. Although this incongruity between hardship to the husband and benefit to the wife is most marked in low income families, the same principle applies in wealthier households. In other words, the man's economic hardship will not prevent a drop in his wife's standard of living – both will be adversely affected. The point to be grasped is that while it is accepted that husbands may suffer financially on divorce, this suffering does not necessarily benefit wives, and it should not be viewed as deriving from some fault in individual wives. The hardship that maintenance payments cause men is quite independent of the life-style it affords to women, yet these two factors have been linked, with the presumption that there is a direct relationship. What needs to be considered is how, in the late 1970s and early 1980s, these two independent factors have been linked to form such a powerful argument against women's rights in family law.

There are undoubtedly a number of factors which have contributed towards this ideological shift or backlash against women. Two significant factors however must be the rise in the divorce rate throughout the 1970s, which has meant that many more people have experienced divorce and even remarriage, and the change in the divorce law in 1971 and in legal practice after *Wachtel* v *Wachtel*[4] in 1973, which made it much more difficult for men to avoid paying maintenance to wives. Prior to 1971 (or 1973 if we take *Wachtel* as the watershed) the conduct of a wife could always be used as a reason to reduce a man's liability to pay maintenance to her. With the new interpretation of divorce as a misfortune befalling both parties this avenue of escape was partially blocked. This shift was symbolically important but also had certain material consequences for some women who could be awarded maintenance even though they were not without some responsibility for the breakdown of the marriage. But in spite of these changes in legal practice regarding conduct,[5] the predominant perception of maintenance is that it remains a gift that must be deserved or merited. Maintenance is not regarded as a right like a wage, it is still viewed as an act of benevolence on the part of the husband. If we consider that family law does nothing to enforce a man's duty to support his wife *during* marriage, it is perhaps not surprising that the legal requirement to support a wife *after* the marriage has broken down creates a sense of resentment, especially if, in the husband's definition, she is not very deserving. This problem was put to me by one Sheffield solicitor[6] who remarked,

> 'I can say this that generally speaking when I ever act for a man I
> am in danger of losing him, he can't believe [laughter] . . . I

always have extreme difficulty in explaining to men that they are going to get caught for maintenance. Generally speaking they don't believe I can be right. So half my task when I'm acting for a man is to keep him, to stop him going elsewhere because I'm no good.'

Another solicitor illustrated the often unspoken but vitally important moral element to any entitlement to maintenance.

'What about, for instance, the wife of a well-to-do Sheffield company director who never worked whilst they were married for twenty years and who is then left by the husband, who goes off with another woman, and she has to support herself on his income? Is she, suddenly, years after the divorce, to have to go off to social security? The answer is no. On the other hand you might get other women who play, for instance, play as fast and loose as the husband did, and still drawing maintenance and doing a bit of work on the side, whose obvious moral entitlement is obviously considerably less. Where do you draw the line?'

Private family law cannot eradicate this moral element because although marriage is a legal contract it is also a personal relationship and legislation cannot override the emotional resentment engendered by paying money to a person towards whom only antipathy is felt. What needs to be examined however is why the discontentment that this causes is focused on individual ex-wives rather than on the economic vulnerability of all women or on the structure of private law which reinforces women's economic dependency on men.

There is a confusion here between the 'moral worth' of individual women and the structural dependency of the majority of women. Because a woman is in an economically inferior position and needs to look to men for support when she has children she is reconstructed as a parasite and a burden; if she happens to be angry, bitter, awkward, or obstructive as well then a perfect case of sympathy for the poor husband is constructed.

In the interviews with solicitors in Sheffield I found that this was precisely how the issues were understood. For example,

'I also feel that very often the law works unjustly toward the husband, where his wife can run off with another man, take the children with her, subsequently terminating that relationship with the other man, and the husband can be forced into a situation where he has to sell his house and then support his wife and children through no fault of his own.'

Of course not all solicitors were simply sympathetic to the men, for example,

'[Brain surgery] is the only answer with many men, you know, because they are little more than animals. They see life in a very narrow and very selfish aspect, you know. They earn whatever they can, stick to as much of it as they can and pay out as little as possible to the wife and the children, and they don't give a damn. And they go on from one woman to another.'

The point that needs to be made, however, is that neither of these stereotypes is an adequate basis for reforming the law and yet it appears that the stereotype of the undeserving 'alimony drone' has in fact been most influential in this respect.

One of the main problems with the recent debate over maintenance is precisely that the issues have been depicted as a conflict between husband and wife or more generally men and women. This tends to ignore two other important dimensions. First that the stereotype drones are not just wives but also mothers and second that marriage is not only a legal contract between individual men and women but also between them and the state.

Wives or mothers

The terms 'mother' and 'motherhood' carry important ideological messages in our culture. Some of these messages are being challenged by feminists because they presuppose that women should have sole responsibility for child care and that looking after children is women's only natural function and ambition. Nonetheless, the concept of 'mother' is important to this debate because it creates a picture of women in relation to children rather than in relation to men. This is significant because as soon as children are attached to women such that they become identified as 'mothers' rather than 'wives', stereotypes of drones and parasites become culturally unacceptable. This process was evidenced in the interviews with Sheffield solicitors. Individuals who, on the one hand, subscribed to the idea that marriage should not be a 'meal ticket' for wives, or who thought the pendulum of law reform had swung too far, presented a very different analysis when children were added to the equation of husband and wife. Consider for example the following statements.

'That is looking at it from the wrong point of view. You have got to look at it from the children's point of view. . . . The law doesn't give *her* a prior claim to the matrimonial home, it gives the children a right to remain in circumstances to which they are used and which is in their best intersts. And I firmly believe that that is the proper thing to do, because the last thing to look at where the children are involved is what is the best for the husband or the wife or whether it is unfair to them or not.'

And

'Yes, I think it is unfair but it is a fact of life. I mean there are lots of unfair disadvantages or advantages that one sex has over the other. But I think which ever way you look at it, it is right that the wife should have custody by and large because she will be the one used to, you know, washing clothes, cooking etc. . . . So I think it's a fact of life simply and I sympathize with men, it must be dreadful . . . but when you explain it to most men, when you explain the pros and cons, very very few actually walk out saying the law is biased against them. Most just see it as a fact of life.'

Once these solicitors started to think about mothers and children they appreciated the structural position of women in the family and they also recognized that many recent reforms to the law have been directed towards protecting children and only indirectly the mothers, who generally have the custody of children. There was a tendency however to ignore the fact that these mothers were the same women who were the undeserving, drone-like wives who were divorcing their husbands.

Marriage and the state

The perception of marriage as a private contract between a man and a woman obscures the role of the state in establishing the nature and terms of that contract. Indeed the role of law and public policy in reproducing women as dependents of men becomes quite invisible. Yet it is both law and public policy that insist that married or cohabiting women look first to men for financial support if they cannot be self-sufficient. Only when individual men fail to provide will the state give any financial assistance to such women and then the provision is at supplementary benefit level which was never intended to be a long-term source of income for women and children. Current trends in family law that reduce a wife's right to claim maintenance from her ex-husband are objectionable, not on the grounds that many women will lose a large source of income, but on the grounds that whilst men's private liabilities are being reduced, there are no plans to improve or supplement existing state benefits for women who cannot lift themselves out of the poverty trap.

While there is now legislative support for reducing men's private law liability, there is no intention to increase expenditure on the welfare state or to improve women's employment. That this might cause problems for women seems to go unremarked. The following responses from the sample of Sheffield magistrates[7] who were interviewed on their matrimonial jurisdiction tended to reflect this rather short-sighted policy.

Table 3   **Sheffield magistrates' views on changing maintenance law**

	women (%)	*men* (%)	*total* (%)
in favour of introducing time limits on maintenance orders	60	50	55
in favour of introducing time limits in order to encourage wives to find employment	93	25	58
not in favour of maintenance for wives as a life-time commitment for husbands	73	63	68
in favour of increasing welfare provisions to dependents when marriage fails	40	37	39

These magistrates were in favour, generally speaking, of reducing husbands' liabilities but against increasing public sources of income maintenance. Clearly the women magistrates expected wives to work for a living. They were perhaps unaware of the difficulties facing working-class women with children looking for work in a climate of severe national unemployment. But the men magistrates were particularly interesting because although the majority did not think men should pay maintenance as a life-long commitment, neither did they think women should go out to work; nor did they think state benefits should be increased. This of course raises the question of how women can get any kind of income to live on at all.

Solicitors in Sheffield tended to share the magistrates' view on state benefits for separated wives. Often quite at variance with their statements about parasitical wives, they insisted that men should support their dependents *if* the alternative was the 'public purse'.

> 'It seems to me that you've got to look at the available income of the parties as a result of their legitimate earning capacity and not as a state handout. I'm not in the job of encouraging the state to pay more and letting husbands off, which is so often what it comes down to.'

Of course not all solicitors shared this perspective but it is important to recognize that sympathy for husbands who had to pay maintenance to wives was abruptly curtailed if a reduction of his liability meant that tax-payers' money was involved. In other words, social class is an important, although often invisible, feature of the debate on maintenance.

There is also another complicating dimension to this issue. While on the one hand it is generally held to be a 'good thing' if husbands do not have to pay maintenance to drones, yet it is not a good thing if the public provision replaces private provision because this induces irresponsibility in men. Hence the reduction of liability through private law is good, but the reduction of liability through public law heralds untold evils and threatens the very fabric of society. Take, for example, the following comment from a Sheffield solicitor:

> 'Yes, well quite, I mean it is obvious what would happen isn't it. People would just waltz off when they felt like it. It would make marriage even less stable than it is at the present time or even more unstable and it would be yet another quasi-socialist idea . . . method of breaking society down. Weakening responsibility, weakening the human race . . . all very bad, assuming the human race is to carry on. Whether that is a good thing is a different question which we haven't been asked.'

Not all solicitors felt as strongly as this but many of them, and certainly a major proportion of the Sheffield magistrates, voiced this fear to varying degrees. Yet it is not a fear that is voiced in connection with changes to private law and it would appear that this is because such changes are deemed mainly to benefit middle-class men, who do not fit into our cultural stereotypes of irresponsibility. It may also be that middle-class wives are thought to have more financial resources so that they will not turn to state benefits and public funds.

If reasonable state benefits are withheld from women who are divorced or separated; if ex-husbands' liabilities are to be gradually eroded; and if women's wages or opportunities to engage in waged work continue to be limited, only one method of economic survival presents itself. In the words of another Sheffield solicitor.

> 'It's a funny business our matrimonial law. He's more or less supposed to have taken her on for life, for better or for worse, despite the divorce law, and theoretically the only thing that lets him off the hook is when she remarries. And so I always advise my male clients who are in the position to pay more money to the wife . . . as a joke (I don't mean it seriously because if you give her too much she may think she's on to a good thing and hang on to it), but I always say send her expensive perfumes, offer to babysit for her and get her, you know, send her out to dances, you know, send a car for her to take her because the sooner she's off your hands and into somebody else's the better. You know, I say the last thing you want to do is to be upsetting her all the time so that she is perpetually going around weeping and looking [so] awful that nobody else will look at her. You know, you've got to try to strike a nice balance so that she's happy and attractive and then somebody else will take her because theoretically she's on his back until she remarries.'

In this solicitor's account your sympathy is drawn to the poor husband who has this awful burden from which he needs to be freed. What is hidden is why and how his wife became financially dependent on him in the first place, and how this in turn justifies her being identified as a burden. Attention is not drawn to her vulnerable economic status but to the desirability of off-loading her (suitably happy and attractive) onto someone else. And then perhaps the cycle can repeat itself. Whilst she is happily remarried she can repay her keep in kind (i.e. housework, child care, sex) but should this marriage also fail she will become a burden again, to be passed on, it is hoped, to another man *ad infinitum* or until she becomes too unattractive to be parcelled out in this way. But whilst remarriage may appear to be a short-term solution to the poverty of single parent families, it does nothing to address the underlying problem of women's economic dependence on men which fosters that poverty.

The problem of divorce

What the Sheffield solicitors and magistrates did not see, and what is also absent from recent debates on maintenance, is that the problems of divorce stem from the problems of marriage. Of course divorce exacerbates these problems by creating a good deal of misery and financial hardship, but the issues that cause so much grievance in law arise not from the nature of divorce, but from the nature of marriage. There is a continuity from marriage to divorce because the sexual division of labour that is celebrated as natural and desirable during marriage is precisely the basis of the main conflict upon divorce (Delphy 1976). Yet while marriage is celebrated we tend to censure individuals (particularly wives) who cannot instantly abandon a married life-style and all its consequences the moment they divorce. This continuity between marriage and divorce is also reflected in the way in which both are regarded as personal, private, individual events. A quick perusal of all the policy documents and legislation on the family, marriage, and divorce should disabuse anyone of this view.[8] However, divorce is still seen as a private, individual problem (even if it has social consequences) with the result that solutions are offered at an individual level (i.e. re-marriage). If we look at the development of divorce law in this century we can see that family law has simply shifted the hardship of divorce back and forth between individual husbands and wives. The problem of divorce is thus contained within the private sphere, it does not become a public issue except in as much as it attracts public alarm and condemnation. The law, which defines the terms of marriage and provides an exit from marriage, remains invisible in this debate. The welfare state will provide, but only an inadequate safety net for the poorest families; otherwise these problems are defined as private and a solution is left to private law. But private law is increasingly revealed as inadequate to this task which is why there is the current crisis over maintenance and the growing conflict over the custody of children. In the early 1970s Morris Finer (1974) recognized that there was a vital third system of family law, namely the DHSS, and his committee made a number of radical suggestions for improving public provision for single parents. As private law in the 1980s continues to fail to provide adequately for marriage breakdown, and as the divorce rate rises, it is increasingly necessary to think again in terms of abolishing private forms of maintenance and replacing them with newly conceived public sources of income maintenance for women. Moreover, we should be critical of legislative changes that only tinker with the family law to the detriment of women and that are not combined with more progressive changes to our system of state benefits, changes that could provide women, with or without children, with some degree of financial independence from men. The advent of widespread divorce has made the concealed poverty of women in the family visible, and it is most important that the emergence of this as a social problem requiring redress is not deflected by an identification of the problem as a bias in law against husbands or as the fault of individual women.

Notes

1 The Conservative Party's secret plans for the family were reported in *The Guardian* on 17 and 18 February, 1983. *The Guardian* reported that the Cabinet had formed a committee to consider ways of restructuring the welfare state. Amongst suggestions made were an examination of 'what more can be done to encourage families . . . to reassume responsibilities taken on by the state, for example, responsibility for the disabled, elderly, unemployed 16-year-olds', and ways to 'encourage mothers to stay at home' (*The Guardian*, 17 February, 1983, p.4f).
2 See for example Coote and Campbell (1982) for an outline of the contemporary position of women in the UK.
3 I am grateful to Jenny Levin for this idea.
4 *Wachtel* v *Wachtel* [1973] Fam. 72 was a major case in the development of case law after the introduction of the 1969 Divorce Reform Act in 1971.
5 How extensively the issue of conduct has been disregarded is open to speculation. Barrington Baker *et al.* (1977) have thrown some light on how registrars view conduct and my own research on magistrates in Sheffield (Smart 1984) indicates that conduct is not a dead issue.
6 In the course of my research in Sheffield from 1980 to 1982, I interviewed thirty-four solicitors who did mostly matrimonial work.

For a detailed discussion of these interviews see my PhD thesis, 'Law and the Reproduction of Patriarchal Relations', Sheffield University Library.
7 In addition to the interviews with solicitors I also interviewed thirty-one magistrates who sat regularly on the Sheffield domestic panel. For more information on these interviews consult my PhD thesis as in note 6.

References

Barrington Baker, W., Eekelaar, J., Gibson, C., and Raikes, S. (1977) *The Matrimonial Jurisdiction of Registrars*. Centre for Socio-Legal Studies, Wolfson College, Oxford: SSRC.

Blom-Cooper, L. and Drewry, G. (1976) *Law and Morality*. London: Duckworth.

Brophy, J. and Smart, C. (1981) From Disregard to Disrepute: The Position of Women in Family Law. *Feminist Review* 9: 3-16.

Coote, A. and Campbell, B. (1982) *Sweet Freedom*. London: Picador.

Davis, G., Macleod, A., and Murch, M. (1983) Divorce: Who Supports the Family? *Family Law* 13(7): 217–24.

Delphy, C. (1976) Continuities and Discontinuities in Marriage and Divorce. In S. Allen and D. Leonard Barker (eds) *Sexual Divisions and Society*. London: Tavistock.

Finer, M. (1974) *Report of the Committee on One Parent Families*, vol. I. Cmnd 5629, London: HMSO.

Graham Hall, J. (1968) *Report of the Committee on Statutory Maintenance Limits*. Cmnd 3587, London: HMSO.

Maclean, M. (1982) Financial Consequences of Divorce. Impact on the Ongoing Family. Oxford: Wolfson College.

Maclean, M. and Eekelaar, J. (1983) Children and Divorce: Economic Factors. Paper presented to the British Association for the Prevention and Study of Child Abuse and Neglect, Cambridge.

Marsden, D. (1969) *Mothers Alone: Poverty and the Fatherless Family*. London: Allen Lane.

Reiss, E. (1934) *The Rights and Duties of English Women*. Manchester: Sherratt and Hughes.

Smart, C. (1984) *The Ties That Bind*. London: Routledge and Kegan Paul.

CHAPTER 2

Changing women's claims to maintenance

Hilary Land

In our society all individuals have claims to economic support from their families, the state, or from the labour market – or from a combination of the three. During the past century the claims to maintenance individuals may make on these systems have changed as a variety of state social assistance and social insurance schemes have been developed, the formal labour market has become more extensive, and liabilities within families less extensive. However, the patterns of men's and women's claims to maintenance have remained different both in the legislation and in practice. In spite of the reforms of the 1970s men have greater access to state benefits than women although the eligibility rules and level of benefit to which they are entitled continue to be constrained by the desire to maintain their incentives to take paid employment. In contrast, women are expected to rely on their families for support, in particular their husbands. The conditions under which women, particularly married women, can claim maintenance from the state have been determined not by a desire to sustain their incentives to take waged work but by a concern that they will continue their unwaged work of caring for their families. The new Matrimonial and Family Proceedings Act 1984 considerably reduces a woman's claims to maintenance on her husband once marriage has ended. This will not necessarily reduce inequalities between men and women nor provide women with greater economic security because, as I shall argue in this paper, this is being done in the context of inadequate state support, particularly for families with young children and women's inferior access to jobs and decent wages.

During the 1970s major reforms were made in the British social security system and some improvements were made for women. In the national insurance scheme women are now treated more as individuals and less in terms of their marital status. For example, contribution rules for pensions are no longer tougher for married women, the married women's option has ended, and those paying the full contribition now get the full benefit rate instead of only two-thirds. Even in the supplementary benefit scheme from November, 1983 a married woman has been able to claim benefit if she is named as the main breadwinner. However, these improvements are not so impressive when looked at against other major changes in the national insurance scheme that have occurred since 1980.

First, short-term benefits are now taxed; short-term sickness benefits have *no* dependent's benefits for men or for women, and there are no earnings related supplements to sickness, unemployment, or maternity benefits. In other words, women have been given more rights within the national insurance system but those rights are worth less in cash terms. Second, administrative rules have been changed and these affect women far more than men. For instance, in order for them to claim unemployment benefit parents of small children may be required to produce evidence that adequate child care arrangements can be made should a job be found. Third, increasing numbers of part-time workers (the majority of whom are women) are excluded from the national insurance scheme altogether because they are defined as 'non-employed' (i.e. earning less than a quarter of male average wages). In 1977, official estimates stated a fifth of part-time women workers were defined as 'non-employed', but by 1981 the proportion had grown to two-fifths.[2] In any case even those part-time workers who have paid contributions may find that they are deemed ineligible for benefit because they are not available for full-time work.

Even if the impact of the reforms of the 1970s had not been subsequently eroded in this way, fundamental changes in our social security scheme are necessary if women's needs are to be met. First and foremost, an *adequate* scheme of family allowances or child benefit is needed. The wages system does not and cannot take account of variations in the needs of workers because it has other functions such as the allocation of workers between jobs requiring different skills. The level of wages is the product of various factors including the bargaining strength of particular groups of workers. Over fifty years ago Eleanor Rathbone eloquently spelt out the inadequacies of the wages system as a means of meeting family needs and her analysis still stands (Rathbone 1924). A child benefits scheme which more nearly met the basic needs of a child would be expensive for it would mean increasing the current level three or four-fold. However, as a start it would be possible to double them by using the revenue gained if the married man's tax allowance were abolished.[3] The assumption on which this allowance is based is that marriage turns every woman into a dependent and while this had some basis in reality at its inception[4] this is no longer so. Today the majority of married women have paid employment throughout most of their working lives and make a substantial contribution to the economic support of the household.

Second, both the social insurance and social assistance schemes are still based on the assumption that there is only one breadwinner in the family although since November, 1983 exceptionally this may be a woman. However, acknowledging women as breadwinners does nothing to recognize that in the vast majority of households *both* men and women contribute to the economic support of their families[5] and that the interruption of a woman's earnings may be as serious as an interruption in her husband's. The aggregation rule in the supplementary benefit scheme means husband's and wife's resources are both taken into account when assessing entitlement to benefit. Since 1979 single parents (mainly single mothers)[6] have their children's income (usually maintenance from their fathers) aggregated with theirs if it exceeds the amount of the scale rate for children of that age. In other words women on supplementary benefit may be forced to be dependent on their children, or indirectly the father of their children, even when the marriage is over. It also means that more generous maintenance payments for children does nothing to improve the standard of living of those living in single parent households and dependent on supplementary benefit as nearly half of them are.

Women then are still not treated as individuals in their own right in all circumstances although the recent reforms have made some improvements. However, the strategy of treating women as individuals *like* men can only be partially successful in meeting women's needs. Individualism is a creed that fails to recognize the needs of those (mainly women) who care for and about others besides themselves. Their caring responsibilities may affect their availability for paid work, but the social security system barely recognizes this. For example, those responsible for children or elderly relatives may have their earnings temporarily interrupted because their charges are ill. However they can claim no benefit as they would be able to do in many other countries. If a carer gives up paid employment more permanently only men and single women are eligible for the invalid care allowance. Married women have no claims on the state in these circumstances: they are still expected to look to their husbands for support.

Similarly improvements in women's access to the labour market have been limited because their responsibilities as wives, mothers, and daughters have changed very little. Marriage still has different meanings for men and women. Men take on an obligation to provide economic support for a wife and children and are expected to take paid employment in order to do so. In return, Carol Smart points out in Chapter 1, women provide care for children, sick or elderly relatives, and, of course, their able-bodied husbands. This is expected to take precedence over their activities in the labour market. Although, as already mentioned, the life-long responsibility of a man to maintain his wife even after divorce is currently under review, and likely to be reduced, there is no parallel reappraisal of a wife's side of the contract. The work of caring is little recognized and is undervalued as work. While there are many dimensions to caring, some very positive and rewarding, it is nevertheless an activity that takes time and energy and constrains other activities inside and outside the home. In particular the ability to earn money or the opportunity to enhance earning capacity is substantially reduced.

The care of children, sick or infirm relatives, and husbands determines whether or not a woman has paid employment, the time of day (or night) and the number of hours she works, and the location of that work. Seven out of eight part-time employees are married women and the big increase in the 1970s in the number of married women taking paid employment is accounted for almost entirely by the increase in those with part-time jobs. Full-time employment is rarely combined with children of pre-school age: only 5 per cent do so, a percentage that has remained constant since the beginning of the 1970s. More mothers with older children have paid employment but school hours limit their availability for employment, too.

In Britain the most dramatic increase in economic activity has been amongst middle-aged married women. Over two-thirds are now economically active and this means Britain has the highest economic activity rates for 45-54-year-old married women in western Europe. (The middle-aged full-time housewife is not as common as the rhetoric would lead us to believe.)[7] Nevertheless, their work in the labour market is still constrained by their caring responsibilities and half have only part-time employment (OPCS 1981). There are estimated to be about one and a quarter million handicapped people living in the community and many of them are receiving a large amount of support from relatives, mainly female relatives. Half of all severely handicapped elderly live with one of their children. A recent study by the Policy Studies Institute found that on average a woman caring for an infirm relative living in the same household was spending on average four and a half hours per day caring for that person, compared with thirteen minutes by her husband (even though in some households it was *his* mother being cared for) (Nissel and Bonnerjea 1983).

Finally, it should not be forgotten that a man may directly constrain his wife's earning activities. For example, a national study in the mid-1960s found that one in six married women who did not do paid work said they did not do so because of their husband's needs or wishes. The proportion today may be smaller but it is still the case that when a man becomes sick or unemployed it is more likely that his wife will give up rather than take up paid employment. This is partly because the British social security system does much to discourage the wives of sick or unemployed men from earning[8] but also partly so as not to undermine the view that it is the *man* who should provide the main economic support for the family.[9] A man's career usually takes precedence over that of his wife, so that decisions, for example to move location, are much more likely to be made in order to enhance his career than hers. Furthermore such a move may well *damage* her position in the labour market. In addition, there are numerous ways within the home in which women enhance their husbands' earning capacity either in the short term or long term, or both. Janet Finch's recent book documents the myriad ways in which women are incorporated into their husbands' jobs (Finch 1983). This is unlikely to enhance their own marketable skills because the ways in which they help are largely unacknowledged and invisible. Women invest in their husbands' careers and in many respects this is a sensible strategy because as long as the marriage lasts and is amicable, they will benefit too. It should however be noted that the benefits may not be shared equally (see Pahl, Chapter 3; Land 1983), and such a strategy is disastrous if the marriage breaks down. Moreover, while it is true that a woman's standard of living is determined by her husband, it is also often true that *his* is dependent on her activities both inside and outside the home. It may well be that some divorced men resent their ex-wives because of their drop in standard of living which is not caused entirely by the actual payment of maintenance. For men to acknowledge that would be to begin to admit the value of and their dependence on their wives' contribution to the marriage. However, unless this *is* admitted fully, marriage will continue to impair a woman's ability to be 'self-sufficient'.

It is in this context that a woman's claim on a former husband's occupational pension needs to be considered. The Occupational Pensions Board and, more recently, the Law Commission recommended that the courts be empowered to deal with such claims (the former at the time of decease of the divorced spouse, the latter at the time of divorce). However, the Bill currently before Parliament makes no specific mention of pension rights. Since the Social Security Pension Act 1975, widows' pensions must be provided if an occupational scheme is to be recognized for the purposes of opting out of the state scheme, so on divorce a woman is giving up the possibility of a survivor's pension. If she does not remarry then the chances of generating for herself a pension over and above the basic state pension are not good. A part-time employee does not usually have access to an occupational scheme[10] and if she has had children she is likely to have had a break in paid employment.[11]

Between now and the end of the century the number of divorced women over retirement age is estimated to increase threefold and widows will still outnumber all other female pensioners. Who has claims on a divorced person's survivor's pension is an important issue and it is not clear that either equity or need requires that the last wife gets all. For women the issue of pension rights on losing or changing a marriage partner is as important as the issue of the pension rights of those who change jobs. The Secretary of State to the DHSS set up an enquiry into the transferability of pensions for the mobile worker at the end of November, 1983, but has not taken the opportunity to review pension rights on divorce. However Lord Hailsham has subsequently said that he intends to issue early in 1984 a consultation document on the question of the appropriation at divorce of occupational pension rights.[12]

The Scottish Law Commission, unlike their English counterparts, did raise the question of achieving an 'equitable adjustment of the economic advantages and disadvantages arising from the marriage' but thought it too vague an objective on which to base policy (see Clive, Chapter 12). It would indeed be a difficult exercise to quantify how each spouse's earning patterns may have differed if they had not married, but it would be interesting to try. Basing a woman's claims to maintenance on her husband, on the grounds that she has a right to compensation for a reduction in her earning capacity or the right to some return on her investment in her husband's earning capacity and occupational pension rights, seems to me, as a feminist, to be far more attractive in principle than claims to maintenance based on defining a woman as a dependant. Of course, it has to be acknowledged that even if this were practically possible, it would be a strategy with limitations. It would not meet the needs of those (mainly women) left alone with the responsibility of caring for children because, as I have stated above, many men's wages and even more women's wages are too low adequately to support one household with dependent children, let alone two.[13] Nevertheless, such an exercise might draw attention to the differential impact marriage has on men's and women's earning opportunities and capacities, and might begin to lead to a reappraisal of the value of the work women do within marriage. At the very least it would require that this be acknowledged and would raise the question of the extent to which men as individuals benefit and hence should pay, compared with the benefits to wider society. This leads back to the issue of the state's share of responsibility to provide benefits and services to support children, the sick, and infirm.

It is also important to consider how the structure of the labour market might be changed to accommodate better the needs of those workers who have caring responsibilities. Unless this is done, those who have such responsibilities, be they men or women, will have weaker access to jobs and wages. Currently these responsibilities conflict with the demands of paid work. A shorter working day would help to reduce this conflict. If this were to mean lower earnings then the inadequacies of the wage system and the low level of child support would be exposed more starkly. More and better child care provision, for example, is important as a means of enabling mothers to take paid employment but it is not a complete answer. Although I would argue for more collective services providing care for children and sick or infirm adults, I do not envisage a society in which we do not as individuals have caring responsibilities for some or most of our lives. I would not wish to argue either that everyone – women or men – should be paid to stay out of the labour market for those periods when they have such responsibilities. Improved access to the labour market is also important because wages are regarded differently from money received from the state or the family. For example, one of the official advertisements for the Community Enterprise Programme in 1983 stated: 'Give a person a dole cheque and they feel like a statistic. Give a person a job and they feel like a human being.' Money received from a member of the family may be felt to be even more damaging to a person's self-respect and sense of independence. This is an issue for men as well as for women as growing numbers of men are being thrust back on their families as long-term unemployment exhausts their claim to insurance benefit and their claim to supplementary benefit is assessed in relation to their wife's earnings. If they do not or cannot claim benefit, they are not counted among the unemployed: they are not even a statistic.[14] In the 1930s, when the household means test forced parents to be dependent on their adult children, some Labour MPs argued that men should be allowed some residual claim on the state even when their unemployment was exhausted. They called this 'dignity money'. (They were not so worried about the dignity of married women.) Whatever the ideological basis for distinguishing between money received from employers, the state, or family, in practice there are fewer strings attached to wages. Since the Truck Acts of the nineteenth century, employers cannot determine how a worker spends his or her money. The state and the family, mainly husbands, can and sometimes do and if it is being 'mis-spent' may withhold it. As long as there are these differences, whether in perception or in reality, then access to more generous state benefits is not necessarily a desirable *alternative* to improved access to the labour market and to wages.

Women's claims to maintenance on the state, the family, and the labour market are still in the process of changing. I have argued in this chapter that a woman's claims on one system should not be altered without regard to the strength of her claims on the other systems because all three are closely interrelated. It is regrettable therefore that the English Law Commission's terms of reference when asked to look at the financial consequences of divorce excluded a close look at these relationships (Law Commission 1980).[15] In principle it is desirable that, as the Commission recommended, women should not be defined or indeed define themselves, as lifelong dependents on their husbands. In the short run, however, the new 1984 divorce legislation, which will reduce a woman's claims on her husband (even though, for most,[16] these hardly added up to 'a meal ticket for life') at a time when retraining opportunities are limited; jobs, even for skilled women, are scarce; and workers with children are at a disadvantage, will increase their risk of poverty. Much will depend on how broadly the courts interpret the requirement that in determining maintenance they should have regard to

'the income, earning capacity, property and other financial resources which each of the parties to the marriage has or is likely to have in the foreseeable future, including in the case of earning capacity any increase in that capacity which it would in the opinion of the courts be reasonable to expect a party to the marriage to take steps to acquire'

as well as to the contributions made by each of the parties to the welfare of the family, including any contribution made by looking after the home or caring for the family.[17] How fully will the courts take account of the differential access men and women have to the labour market, particularly when assessing the length of time maintenance should be paid in order to allow an adjustment to independence to be made 'without undue hardship'?[18] More important, these changes alone can do little to improve access to jobs and wages in practice. Only when women's caring responsibilities are shared differently between the family and the wider community will this become a real possibility. This requires a much more fundamental reappraisal of the marriage relationship and the responsibilities arising from it than has been made so far.

Notes

1 Matrimonial and Family Proceedings Act 1984, s.3.
2 Department of Employment, *New Earnings Survey,* 1982, London: HMSO, 1983, Introduction. The 1981 new earnings survey excluded two-fifths of part-time female employees because they earned below the national insurance limit. House of Lords, Select Committee on the European Communities, *Voluntary Part-Time Work* (216) 19th Report, Session 1981–82, London: HMSO, 1982, p. 131. (Evidence from the Department of Employment.)
3 The annual cost in foregone revenue is currently over £3 billion.
4 When the additional personal allowance was introduced for married men in 1918, tax-payers belonged to the middle and higher income groups in which it was common for a woman to give up paid employment when she married.
5 In 1980 62 per cent of married women were economically active and contributed on average 28 per cent to the household income.
6 Eight out of nine of the 900,000 single parent households comprised mothers and children in 1980.
7 There are a million married women without paid employment who

do not have caring responsibilities and who are not incapacitated in any way; 90 per cent of them are over forty years old.

8 The earnings disregard for a wife of a sick or unemployed man are very low. If she earns more than £4 a week then her husband has his benefit reduced, so unless she can earn enough to support the whole family it is not worth while continuing her paid work.

9 In a recent in-depth study of unemployed men and women and their families, Colin Bell and Lorna McKee noted the strength of the view that it *ought* to be the man who provides for the family (Bell and McKee 1983:23).

10 72 per cent of establishments in a national survey had a firm's pension scheme but only 20 per cent admitted part-timers (see Hunt 1981).

11 The state scheme since 1978 protects her basic pension rights during the period of looking after children and if she has an incomplete contribution record herself she can use her former spouse's record to entitle her to the basic pension. However, divorced spouses cannot use each other's contributions to acquire the earnings-related component of the pension in the way a married couple can.

12 Reported in letter from Frank Field, *Guardian*, 23 December, 1983.

13 In over 90 per cent of divorces with children, it is the mothers who get custody.

14 Since December, 1982, the official number of unemployed is based on the number claiming benefit, not as previously the number registered as unemployed. This means that those not eligible for benefit, namely the school leavers, many married women and many of the unemployed who after twelve months have exhausted their right to insurance benefits do not appear in this number. As a result of this change between 0.5 million and 1.0 million unemployed have 'disappeared'. In July, 1983, 1.1 million adults in the UK had been unemployed for more than twelve months.

15 See Law Commission (1980: para. 3). The Law Commission in its Report acknowledged that it did not think there is any real dispute that the most serious problems faced by the majority of single parent families are caused by economic factors and that changes in the private law can do little if anything to alleviate the hardship and deprivation they experience (Law Commission, *The Financial Consequences of Divorce*, HC 68, 1981, para. 5).

16 Only 6 per cent of divorced women relied solely on their husbands' maintenance in 1980. This compares with over 300,000 single parents receiving supplementary benefits.
17 Matrimonial and Family Proceedings Act 1984, part II, s. 25 (2) (a) and (f).
18 Matrimonial and Family Proceedings Act 1984, part II, s. 25A (2).

References

Bell, C. and McKee, L. (1983) Marital and Family Relations in Times of Male Unemployment. Paper given at SSRC workshop on Employment and Unemployment, November.
Finch, J. (1983) *Married to the Job*. London: Allen & Unwin.
Hunt, A. (1981) Women and Underachievement at Work. EOC Bulletin No. 5. Spring
Land, H. (1983) Poverty and Gender, the Distribution of Resources Within the Family. In M. Brown (ed.) *The Structure of Disadvantage*. London: Heinemann.
Law Commission (1980) *Financial Consequences of Divorce: The Basic Policy, A Discussion Paper*. Cmnd 8041. London: HMSO.
Nissel, M. and Bonnerjea, L. (1983) *Family Care for the Handicapped Elderly: Who Pays?* Policy Studies Institute.
Office of Population Censuses and Surveys (1981) *General Household Survey 1979*. London: HMSO.
Rathbone, E. (1924) *The Disinherited Family*. London: Allen & Unwin.

CHAPTER 3

The allocation of money within the household

Jan Pahl

This chapter will present preliminary results from a study of the control and allocation of money within households.[1] The aim of the study was to explore the ways in which money is allocated within households, focusing on that particular household type which consists of a married, or as-married couple, with at least one dependent child. A better understanding of the ways in which money is controlled and allocated within the family has relevance both for those who are interested in the sociology of the family and for those who are concerned with the impact of social and economic policies on family life. Traditionally the family has been construed as a sort of black box, within which the resources acquired by individuals are assumed to be shared with members of the same family living in the same household. One aim of this chapter is to open up this black box, in order to investigate some of the social processes involved in the flows of money within households. Money enters the household in a number of different forms, for example, as wages and salaries, as social security payments, as gifts, interest on savings, or rent from property owned. It leaves as payment for the whole range of house-hold expenditure, in the form of cash and cheques, hire purchase and credit card payments, and so on. Thus both at the point when it enters and at the point when it leaves the household it is effectively in the hands of individuals. What happens between these two points? What form do flows of money *within* the household take?

There are many definitional problems involved in this topic, above all in the question of the unit with which we are concerned. Should this be 'the household', 'the family', or 'the couple'? The fact that it is so difficult to differentiate these different units for the purpose of exploring flows of money is itself significant. 'The household' has been defined as 'all those people who live at the same address, having meals prepared together and with common housekeeping' (Central Statistical Office 1980). Thus the household is primarily an economic unit, in which common residence plays a significant part; it is also a bureaucratic unit, one which is central to census and survey analysis. On the other hand, 'the family' is primarily a kinship unit; common residence is not necessarily a significant characteristic, and the normal 'laws' of economics do not necessarily apply. 'The family' is an ideological and normative concept, and any definition has to take into account not only its biological and kinship aspects, but also cultural, institutional, and personal elements. Third, there is 'the couple'. In this discussion we are concerned only with those couples where some sharing of resources takes place on a regular basis, and such couples most commonly take the form of two people living together in a married, or marriage-like state. A couple with their dependent children form one type of family and one type of household, but there are many other versions of both.

One problem with our topic is a product of the unclear distinctions between household, family, and couple (Harris 1981). There are large areas of overlap and yet important differences in meaning. For example, it is commonplace to say that 'money enters the household', but inappropriate to say that 'money enters the couple'. Yet many couples cherish the idea that individual income pertains to the unit: they will say 'It's not my money or her/his money – it's our money' and their sharing of money represents for them their love for each other and their sharing of life together. This view of our topic emphasizes the community of interest among members of units and their mutual agreement to share resources. A contrasting analysis emphasizes the possibility of a conflict of interest among members of households, families, or couples, a conflict which can express itself in the form of conflict over resources such as time and money. In looking at patterns of allocation of money we can see yet another instance of the ways in which 'his' marriage may be very different from 'her' marriage (Bernard 1973).

Implications for policy

The idea that the household is a unit and that those who bring money into the unit will share it with other household members has had the effect both of creating the idea of the single breadwinner who will bring home and share the 'family wage', and also of providing few remedies for dependents who do not receive their share of the household income (Land 1980, 1981; Pahl 1980).

There are a number of specific policy areas in which assumptions are made about the allocation of money within the household, but where evidence is either lacking, or is contradictory, or it suggests that the assumptions being made are based on false premises. Let us consider some of these policy areas. The examples are taken from the UK, but it is likely that other countries could provide similar instances of the general points which are being made.

The measurement of poverty

Most work on poverty takes it for granted that all the members of any one household have the same standard of living, and that they all receive equal, or at least equitable, shares of the income of the household. However, studies of women whose marriages have broken down, and who are living on supplementary benefit, report a sizeable proportion as saying that they are 'better off' on supplementary benefit than they had been when living with their husbands. This proportion varies from 18 per cent (Houghton 1973) to 31 per cent (Evason 1980) and a third (Binney, Harkell, and Nixon 1981; Marsden 1969). Since supplementary benefit levels are usually taken to represent the poverty line in Britain these findings imply that these women, and probably their children, had previously been living below the poverty line. At the present time it is probably not practicable to assess poverty on an individual basis; however, it is important to remember that assessment on a household basis means the concealment of much 'hidden poverty', the product of the inequitable allocation of money within 'income units'.

Taxation

British taxation policy, similarly, regards husband and wife as one unit. This has many consequences. For example, it is assumed that a decrease in direct taxation can be matched by an increase in indirect taxation. This implies that the flow of money within households is being seen as completely unimpeded, so that those whose income increases because less tax is being deducted will automatically transfer their additional income to those who have to spend more because prices have risen. The evidence on this point is contradictory. It comes mainly from studies of 'housekeeping allowances', though as we shall see, this particular allocative pattern is just one among many ways in which households organize their finances. Several studies have suggested a lag between, on the one hand, increases in wages and prices and, on the other hand, increases in housekeeping allowances.

Policies relating to household formation and dissolution

There are many different dimensions to the formation of households; these may include sharing accommodation, eating meals together, pooling money for housekeeping expenses, entering into a sexual relationship, spending leisure time together, helping other household members with domestic work. When the idea of a 'household' is being used, for example in deciding whether or not a woman is entitled to supplementary benefits, it often appears to be assumed that all these aspects of an individual's life change simultaneously; either a person is in a household or she/he is not. Yet in reality people may eat together regularly without sharing accommodation, may have a sexual relationship without pooling their money. We do not, at present, know what are the social processes involved in household creation. Is there a typical sequence of events in which people 'form a household' along one dimension of their lives before amalgamating along another dimension?

My own study of abused women who had been assaulted by their husbands showed how hard it is to identify a precise moment at which any one marriage breaks down (Pahl 1978, 1984). One couple lived separately, but still regularly ate and slept together and the man gave the woman money for his keep. Another couple lived together, for lack of any alternative accommodation, but a court order forbade the woman to prepare food for the man, and forbade the man to enter the woman's bedroom. Should either of these two couples be defined as a 'household'? The answer is important not only for the purposes of enumeration, but also in deciding to whom social security benefits should be paid.

That study suggested that some women chose to live as single parent families in order to have control of the financial resources of the household, even though they knew this would mean a lower income coming into the household. How general are the social forces which precipitate such a decision? How easy is it to define whether a group of people, or a couple, do or do not comprise a household?

39

Such questions would surely be illuminated by a greater understanding of the relationships between patterns of allocation of money and all those other elements which at present combine together in our very broad definition of 'household'.

The payment of wages and salaries

There are a variety of links between the ways in which money enters households and the ways in which it is distributed within the household. Thus, for example, an earner's basic pay may be defined as money for domestic consumption by the household as a whole, while bonus pay or overtime earnings are more likely to be seen as for individual consumption and as for the sole use of the individual who earned the money (Tunstall 1962). Gray, in her study of housekeeping systems in Edinburgh, showed that the allocative system adopted within the household affected attitudes to earnings. She demonstrated that, in households where the husband handed the whole of his wages over to his wife, he was less likely to earn money from overtime work than were those husbands who gave their wives a fixed housekeeping allowance; in the latter case extra earnings were retained by the husband and so there was a greater incentive for him to do overtime (Gray 1979).

Patterns of allocation of money

There is an infinite variety of different allocative systems within the great variety of types of households. The chapter will differentiate four different types of allocative system. In reality, the proposed typology represents points on a continuum of allocative systems, but previous research suggests that the typology has considerable validity both within Britain and in other parts of the world. Two criteria are central in distinguishing one system from another: these are, first, each individual's responsibility for expenditure between and within expenditure categories, and second, each individual's access to household funds, other than those for which he or she is responsible.

The whole wage system

In this system one partner, usually the wife, is responsible for managing all the finances of the household and is also responsible for all expenditure, except for the personal spending money of the other partner. The personal spending money of the other partner is either taken out by him before the pay packet is handed over, or is returned to him from collective funds. If both partners earn, both pay packets are administered by the partner who manages the money. Where a whole wage system is managed by a husband, his wife may have no personal spending money of her own and no access to household funds.

The allowance system

In the most common form of this system the husband gives his wife a set amount, which she adds to her own earnings if she has any; she is responsible for paying for specific items of household expenditure. The rest of the money remains in the control of the husband and he pays for other specific items. Thus each partner has a sphere of responsibility in terms of household expenditure. If a wife does not earn she only has access to the 'housekeeping' allowance and, since this is allocated for household expenditure, she may feel that she has no personal spending money of her own: the same phenomenon can also be seen in the case of the whole wage system where the wife is responsible for all family expenditure but has no personal spending money. The allowance system has many variations, mainly because of the varying patterns of responsibility. At one extreme a wife may only be responsible for expenditure on food; at the other extreme she may be responsible for everything except the running of the car and the system may come close to resembling the whole wage system. The allowance system is also known as the 'wife's wage' and the 'spheres of responsibility' system, while the whole wage system is sometimes called the 'tipping up' system (Barrett and McIntosh 1982).

The shared management or pooling system

The essential characteristic of this system is that both partners have access to all or almost all the household money and both have responsibility for management of the common pool and for expenditure out of that pool. The partners may take their personal spending money out of the pool. On the other hand one or both of them may retain a sum for personal spending; when this sum becomes substantial the system begins to acquire some characteristics of the independent management system, which is described below.

The independent management system

The essential characteristic of this system is that both partners have an income and that neither has access to all the household funds. Each partner is responsible for specific items of expenditure, and though these responsibilities may change over time, the principle of keeping flows of money separate within the household is retained.

The political economy of the household

Distinguishing different types of allocative system is, however, only a beginning. What are the variables which determine the allocative system adopted by any one couple at any one time? What are the implications for the couple as a whole, and for individuals, of adopting one system rather than another? The rest of this chapter considers these issues, drawing on the first results from an empirical study of the allocation of money. The study involved interviewing 102 married couples, all with at least one child under sixteen. The couples were randomly selected from age-sex registers held by health centres in Kent. The respondents were interviewed both together as a couple, and separately at the same time but in different rooms. The interviews covered patterns of income and expenditures, transfer of money within the household, standards of living, and the relationship between husband and wife with particular reference to the control of money and power in decision-making.

In the course of the joint interview the way in which each couple organized its finances was classified into one of the four allocative systems outlined above. *Table 4* sets out the proportions of couples who fell into each of the four categories. The table also compares these findings with data from a study carried out by the Family Finances Group at the University of Surrey. This study was based on a postal survey in which a questionnaire was sent to married couples selected at random from electoral registers throughout Britain. The University of Surrey study used the same typology of allocative systems, so the results make it possible to set the data from Kent in a broader context (Evans *et al.* 1983).

It is interesting to see how similar are the results from the two studies. The main difference is in the numbers falling into the 'independent management' category. However, tabulations of the University of Surrey data, which plotted patterns of allocation of money by region of Britain, showed that the independent management

Table 4   **Frequency of four types of allocative system**

	Pahl study (Kent 1982–83) (%)	University of Surrey study (Britain 1983) (%)
whole wage system	14	18
allowance system	22	24
pooling system	56	54
independent management	9	4
total	100	100
number	102	250

system is more commonly found in the south-east of England, so this result should not be unexpected.

When the research began it was hypothesized that the main variables determining a couple's choice of allocative system would be the income level of the couple, the source of their income, their employment pattern, and their life cycle stage. Other variables, expressing various aspects of culture and ideology, were also found to be important, but these require more extensive discussion than space permits.

Couples with low incomes, whether the money was drawn from employment or from social security, were likely to adopt the whole wage system managed by the wife. Higher household incomes seemed to be associated with the allowance system and a greater involvement of the husband in the management of the family finances. Higher income levels, however, were also the point at which pooling systems became common. It is likely that a couple's choice of allocative system at these higher income levels reflected normative assumptions about the nature of marriage. *Table 5* relates allocative system to net household income; a similar pattern emerged if the social class of the husband replaced net household income. This association between income level and choice of allocative system has been confirmed by researchers from other parts of Britain and from other countries (e.g. Edwards 1981; Gray 1979; Hunt 1978; Rubin 1976; Sharma 1980; Stebbing 1982; Whitehead 1981.) It seems that when money is short, so that managing it becomes difficult, women are likely to be responsible for household finances.

The source of the household income is another significant variable. This heading covers both whether the income is drawn from employment or social security and whether it is earned by one or both

The State, the Law, and the Family

Table 5 **Allocative system by household income**

	Net household income		
	under £135 per week (%)	£135+ per week (%)	all sample (%)
whole wage system	21	3	14
allowance system	13	35	22
pooling system	56	55	56
independent management	10	8	9
total	100	101[1]	101[1]
number	62	40	102

[1]Because of rounding, not all total percentages add up to 100.

spouses. As *Table 6* shows, when social security was the source of a couple's income, it was more likely that they would adopt the whole wage system; this association has been found in other studies (Land 1969). It may be that the link between social security and the whole wage system is a product of low income rather than of income source. However, the interview material suggested that people did feel differently about money acquired from social security. Some respondents felt ashamed or resentful about being dependent on the state, and husbands tended to see this money as pertaining to the family as a unit, in contrast to earnings, which were more likely to be seen as belonging to the person who earned them.

Table 6 **Allocative system by source of income**

	income mainly or entirely from earnings (%)	income from social security (%)
whole wage system	10	46
allowance system	22	18
pooling and independent management	68	36
total	100	100
number	91	11

Whether or not a wife earned in her own right also had an effect on financial arrangements, as *Table 7* shows. Overall the pooling system was more common than any other, but the allowance system was particularly likely to be found when the husband was the only earner in the household. Pooling and independent management systems were more common when both spouses were in employment.

Table 7 **Allocative system by employment pattern of couple**

	both employed or wife only[1] (%)	only husband employed (%)	neither employed (%)
whole wage system	10	10	46
allowance system	16	30	18
pooling and independent management	75	60	36
total	101[2]	100	100
number	51	40	11

[1]Includes one couple where only the wife was employed.
[2]Because of rounding, not all total percentages add up to 100.

The complexity of the relationships between different patterns of employment and different financial arrangements were brought out by Edwards in her study of fifty Australian families:

'In lower income families, particularly where the wife did not earn, the wife was more likely to manage the finances. If the wife did earn either she managed the finances herself or she and her husband did so jointly. At higher income levels, if the wife did not have paid employment, the husband was likely either to manage the finances himself or to give his wife a housekeeping allowance. At higher income levels, if the wife did earn, either a shared management system or an independent management system was likely; the latter form of financial management was more likely if the wife made a significant contribution to family income.'

(Edwards 1981:132)

When the research began it was hypothesized that the choice of allocative system would reflect the life cycle stage of the couple, with couples altering their systems as their levels of income, responsibilities, and sources of income altered. The results showed that few couples ever changed from one system to another. Instead it seems as if many couples adopted a system on marriage, without really being aware of consciously choosing to organize their finances in one way rather than another. The choice of system seemed to reflect current ideologies about the nature of marriage in general and about specific gender roles within marriage.

The results from this and other studies suggest that the allowance system is more commonly found among older couples, while younger couples tend to manage their money jointly. This joint management may simply take the form of a pool from which both draw money as it is needed or it may incorporate the concept of 'housekeeping money' which the wife draws from the pool. Many pooling husbands commented that they saw the pooling as expressing an ideal of equality between themselves and their wives. *Table 8* makes a comparison between the couples in the study and their parents and provides further evidence that there has been a change taking place over the last thirty years from the allowance system to the pooling system.

Table 8 **Allocative systems of parents of study couples and of the study couples themselves**

	wives' parents	husbands' parents	study couples
whole wage (wife)	24	16	14
whole wage (husband)	2	4	0
allowance system	31	45	22
pooling system	11	11	56
independent management	2	1	9
don't know	30	23	0
total	100	100	101[1]
number	102	102	102

[1]Because of rounding, not all total percentages add up to 100.

It seems that patterns of allocation of money reflect normative assumptions about the nature of gender relationships. These expectations may be embedded in the socialization of husband or wife or both; they may be held to by the couple's social network or the local community or they may arise out of the occupational structure of the local labour market. Edwards suggested that many wives perceived their husbands as being 'rightfully' in control of family finances, and there is a substantial body of evidence testifying to the deferential dialectic in which wives are seen as subordinate to their husbands, largely because of their financial dependence (Bell and Newby 1976; Edwards 1981; Hunt 1980). Work in the USA has shown that 'contemporary' attitudes towards the female role are associated with a greater involvement by the wife in the management of family finances (Green and Cunningham 1975). British community studies have documented the ways in which the expectations of occupational cultures can be translated into patterns of allocation of money within the household: thus a strongly male occupational culture may express itself in heavy drinking after work which necessitates male control of finances, while in areas of traditional female employment women are more likely to control household finances (Dennis, Henriques, and Slaughter 1956; Humphreys 1966; Jephcott, Sear, and Smith 1962; Kerr 1958; Mays 1954; Tunstall 1962).

Conclusion

Other contributors to this book have documented the links beween inequalities within marriage and gender inequalities in the wider society. These inequalities can be mutually reinforcing. The pattern is complicated and there are many different dimensions. For example, married women gain power if they earn in their own right and this increase in power is likely to be reflected in increased control of money. On the other hand, women are also likely to control money when it is short, but this does not reflect increased power on their part so much as the decreased spending power of the household as a whole. In isolating out the separate strands of this argument money can be seen as a 'tracer' reflecting different dimensions of inequality at the same time as it reinforces these inequalities (see also Barrett and McIntosh 1982; Gillespie 1972; Pahl 1983).

A consideration of flows of money within households shows that it is misleading to regard households as single units whose members are in the same social structural position. Inequalities in the wider society tend to be translated into inequalities within marriage. Even in households where money was said to be pooled and managed jointly there were large variations in the ways in which money was perceived. A wife who was not earning was less likely to regard pooled money as being for her personal use, even though her husband might urge her to regard it as rightfully hers in recognition of her unpaid work in the home. One effect of this was shown in the amounts spent on leisure activities: on the whole wives spent less on leisure than husbands, especially at lower income levels.

There are important implications for financial arrangements when marriages break down. The fact that a substantial minority of wives report that they were 'better off' on supplementary benefit than they had been when living with their husbands suggests that disputes over the allocation of money often accompany the breakdown of a marriage. It is not clear whether the inequitable allocation of household resources is a cause or an effect of breakdown. However, the consequences are that women who are contemplating or going through with a divorce may have severe financial problems. They are likely to have used up their savings and to have been skimping for some time on expenditure on such things as clothes for themselves and the children. It is important both to settle accounts between the parties as quickly as possible and to settle accounts in a way that recognizes the less powerful financial position of wives within marriage.

Notes

1 The research on which this paper is based was funded by the Social Science Research Council and the Joseph Rowntree Memorial Trust. It was carried out between 1981 and 1983 and was based at the University of Kent. This chapter presents the first, preliminary results: more detailed and more extensive results will be available in the future.

References

Barrett, M. and McIntosh, M. (1982) *The Anti-Social Family*, London: Verso Editions.

Bell, C. and Newby, H. (1976) Husbands and Wives: The Dynamics of the Deferential Dialectic. In D. Leonard Barker and S. Allen (eds) *Dependence and Exploitation in Work and Marriage*. London: Tavistock.

Bernard, J. (1973) *The Future of Marriage*. New York: Bantam.

Binney, V., Harkell, G., and Nixon, J. (1981) *Leaving Violent Men: A Study of Refuges and Housing for Battered Women*. London: Women's Aid Federation (England).

Central Statistical Office (1980) *Social Trends No. 11*. London: HMSO

Dennis, N., Henriques, F., and Slaughter, C. (1956) *Coal Is Our Life*. London: Eyre and Spottiswoode.

Edwards, M. (1981) *Financial Arrangements within Families*. Canberra, Australia: National Women's Advisory Council.

Evason, E. (1980) *Just Me and the Kids*. Equal Opportunities Commission for Northern Ireland.
——(1982) *Hidden Violence*. Belfast: Farset Press.
Evans, J. *et al.* (1983) *Marriages and Money: Forms of Financial Arrangement within the Family*. Mimeo. University of Surrey, Department of Sociology.
Gillespie, D. (1972) Who Has the Power? The Marital Struggle. In H.P. Dreitzel (ed.) *Marriage and the Struggle of the Sexes*. New York: Collier-MacMillan.
Gray, A. (1979) The Working Class Family as an Economic Unit. In C. Harris (ed.) *The Sociology of the Family*. University of Keele, Sociological Review Monograph.
Green, R.T. and Cunningham, I.C. (1975) Feminine Role Perception and Family Purchasing Decisions. *Journal of Marketing Research* XII: 325-31.
Harris, O. (1981) Households as Natural Units. In K. Young, C. Wolkowitz, and R. McCullagh (eds) *Of Marriage and the Market*. London: CSE Books.
Houghton, H. (1973) *Separated Wives and Supplementary Benefit*. London: DHSS Social Research Branch.
Humphreys A. J. (1966) *New Dubliners: Urbanisation and the Irish Family*. London: Routledge & Kegan Paul.
Hunt, P. (1978) Cash Transactions and Household Tasks. *Sociological Review* 26 (3): 569-80.
——(1980) *Gender and Class Consciousness*. London: Macmillan.
Jephcott, P., Sear, N., and Smith, J. (1962) *Married Women Working*. London: Allen & Unwin.
Kerr, M. (1958) *The People of Ship Street*. London: Routledge & Kegan Paul.
Land, H. (1969) *Large Families in London*. London: Bell.
——(1980) The Family Wage. *Feminist Review* 6: 55-78.
——(1981) *Parity Begins at Home*. EOC/SSRC Joint Panel on Equal Opportunities. Manchester: Equal Opportunities Commission.
Marsden, D. (1969) *Mothers Alone*. Harmondsworth: Allen Lane, Penguin Press.
Mays, J.B. (1954) *Growing up in a City*. Liverpool University Press.
Pahl, J. (1978) *A Refuge for Battered Women*. London: HMSO.
——(1980) Patterns of Money Management within Marriage. *Journal of Social Policy* 9 (3): 313-35.
——(1983) The Allocation of Money and the Structuring of Inequality within Marriage. *Sociological Review* 31 (2): 237-62.

——(1984) *Private Violence and Public Policy*. London: Routledge & Kegan Paul.

Rubin, L.B. (1976) *Worlds of Pain: Life in the Working Class Family*. New York: Basic Books.

Sharma, U. (1980) *Women, Work and Property in North-West India*. London: Tavistock.

Stebbing, S. Personal communication. See also S. Stebbing (1982) Some Aspects of the Relationship between Rural Social Structure and the Female Sex Role. Thesis for University of London PhD degree.

Tunstall, J. (1962) *The Fishermen*. London: MacGibbon & Kee.

Whitehead, A. (1981) 'I'm hungry, Mum.' The Politics of Domestic budgeting. In K. Young, C. Wolkowitz, and R. McCullagh (eds) *Of Marriage and the Market*. London CSE Books.

CHAPTER 4

Legal ideologies, patriarchal precedents, and domestic violence

Michael D. A. Freeman

Introduction

In the last dozen years there has been considerable interest in the problem of violence against women (Binney, Harkell, and Nixon 1981; Borkowski, Murch, and Walker 1983; Bowker 1983; Davidson 1978; Dobash and Dobash 1980; Freeman 1979; Gelles 1974 and 1979; Langley and Levy 1977; Martin 1976; Moore 1979; Pagelow 1981; Pizzey 1979; Pizzey and Shapiro 1982; Schechter 1983; Straus, Gelles, and Steinmetz 1980; Walker 1979; Wilson 1976, 1983). One response to this concern has been the development of various legal remedies designed to provide women with protection and relief. There is, however, no indication that the legal remedies are efficacious or that they are contributing to the conquest of, what all agree is, a severe social problem. Does this reflect on the limits of effective legal action or are we faced with an ambivalent form of social deviance – a form which is not susceptible to eradication through legal means so long as the law reflects an ideology supportive of the behaviour? Can the law provide solutions to the problems of violence against women when it constitutes part of that problem? In many areas, as Klein notes, 'the law *itself* constitutes the harm' (1981:66).

This article investigates this problem using, as a case study, English law and practice, appropriately since the private ills of battered women were recognized as a public problem in England before they were recognized elsewhere (Freeman 1977; May 1978). Furthermore, remedies developed in England to tackle the problem have provided a model for other legal systems. I argue that the legal system is a cultural underpinning of patriarchy. Though mindful of the dangers of developing conspiratorial models (see Coward 1983; Rowbotham

1981), I show in this article how the English legal system is permeated by ideological considerations that express the subordination of women to the patriarchy.

The debate about violence against women needs to be removed from deliberations about strategies for social, including legal, intervention and placed firmly within the arena of sexual politics. Violence by husbands against wives should not be seen as a breakdown in the social order, as orthodox interpretations perceive it, but as an affirmation of a particular sort of social order. Looked at in this way domestic violence is not dysfunctional; quite the reverse, it appears functional. But violence against women must not be viewed as an abstract, unproblematic concept. Nor can it be taken out of its historical context and perceived as some kind of transhistorical activity. It must be considered in a particular cultural context.

The position of women in England today

In *Capitalism, the Family and Personal Life*, Zaretsky has described how the family and the familial role of women became idealized, the home became a refuge from the demands of capitalist society, 'a separate realm for the economy' (1976: 30; see also Foreman 1977) – a private place to which people, but especially men, could withdraw. In Lasch's graphic phrase, the family became a 'haven in a heartless world' (1977: 6). 'The family', Lasch has written, 'found ideological support and justification in the conception of domestic life as an emotional refuge in a cold and competitive society' (1977:6). But the home became not only a 'walled garden' but also a 'stifling menagerie' (Davidoff, L'Esperance, and Newby 1976: 163). Man became the breadwinner; his wife the dependent home-maker. The ideology encapsulated by this was adopted first by the middle classes and only later by working-class people. That we can speak of 'the family' today as a single entity is in major part the product of the gradual bourgeoisification of the working class who, as Barrett puts it, 'acknowledged the moral legitimacy of the bourgeoisie by adopting its family structure' (1980: 203; see also Flandrin 1979). Poster has described this as 'one of the unwritten aspects of the political success of bourgeois democracy' (1979: 196).

The position of women in British society today is closely related to their role within the family. An understanding of women's oppression accordingly requires a description and analysis of the position of women in today's privatized family. As McIntosh has observed, 'ultimately the very construction of men and women as separate and opposed categories takes place within, and in the terms of, the family' (1979: 154). Women are expected to be dependent on men. Their role is geared to the household. They are responsible for child care, as well as for the care of the aged and handicapped. Their domestic labour is seen as non-productive, not real work. Women, particularly married women, have to be housewives: if they do not carry out the service roles depicted here they are 'bad' housewives, but housewives nevertheless. Furthermore, as Millett notes, 'sex role is sex rank' (1969: 343). As long as woman's place is defined as separate, a 'male-dominated society will define her place as inferior' (Brown *et al*. 1971: 873).

In fact most women are also engaged in remunerative employment. For well over a century, women have constituted about one-third of the formal labour force in Great Britain; 32 per cent of women in paid employment in Britain work part-time (*Social Trends* 1984: 60). Women workers are not dispersed throughout all sectors of the economy, but are heavily concentrated in four occupational groups: clerical workers, service, sports, or recreational workers (mainly cooks, canteen assistants, and office cleaners); professional and technical workers such as teachers and nurses; and shop assistants. It is noticeable that women are over-represented in work which resembles domestic work in the house: ideological divisions within the family are reproduced in the labour market. To Alexander (1976: 59), this represents an extension of the division of labour in the patriarchal family. Nor is this new: Pinchbeck's evidence from the early Victorian period indicates similar work patterns (1977: Appendix) and Clark's *Working Life of Women in the Seventeenth Century* (1919) suggests that even where goods were being produced in the household there was a division of labour along gender lines. The ideology of gender and divisions of work tasks antedate capitalism. Capitalism is nevertheless a watershed, for it divided the work force into wage-earners and those dependent upon the wage of others. In Barrett's words, 'capitalism did not create domestic social relations in which pre-existing divisions were not only reproduced but solidified in the wage-labour system' (1980: 182). Divisions of work tasks along gender lines also exist in so-called 'socialist' countries such as the Soviet Union, Czechoslovakia (Heitlinger 1979), and China (Croll 1978).

In trying to understand the position that women occupy in the labour market as a secondary labour force (Barron and Norris 1976), it is difficult to avoid the conclusion that family structure and the ideology of domestic responsibility are significant factors. Barrett puts it this way:

'It is clear . . . that women's involvement in the highly exploited areas of part-time work and home-work is the direct consequence of their responsibility for child care. This type of work is not only most convenient for a worker with responsibility for children, it is often (in the absence of nursery or after-school provision) literally the only work available. In addition to this, the categories of work primarily undertaken by women have clearly been constructed along the lines of an ideology of gender which poses servicing and caring work as pre-eminently "feminine". Furthermore, the construction of a family form in which the male head of household is supposedly responsible for the financial support of a dependent wife and children has militated against demands for equal pay and equal "right to work" for women. The "right" of married women to take jobs at the expense of male workers has frequently been explicitly challenged .... Family responsibilities play a direct role in the structure of women's wage labour and in setting limits on women's participation.

(Barrett 1980: 157-58)

But the process is not one way. The weak position of women on the labour market has the effect of reinforcing their subordination in the home. The notion of the 'family wage' has as its concomitant female dependence. A privileged male wage has usually meant an under-privileged female one. Women's wages are generally seen as supplementary to those of husband wage-earners, even by many women themselves.

The family wage notion is usually justified in terms of the sexual division of labour. Thus, it is said to rest on a fair distribution of responsibilities between the sexes, to uphold complementarity of roles. But the sexual division of labour is, as Molyneux notes, 'more than a mere technical division in that it helps to enforce relations of domination and subordination creating structures of privilege and discrimination' (1979: 24). Women are expected to perform household duties even when they are employed on the labour market. Most are poorly paid. These two considerations together act as a deterrent to women seeking remunerative employment and encourage them to seek fulfilment in the home. Female unemployment is also frequently justified by invoking the family wage notion: family income should be provided by its 'head'. An effect of this ideology is that women are not expected to enter the labour market but to become housewives and mothers, or at best part-time workers earning 'pin-money'. Both their formal and informal education tends to be oriented toward these skills and expectations (David 1980). This in turn is reinforced by the sexual division of labour which, as already noted, allocates women in the main to jobs designed to utilize their 'natural', 'feminine' capabilities.

The law and ideological practice

Where does the legal system fit into this? How do its rules, principles, and administration reflect the practice discussed in the previous section? It is common for lawyers to believe that the law does not play an active role in regulating family relationships. 'The normal behaviour of husband and wife or parents and children towards each other', wrote Kahn-Freund, 'is beyond the law – as long as the family is healthy. The law comes in when things go wrong' (Eekelaar 1971: 7). In the same book Eekelaar wrote of 'English practice', which, he said, 'has been to refrain from formulating general principles as to how families should be managed' (1971: 76). Seven years later, he wrote in *Family Law and Social Policy* of the law's 'minor role in creating conditions which are hoped to be conducive to the successful creation of families' (Eekelaar 1978: xxvii).

This view completely distorts reality. It is clear that not only does the law serve to reproduce social order, but it actually constitutes and defines that order. The legal form is one of the main modalities of social practice through which actual relationships embodying sexual stratification have been expressed. Law defines the character and creates the institutions and social relationships within which the family operates. The legal system is constantly recreating a particular ideological view of relationships between the sexes, best expressed as an ideology of patriarchalism.

That law operates as a form of ideological practice was propagated by Marx and Engels (Cain and Hunt 1979: Chapter 4) and articulated more fully by Gramsci (1971) and Althusser (1971). Such a view has gained currency in the last decade largely through its propagation by social historians. Hay (1975), Thompson (1975), and others, as well as in the writings of critical legal theorists such as Fraser (1978) and Klare (1979). Law plays a primary and significant role in producing social order. The power of law is as a symbol. This power is based on an ideology of law and an ideology of women supported by law. Relationships between the sexes are expressed 'through the forms of law' (Thompson 1975: 262). One function of ideology is to mystify social reality and to obstruct social change. Law functions, in Gramsci's expression (Boggs 1976: 36-54), as a form of 'ideological hegemony'. For example, it states that women are dependent home-makers and this helps to induce people to consent to this state of affairs, to see it as natural, even just (Peattie and Rein 1983: Chapter 1). Because law has this effect, it acts as a powerful ideological force supportive of social stability. What the law says is so, is 'reality'. The ideology of law is additionally part of its form as a set of principles embodying a notion of rationality. For, as Gouldner has argued, 'freezing ideas and information in words makes it possible to assess more coolly and rigorously the validity of an argument' and this reinforces 'a certain kind of rationality' (1976: 41). The law in relation to women is seen to reflect a rational set of beliefs.

It is important to recognize the power of law as ideology when social engineering efforts to change the status of women are examined. Beliefs in the power of legislation or the results of litigation to effect social reform reflect the pervasive belief in law as a source of social change (see Marris and Rein 1972). But this ignores the ideological power of law to mask social reality and to obstruct real social change. Even the creation of a new corpus of rights for women, as seems to have happened with, for example, equal opportunities or abortion legislation, does not undermine basic sexual hierarchies. The passage of an Act like the Domestic Violence and Matrimonial Proceedings Act of 1976, the victory of Jennifer Davis in a highly publicized case (*Davis* v. *Johnson* 1979), the use of terms like a 'battered mistresses' charter' or 'new rights for women assaulted by their cohabitants', common after a successful piece of litigation, divert potential public consciousness away from the deeper roots of the problem. The power of law is such that by framing the issue in terms of individual rights the real problem is obscured. With domestic violence, as we shall see, the tendency has been to individualize the problem, so that social and psychological analysis has been very much in tune with legal thinking. Both have concentrated on a small sample of known batterers, on 'official deviants' (Box 1981). None of these disciplines has done much to improve the overall position of women.

Women, law, and ideology

A study of the relationship between the law and the family today gives us insight into the modern forms of patriarchy. The law both serves and legitimizes patriarchal power. Many justifications are posited for treating men and women differently in law (Okin 1979). These may rest on sex differences, but usually gender role differences are called upon to justify differential treatment. But the law itself is a major instrumental force in constructing the gender role differences themselves. 'Legal institutions support the ordering of society on a gender role basis . . . The law defines and reinforces gender roles for individuals which do not necessarily have an inevitable connection with sex differences' (O'Donovan 1979: 135). Very few of the rights and duties of husband and wife are laid down in legislation in England, but there is a consensus among lawyers, judges, and governmental bureaucrats about the legal nature of family relationships. Barker comments that 'the lack of specification reflects the totality of the relationship . . . and that it is a relationship of *personal* dependency' (1978: 242). 'Women cannot at one and the same time be married as we understand marriage, and independent,' Wilson (1977: 153) observes, speaking of the cohabitation rule as a particular instance of this 'general principle'.

Women are supposed to be dependent and to lack power and control over themselves. Their domestic work is seen as non-productive. There are ideals to which 'a good wife' must conform. Her status, her standard of living, her expectations, her life-style, and much of her identity are governed by her husband, even by her cohabitant as the law gradually assimilates the rights and obligations of quasi-marital relationships to those of marriage (Freeman and Lyon 1983). Married women are not autonomous individuals, but are defined in legal institutions in terms of marriage.

There is no better illustration of this relationship, particularly since it demonstrates direct intrusion by the state apparatus, than in fiscal policies (Lister 1980) and social security arrangements (Allatt 1981). These affect the economic dependence of women at every turn. Men and women are not treated equally. Both are stereotyped and discrimination is a necessary concomitant, for women do not fit the female stereotype upon which such laws and other institutional arrangements are predicated. Assumptions about the place of married women derive from economic and demographic concerns of the 1930s (Land 1976), though they are rooted in an ideology that developed with industrialization in the nineteenth century. The woman's place is in the home, and this 'cult of domesticity' is supported throughout in the tax and social security systems.

The law in Britain relating to national insurance, pensions, supplementary benefit, sickness and unemployment benefit, family income supplement, and income tax are all based on stereotypical sex classifications that impute a dependent role to women. The system assumes that women's earnings are supplementary to the male breadwinner's, and women and children dependent on the man's income. The social security system strengthens the subordinate position of women as domestic workers inside the family and as a secondary labour force outside it. They are, even with recent reforms, largely excluded from independent rights to benefits because they are assumed to be dependent on their husband's income. Women not conforming to the norm of dependence on men are often relegated to a low level of benefits. At the same time, social security policies nurture the position of women as low-paid, casual, or part-time workers, or even home-workers with low pay and insecurity. Parker and Land have commented that 'in reading the social security legislation it would be hard to deduce that the "typical" family consisting of a man in full-time employment, the woman as a full-time housewife, and two dependent children has been at any point a minority of families' (1978: 342). In fact, few families conform to this stereotype.

In reality many women are not dependent on men. Some are wage-earners who do not need men to support them; and many widows, separated and divorced women, and unmarried mothers do not have and may not want men to support them. But, as Ginsburg notes, 'support of these women by the state has been such as to encourage, if possible, the renewal of dependence on men and to discourage the break-up of marriage by rendering single motherhood less eligible and attractive' (1979: 79). Unsupported women (that is, those not barred by the cohabitation rule) tend to fall back on supplementary benefit but supplementary benefit authorities, and before them the poor law, have consistently attempted to shift the burden of support from the state (or parish) to 'liable relatives'. They have attempted to re-establish economic dependence on husbands and fathers. In fact the authorities have had little success. Thus, the cost to the state of providing benefits where there were 'liable relatives' was £486 million in 1978 and only £35½ million of this sum was recovered from 'liable relatives' (Supplementary Benefits Commission 1979: table 12.8). Not surprisingly, many women are not especially co-operative in helping the authorities to establish paternity or locate a separated husband. The invitation to re-establish dependence is quite properly rejected by many women. This is not entirely true, for when a marriage breaks up there are implicit pressures on a woman to remarry. Having been (if that is the case) a housewife for a number of years, a woman has decreasing value on the labour market. Thus, as Delphy has noted:

'from the woman's standpoint, marriage creates the conditions for its own continuation and encourages entry into a second marriage if a particular union comes to an end. . . . For the majority of women the contrast between the standard of living that they enjoy while married and that which they can expect after divorce simply redoubles the pressures in favour of marriage or remarriage depending on the circumstances.'

(Delphy 1976: 81)

The roots of the social security system are embedded in the Beveridge Report published during the Second World War. Women were not treated equally in this report. Man and wife were seen 'as a team' (Beveridge 1942: 45). The married woman was to be treated as a dependent of her husband, and as entitled to economic support by him, both for herself and their children. Thus, it was argued that 'it should be open to any married woman to undertake [paid employment] as an exempt person, paying no contribution of her own and acquiring no claim to benefit in unemployment or sickness' (Beveridge 1942: 50). Those who opted to contribute were to receive benefits at a reduced rate. For Beveridge, 'maternity [was] the principal object of marriage' (1942: 50) and his proposal that maternity benefits should be higher than normal unemployment or disability benefits (as Wilson notes, 'reproduction was . . . tacitly defined as a disability' (1977: 151)) was adopted by the legislature in 1948, though repealed in 1953. Beveridge's conception of the family 'articulated ideas which already commanded a good deal of support' (Harris 1977: 415).

A number of Beveridge's initiatives have succumbed to recent reforms. Women entering employment now have to pay full contributions and can receive full benefits. The new state pension scheme has introduced protected state pension rights for women: years of 'home responsibility' count as contribution years. There are new maternity rights for women though these are mainly conditional on contributions, continuity, and hours of employment – thus excluding the majority of mothers from them. But increasing formal recognition of equality can obscure discriminatory structures which continue to exist.

For all the reforms, the social security system still embodies the concept of women's dependence on men and emphasizes their maternal and domestic duties. Countless examples remain, two of which will be examined. The most notorious principle of the social security system is the cohabitation rule. It has been described by Ginsburg as 'the implicit reinforcement of patriarchy within the social security system' (1979: 87). The rule – which applies to a wide range of benefits, though criticism tends to centre on its application to supplementary benefits, where it is policed most stringently – states that where a husband and wife live together as members of the same household their requirements and resources shall be aggregated and treated as the husband's. Only he then may claim the relevant benefits. Though this is susceptible to criticism, it is the extension of the rule to men and women who 'live together as a man and wife' that has provoked most censure (Lister 1970). What is meant by 'cohabitation' is not defined in statute or case law. A number of considerations are taken into account in determining whether a man and a woman are living together as man and wife, though more than a lurking suspicion remains that the primary consideration in the minds of officials and investigators is a sexual relationship between the couple. The now defunct Supplementary Benefits Commission itself admitted that 'in the last resort, it is a matter of personal judgement' (DHSS 1971: para. 15).

The cohabitation rule is symptomatic of the ideology structuring family relationships, for it assumes that if a man lives with a woman he supports her. The rule is often justified on the basis that an unmarried couple should not get more favourable treatment than a married man and his wife would. This is in many ways a boot strap argument for it assumes and does not question that marriage should contain a breadwinner and a dependent. In this sense the removal of the cohabitation rule would reveal starkly the dependence and inequality inherent in the marriage relationship. This aside, the way the rule operates, a married woman is treated 'more favourably' than her cohabiting sister. The rule puts women, who are often in tenuous personal and economic circumstances, into a position where it is difficult for them to establish stable and viable relationships with men. It subjects them to widespread invasions of privacy from those policing the system. It is thoroughly anomalous. A man has no obligation to maintain a woman with whom he is living, even if he has fathered children by her, though he may be compelled to support any such children through affiliation payments. A cohabiting woman has no legal means of compelling support. On the other hand, a married man gets a tax allowance for his wife, irrespective of whether there are dependent children: a man receives no tax allowance for the woman with whom he cohabits. The cohabitation rule succours the institution of marriage (in itself a strange moral argument), but undoubtedly also reinforces the ideology of dependence which so permeates the legal system and its administration.

A second example of arrangements that embody notions of dependence is to be found in several statutory provisions governing tax and social security. As already indicated, a married man gets a tax allowance for his wife. It is assumed that a wife 'or some female person' should care for that man's children and do his housework. An additional personal allowance is paid where wives are incapacitated. But married women with incapacitated husbands are denied this additional allowance. As O'Donovan has noted:

'The allowance reflects the assumption that it is a married woman's unpaid job to care for children and that if she cannot do so, her husband is entitled to financial assistance for someone else to perform the job. In contrast, a woman on her own, even if working, is not considered by the courts as in need of an allowance for a substitute childminder'.

(O'Donovan 1979: 145-46)

Similar examples can be found in other social security provisions. The invalid care allowance is not paid to married women. This can only be because they are expected to do such work without compensation. Where additions for adult dependents are given to those who get the allowance, these are limited to a wife or 'some female person . . . who . . . has care of a child or children of the beneficiary's family' (Social Security Act 1975, s.37 (3)): in other words, a male dependent caring for children is excluded. It is also notable, though perfectly consistent with a system which emphasizes women's domestic duties, that a disabled married woman is not eligible for the non-contributory invalidity pension 'except where she is incapable of performing normal household duties' (Social Security Act 1975, s.37 (2)). This test has been described as an 'unjust and illogical anachronism,' (Glendinning 1980: 13). The assumption behind the 'household duties' test is that a married woman is by definition a 'housewife', who is dependent on her bread-winner husband for financial support and whose contribution to the family is the unpaid work she does in the home. Indeed, the 1974 British Government white paper which first proposed a non-contributory invalidity pension for married women says as much (*Social Security Provision for Chronically Sick and Disabled People* 1974). The retention of the 'normal household duties' test is virtually impossible to defend but it limps on, as one of the most stereotypically sexist of social security provisions (Equal Opportunities Commission 1981).

These examples illustrate the way in which fiscal policies and social security arrangements impose a particular structural form, patriarchy, on social relationships between men and women. Sachs discusses the reasoning used by the judiciary in the nineteenth and early twentieth centuries to deny women rights to participate in the professions and in public affairs and demonstrates the use of a strikingly similar ideology. For sixty years the judiciary strongly denied that women were 'persons'. Accordingly, they were denied voting rights, rights to higher education, and other rights. The judges even accepted the absurd argument that 'women were persons for the purpose of legal disabilities but non-persons for the purpose of legal rights' (Sachs 1976: 107). A reversal came in 1929 (*Edwards* v. *A.-G. for Canada* 1930). Sachs (1976: 114) suggests that there is no explanation of the change in terms of judicial reasoning, in 'legal logic'. He and Wilson argue that 'a study of sexism in the legal systems of Britain and the United States . . . explodes the notion that legal systems evolve according to inherent principles of logic and procedure'. They continue:

> 'the structures of the law were part of the wider social structures rather than apart from them. The inequality in public life which the women complained about was as present inside the legal system as outside of it, while the stake which the male judges had in maintaining gender exclusiveness was in some ways more direct than any interest they might have had in maintaining race or class inequality.'
>
> (Sachs and Wilson 1978: 225)

They show how it was the prevailing concept of 'womanhood' that determined how the courts would decide the arguments. The judges put forward a theory of sexual complementarity. Sachs and Wilson argue that this was 'merely a gracious way of explaining subjection' (1978: 52). The judges couched their language, their justifying reasoning in terms of refinement, decorum, and delicacy. They stressed that women were not being deprived so much as exempted. They claimed to be endorsing women's favoured position as elevated spiritual beings. The exemption was said to be based on respect. The clearest statement of this comes in Willes J.'s judgement in the notorious Manchester voters' case, *Chorlton* v. *Longs* (1869). 'Far from being impartial arbiters,' Pearson and Sachs argue, '... the Judges appear to have been part of the very problem the women and their male supporters were complaining about . . . the judges believed in the principle of gender exclusiveness, and said as much, both on and off the Bench' (1980: 401).

The bias in the 'persons' cases that glares at us today was just as clearly impartial justice to the judges and the majority of society 100 years ago. 'What was self-evident truth to feminists, however, was manifest absurdity to most judges' (Sachs and Wilson 1978: 6). How, then, is this particular change to be explained? Sachs argues that 'what had altered was the ideology of the Judges' (1976: 108). It is not necessary here to examine why this had altered. But what the history of the male monopoly cases puts beyond question is the way that judicial reasoning both reflected dominant male interests (it was, for example, important for middle-class men and their status position to have an unemployed wife) and reinforced patriarchalism.

It is not unusual for judicial modes of reasoning to define issues in terms favourable to dominant groups. There can be few better examples of this than Lord Denning's reasoning in the leading divorce case of *Wachtel* v. *Wachtel* in 1973. Earlier, in a lecture at Liverpool University, he had warned of the dangers of women being given equality. He had pointed to, what he saw as, the Roman example (Denning 1960) (see further Freeman 1984). In *Wachtel* v. *Wachtel*, Lord Denning defended the resuscitation of the 'one-third rule' as a starting point for the reallocation of assets on divorce in this way:

'When a marriage breaks up, there will thenceforward be two households instead of one. The husband will have to go out to work all day and must get some woman to look after the house – either a wife, if he re-marries, or a housekeeper, if he does not. He will also have to provide maintenance for the children. The wife will not usually have so much expense. She may go out to work herself, but she will not usually employ a housekeeper. She will do most of the housework herself, perhaps with some help. In any case, when there are two households, the greater expense will, in most cases, fall on the husband than the wife.'

(*Wachtel* v. *Wachtel* 1973: 94)

Of course, this reasoning is totally unrealistic. Most men whose marriages founder do not employ housekeepers. And, even if this argument were relevant, it would not explain why wives are not allowed the value of their housekeeping services. The fact that a wife will not employ a housekeeper hardly seems a justification for cutting down on her share. Lord Denning's reasoning makes a number of assumptions and none of them is right. First, that all women perform household duties and that no men do housework. Second, that only fathers maintain their children. Mothers who do not take remunerative employment, do so in kind rather than in cash. Indeed, they often forgo paid employment and lose promotion to do so. Third, that housework is not real work.

Lord Denning is the most influential of contemporary English judges (see Jowell and McAuslan 1984). He thinks, as do much of the public, that his decisions are some form of 'wives' charter' (Denning 1980). It is as well to remind ourselves of Thompson's insight that 'the dominated and oppressed have often perceived their grievances in legal terms and articulated their needs and interests in terms of rights thought to be promised or owed by law'. In fact, he adds, rather wryly, 'some of them had the impertinence, and the imperfect sense of historical perspective, to expect justice' (1975: 268). Thompson is making the point, expressed throughout this section, that if law is to be effective in its function as ideology it must appear to be just. Indeed, he notes that this cannot be the case where it does not uphold 'its own logic and criteria of equity; indeed, on occasion, by actually *being* just' (1975: 263).

Lord Denning's reasoning in *Wachtel* v. *Wachtel* was not 'just', though other parts of his judgement dealing with a woman's contribution to the welfare of the family and his comments on the effect of adultery on financial provision are instances of actual justice, in Thompson's terms. Lord Denning's reasoning otherwise is an apt example of what Barker (1978) has called 'repressive benevolence'. There have been a number of reforms in the recent past. For example, the duty to maintain now is mutual. But this, like many other changes, remains only formal until women are given substantial equality. Even today, the law refuses to intervene in a married couple's financial relationship when they are living together. It supports the notion that the husband sets the standard of living. The wife, in other words, may be a dependent, but the legal system shows marked reluctance to afford her economic protection during marriage. Conditions of domestic production remain outside the purview of the law.

A limited exception is the rule contained in s. 1 of the Married Women's Property Act 1964 that money derived from an allowance given to the wife by the husband or anything bought with that allowance is shared equally by the spouses. The Act only applies if the housekeeping allowance is provided by the husband. Cases have indicated that if the wife gives her money to her husband for use in the home, she is deemed to give it to him as the head of the family, so that the money becomes his (*Edward* v. *Cheyne* 1888; *Re Young* 1913). It is doubtful, to say the least, that the courts would take such a view today though the cases remain interesting for their ideological assumptions. But it is not only the gender assumption of the 1964 Act that invites critical comment. It is also significant that the Act, despite these assumptions, does nothing to compel a husband to make his wife any allowance. It concentrates instead on penalizing a thrifty wife by compelling her to share half of what she saves, or buys with what she saves, with her husband. In past times women managed the domestic economy (Tilly and Scott 1978). The allowance system itself is thus a relatively recent innovation. The 1964 Act now enshrines it.

Many more examples could be given to illustrate the point. More significant is the fact that in England today (and English law is not untypical) there is but one type of marriage. Its nature is not negotiable. Rights and obligations are fixed by operation of the law, not by agreement between the parties. Weitzman (1974: 1170) has, with considerable justification, described the conception of a single structure for all marriages as 'tyrannical'. I view with some alarm the increasing tendency to treat cohabitation as if it were marriage. It seems that many who avoid marriage because of its ideological notions of subordination and dependence find the consequences attaching to marriage thrust on them whether they like it or not. It is almost as if women were being told that they were not allowed to escape by cohabiting. The extension to relationships outside marriage of 'marriage type' law merely reinforces the outmoded views discussed in this section and transfers their application to settings where they are even less appropriate (Freeman and Lyon 1983). However, it is common to find arguments which support such an extension based on the idea that such an assimilation will protect cohabitants, especially female cohabitants. One of the main 'functions' of family law is often said to be its 'protective function' (Eekelaar 1978: 44). The ideological assumptions underlying protection are worth examining.

Stang-Dahl and Snare (1978) regard claims that the law is a protector of women's integrity as a myth. Referring to the state's role, they use the suggestive phrase the 'coercion of privacy' (1978: 8-26). They see the family as a private prison for women. The state, they argue, need not use formal methods of repression and control when women are constrained by a more primary and informal control within the family. The relegation of women to the private sector, documented in Stang-Dahl and Snare's article, is significant also as it becomes an alternative to granting women greater public rights. Sachs, whose exposure of the myth of male protectiveness has been referred to, draws attention to this idea in his discussion of the Married Women's Property Act of 1882. This allowed married women to retain control over their own property. Sachs argues convincingly that:

'the law went some way towards protecting wives from being abused inside the home; it did not create opportunities for them to be useful outside the home. A curb on spending by husbands was not the same as a licence to earn independently by wives. Thus the destiny of woman as wife rather than as independent person was enhanced rather than reduced by the Act.'

(Sachs and Wilson 1978: 137)

The question must be raised as to whether law protects or controls women. The analogy with measures to protect children, for example, the invention of the juvenile court (Platt 1969) or intelligence testing (Mercer 1974: 328-44), looms large far too often. Child-saving has been a cloak to control a 'problem population' (Spitzer 1975: 642). The Victorian conservative judge, Stephen, understood the meaning of protection. In his mind, 'submission and protection' were 'cor-relative'. 'Withdraw the one,' he argued in *Liberty, Equality, Fraternity*, 'and the other is lost, and force will assert itself a hundred times more harshly through the law of contract then ever it did through the law of status' (Stephen 1873: 289).

Hanmer (1978) has shown how violence or its threat is used to control women both within and outside the home. Women, for example, are taught to avoid certain areas. 'Urban space for women is compartmentalised, to deviate from women's allocated space is to run the risk of attack by men' (1978: 228). The fear of violence, particularly rape, has the effect of driving women to seek protection from men, of making them dependent. There is a certain irony here for women are supposed to feel safer in the company of husbands and boyfriends though the evidence suggests that they are more likely to be attacked or raped by them than by the dangerous strangers whom they are taught to fear. 'Chivalry', Griffin has noted, 'is an age-old protection racket which depends for its existence on rape' (1971: 28). She equates it with the sort of relationship the Mafia established with small businessmen in the United States earlier in this century.

The problematic nature of protection is forcefully to the fore in legislation regulating employment conditions of women (and children), which is usually called 'protective legislation'. Whom does this legislation protect? It was introduced in the nineteenth-century 'reform era', not in all areas of work but rather, it has been argued (Alexander 1976), in areas where women competed with male workers. Coyle has called protective legislation a 'protection racket'. It did not

> 'bring women equal pay, it did not bring equality and it has not provided adequate protection at work . . . The very existence of legislation serves as a recognition of . . . inequality . . . The problem with the current legislation is that it does not genuinely 'protect' women but rather operates paternalistically to reinforce women's conditions of inequality'.
>
> (Coyle 1980: 10)

Why was protective legislation passed? Indeed, why was it that when challenged in the USA it was upheld as constitutional when similar restrictions on male labour were held to violate constitutional rights of personal liberty and liberty of contract?

On the face of it limiting the hours of female labour was not in the immediate interests of capital. But it was of concern that if women were worked too hard they would be unable to produce the next generation of workers. No individual firm would benefit from stopping the exploitation of female labour, 'but the state under pressure from the Ten Hours movement, as well as from elements of the bourgeoisie, was able to restrict hours of work, especially for women and children' (McIntosh 1978: 262). The state, in other words, as the 'ideal collectivity of capitals', had to concede limitations on hours of work to ensure the reproduction of labour power.

Another interpretation of the emergence of protective legislation, sometimes posed as an alternative view and sometimes as a supplementary one, stresses that such legislation was supportive of the interests of male workers. It suggests that working men were fearful that women, being cheaper and more pliable, would infiltrate industry, taking men's jobs and lowering rates of pay for all. Not only would this be a disaster in terms of men's position within commodity production but it would also liberate women from dependence on men and obliterate gender labour divisions in the home. Hartmann argues that women and children in the labour force 'undermined authority relations'. She continues:

> 'Not only were women "cheap competition" but working women were their very wives, who could not "serve two masters" . . . While the problem of cheap competition could have been solved by organising the wage-earning women and youths, the problem of disrupted family life could not be. Men reserved union protection for men and argued for protective labour laws for women and children.' (Hartmann 1980: 15-16)

On the other hand, as Humphries (1981) shows in her study of the 1842 Mines Regulation Act, which she agrees may be an atypical instance, hewers neither individually nor collectively feared competition from female labour and many had an interest in the retention of female and child labour underground as it increased their family's income. Despite this 'male colliers almost universally wanted state intervention to regulate the labour of women and children, and the overwhelming majority of hewers believed that women should be prohibited from working below ground' (1981: 15). She also shows that the other strand in the Hartmann (Hartmann and Markusen 1980) 'patriarchy first' approach, which emphasizes patriarchal privileges in having wives at home, is inconsistent with the realities of collier life. 'Existing theorisations', she concludes, 'have proven inadequate to the understanding of an important historical example.' Her conclusions are rather negative though she draws attention to the contradiction between the exploitation of women workers and the sex role standards prevailing among the bourgeoisie, 'themselves conditions of existence of the *sexual* oppression of women within that class' (Humphries 1981: 28). In so far as this might suggest that the legislation supports the transformation of working-class family structure to something like that found in the bourgeoisie, it reinforces a view presented earlier in this article.

Protective employment legislation is likely to disappear quite soon. In 1979 the British Equal Opportunities Commission (EOC) submitted a report to the Government proposing the removal of much of it governing the conditions of work for women, though retaining it for young people. It argues:

> 'that the hours of work legislation constitutes a barrier – often an artificial one – to equal pay and job opportunities for women. So long as this legislation remains as it is at present, women as workers will be disadvantaged. Therefore we cannot accept the retention of legislation in its present form, because discrimination will continue to arise out of it.
>
> (Equal Opportunities Commission 1979b: 92)

Unfortunately, a number of matters are not unquestioned by the EOC. For example, their report 'poses the question of shift work as a choice for women to make, rather than recognising the economic circumstances which *force* people into the night shift' (Coyle 1980: 7). There is a strong case for making work conditions equal by extending protective legislation to male workers but that is not a likely reform.

Domestic Violence

This is the context within which domestic violence must be located. But it has not been understood in this way by the majority of those investigating the problem or those engaged in finding solutions to it. The result has been that 'solutions' remain superficial. Responses hitherto have made few inroads into the problem.

The most common interpretations of domestic violence individualize it (considered in Freeman 1979). They emphasize that men are violent toward the women with whom they live 'because of some internal aberration, abnormality or defective characteristic' (Gelles and Straus 1979: 561). These characteristics are variegated but include inadequate self-control, often linked to problems of alcoholism, psychopathic personality types, and various undifferentiated types of mental illness. The research tends to look for 'inner traits' rather than social or cultural context. A second view of marital violence attributes it to stress, frustration, and blocked goals. It assumes an uneven distribution of the deviance in the social structure, with violence being more common among those in lower socio-economic strata. The precise causal relationship between the stresses caused by economic conditions and domestic violence is not analysed. The lives of the poor are, of course, more susceptible to public scrutiny and social intervention than those of middle-class people who are better able to preserve their privacy. This theory of wife battering also individualizes the problem. The psycho-pathological model gave us 'sick people'; the environmental stress model posits instead 'a sick society' (McGrath 1979: 17). Both, however, privatize the violent event.

It is of course true that only certain violence is recognized as such. Klein has noted that 'a man's laying hands on a woman can be seen as necessary discipline, proof of manhood, a felony or hideous sin, depending on the relationship (wife, slave, stranger) which itself is socially constructed' (1979: 28). It is a fact of some significance, though one frequently neglected, that some violence against women is regarded as legitimate and not deviant at all. This is the case also with violence against children, for corporal punishment is culturally sanctioned in most societies. Ariès (1962) has shown how, at the time when the conception of childhood evolved, being subject to the infliction of corporal punishment was a badge of inferior status. Dobash and Dobash (1980) have traced the relationship between the growth of the nuclear family and the chastisement of wives. They describe (1980: 56) the period from the sixteenth century until the nineteenth as the 'great age of flogging'. Flogging was used throughout society 'as a means of controlling the powerless: children, women and the lower classes'. Wife beating was acceptable and widespread. At common law a husband was said to have the legal right to beat his wife. The expression 'rule of thumb' is thought to have derived from the belief that he could only use a stick of the thickness of his thumb. Blackstone's rationalization saw a correlativity between the husband having to be answerable for his wife's misbehaviour and his having the power of restraining her by 'domestic chastisement, in the same moderation that a man is allowed to correct his apprentice or children, for whom the master or parent is also liable in some cases to answer' (1765: 444).

Blackstone's formulation was the guide when the first American states formed their wife beating laws in the early nineteenth century. They have since repealed them. In England domestic chastisement is obsolete, though no statute has ever as such repealed the privilege. But throughout the century there are dicta from judges and magistrates affirming its continued existence (Freeman 1979: 178). Most recently, a sheriff in Scotland, having fined a husband for hitting his wife in the face, is reported as having remarked, 'It is a well known fact that you can strike you wife's bottom if you wish, but you must not strike her on the face.' He expressed support for the ancient principle that 'reasonable chastisement should be the duty of every husband when his wife misbehaves' (*Ms*, August 1975: 4).

It is not merely that wives have long been legitimate victims of domestic chastisement. They have been, and remain in England today, liable to forced sexual intercourse by their husbands, which in law is not regarded as rape (Freeman 1981: 8). John Stuart Mill commented on this over 100 years ago that

> 'a female slave has (in Christian countries) an admitted right . . . to refuse to her master the last familiarity. Not so the wife [whose husband] can claim from her and enforce the lowest degradation of a human being, that of being made the instrument of an animal function contrary to her inclination.'
>
> (John Stuart Mill 1869: 32)

So long as marital rape is considered legitimate, it is difficult to see how violence against women in the home can ever be eliminated. There is now a proposal in England to qualify the husband's immunity from prosecution. Marital rape, it is proposed, is to become a crime but only where the spouses are living separately (Criminal Law Revision Committee 1984). The Committee in its working paper of 1980 had suggested that a prosecution should require authorization from the Director of Public Prosecutions but this proposal has been dropped. Marital rape is still to be regarded as different from other rape: as such the proposal may be criticized.

Attitudes described here permeate not just the courts but the helping professions and the police as well. According to Nichols, case-workers often uphold a position that 'supports a belief that the wife encourages, provokes or even enjoys abusive treatment' (1976: 27). As far as the police are concerned, what they tend to call euphemistically 'domestic disturbances' take up considerable time and the 'role of the police is a negative one. We are,' the Association of Chief Police Officers told the House of Commons Select Committee on Violence in Marriage, 'after all dealing with persons bound in marriage, and it is important, for a host of reasons, to maintain the unity of the spouses.' They go on to express their approval of the provision of refuges for battered wives, but add 'every effort should be made to re-unite the family' (House of Commons 1974-75: 366, 369). They and many social workers also seem to take it for granted that preserving family relationships is a desirable goal. Often it seems that social workers particularly are concerned that a family should be kept together for the sake of the children. Many helping professionals are imbued with a belief that an intact family is preferable to a broken one regardless of the quality of the relationship within it.

Conclusion

Violence against wives has been described by a leading English judge (Sir George Baker in *Davis* v. *Johnson* 1979: 283) as 'domestic hooliganism'. There is no evidence that it is more prevalent today than in the past. But contemporary society recognizes it as a problem. It looks to the legislature, the courts, the helping professions, and the police to root it out. Some contemporary observers, Pizzey being a prime example, see the remedy as lying with the medical profession and not, for example, in courts of law because, she argues, 'the men act instinctively, not rationally' (House of Commons 1974-75: 2). But given the position of women in society the behaviour of violent husbands is rational, if extreme. It is not necessary for husbands to have formal rights such as to chastise their wives. That they once had this right and exercised it is sufficient. It helped to form and then to reinforce an ideology of subordination and control of women. The ideology remains imbricated in the legal system even if one of its grosser manifestations has virtually disappeared. Wife battering remains one of its legacies and if this too is to go the ideology must be dismantled. The legal system has been committed to a patriarchal ideology. It is this that must be challenged if violence against women is to diminish and ultimately to cease. It is a challenge for which resistance can be expected, for the stakes are high and there are considerable vested interests in the *status quo*. Success is important for through it will come improvement of the position of women in the home, in the economy, and in society in general.

References

Alexander, S. (1976) Women's Work in Nineteenth Century London: A Study of the Years 1820–50. In J. Mitchell and A. Oakley (eds) *The Rights and Wrongs of Women*. Harmondsworth: Penguin.
Allatt. P. (1981) Stereotyping: Familism in the Law. In B. Fryer *et.al.* (eds) *Law, State and Society*. London: Croom Helm.

Althusser, L. (1971); Ideology and Ideological State Apparatuses. In *Lenin and Philosophy and Other Essays*. London: New Left Books.

Ariès, P. (1962) *Centuries of Childhood* (translated from French). London: Jonathan Cape.

Barker, D.L. (1978) The Regulation of Marriage: Repressive Benevolence. In G. Littlejohn, J. Wakeford, B. Smart, and N. Yuval-Davis (eds) *Power and the State*. London: Croom Helm.

Barrett, M. (1980) *Women's Oppression Today*. London: Verso Books.

Barron, R. and Norris, G. (1976) Sexual Divisions and the Dual Labour Market. In D.L. Barker and S. Allen (eds) *Dependence and Exploitation in Work and Marriage*. Harlow: Longman.

Beveridge, Sir W. (1942) *Social Insurance and Allied Services*. Cmd 6404. London: HMSO.

Binney, V. Harkell, G., and Nixon J. (1981) *Leaving Violent Men*. London: WAF, England.

Blackstone, Sir W. (1765) *Commentaries on the Law of England*. London: Tegg.

Boggs, C. (1976) *Gramsci's Marxism*. London: Pluto Press.

Borkowski, M., Murch, M., and Walker, V. (1983) *Marital Violence*. London: Tavistock.

Bowker, L. (1983) *Beating Wife-Beating*. Lexington: Lexington Books.

Box, S. (1981) *Deviance, Reality and Society*. London: Holt, Rinehart & Winston.

Brown, B., Emerson, T.I., Falk, G., and Freedman, A.E. (1971) The Equal Rights Amendment: A Constitutional Basis for Equal Rights for Women. *Yale Law Journal* 80: 891–985.

Cain, M. and Hunt, A. (1979) *Marx and Engels on Law*. London: Academic Press.

Clark, A. (1919) *Working Life of Women in the Seventeenth Century*. London: G. Routledge.

Coward, R. (1983) *Patriarchal Precedents*. London: Routledge & Kegan Paul.

Coyle, A. (1980) The Protection Racket. *Feminist Review* 4: 1-12.

Criminal Law Revision Committee (1984) *Sexual Offences*, 15th Report, Cmnd 9213. London: HMSO.

Croll, E. (1978) *Feminism and Socialism in China*. London: Routledge & Kegan Paul.

David, M. (1980) *The State, The Family and Education*. London: Routledge & Kegan Paul.

Davidoff, L., L'Esperance, J., and Newby, H. (1976) Landscape with Figures: Home and Community in English Society. In J. Mitchell and

A. Oakley (eds) *The Rights and Wrongs of Women*. Harmondsworth: Penguin.

Davidson, T. (1978) *Conjugal Crime*. New York: Ballantine.

Delphy, C. (1976) Continuities and Discontinuities in Marriage and Divorce In D.L. Barker and S. Allen (eds) *Sexual Divisions and Society*. London: Tavistock.

——(1977) *The Main Enemy* (translated from French). London: Women's Research and Resources Centre.

Denning, Lord (1980) *The Due Process of Law*. London: Butterworths.

——(1960) *The Equality of Women*. Liverpool: Liverpool University Press.

Dobash, R. and Dobash, R. (1980) *Violence Against Wives*. Shepton Mallett: Open Books.

DHSS (1971) *Cohabitation*, Report by the Supplementary Benefits Commission. London: HMSO.

Eekelaar, J. (1971) *Family Security and Family Breakdown*, Harmondsworth: Penguin.

——(1978) *Family Law and Social Policy*. London: Weidenfeld & Nicolson.

Equal Opportunities Commission (1979a) *Third Annual Report*. London: HMSO.

——(1979b) *Report on Health and Safety Legislation: Should We Distinguish Between Men and Women?* London: HMSO.

——(1981) *Behind Closed Doors*. London: HMSO.

Flandrin, J.-L. (1979) *Families in Former Times* (translated from French). London: Cambridge University Press.

Foreman, A. (1977) *Femininity as Alienation*. London: Pluto Press.

Fraser, A. (1978) The Legal Theory We Need Now. *Socialist Review* 40-1:147-88,

Freeman, M.D.A. (1977) Le Vice Anglais? – Wife Battering in English and American Law. *Family Law Quarterly* 11: 199-251.

——(1979) *Violence in the Home – A Socio-Legal Study*. Farnborough: Gower Press.

——(1981) But if You Can't Rape Your Wife, Who[m] Can You Rape? *Family Law Quarterly* 15: 1–29.

——(1984) Family Matters. In J. Jowell and J. McAuslan (eds) *Lord Denning and the Law*. London: Sweet & Maxwell.

Freeman, M.D.A. and Lyon, C.M. (1983) *Cohabitation Without Marriage: An Essay in Law and Social Policy*. Aldershot: Gower Press.

Gelles, R. (1974) *The Violent Home*. Beverly Hills: Sage.

——(1979) *Family Violence*. Beverly Hills: Sage.

Gelles, R. and Straus, M. (1979) Determinants of Violence in the Family: Toward a Theoretical Integration. In W.R. Burr and R. Hill (eds) *Contemporary Theories About the Family – Research-Based Theories*. New York: Free Press.

Ginsburg, N. (1979) *Class, Capital and Social Policy*. London: Macmillan.

Glendinning, C. (1980) *After Working All These Years*. London: The Disability Alliance.

Gouldner, A.W. (1976) *The Dialectic of Ideology and Technology: The Origins, Grammar and Future of Ideology*. London: Macmillan.

Gramsci, A. (1971) *Prison Notebooks* (translated from Italian). London: Lawrence and Wishart.

Griffin, S. (1971) Rape – the All-American Crime. *Ramparts* 10: 26-35.

Hanmer, J. (1978) Violence and the Social Control of Women. In G. Littlejohn, B. Smart, J. Wakeford, and N. Yuval-Davis (eds) *Power and the State*. London: Croom Helm.

Harris, J. (1977) *William Beveridge: A Biography*. Oxford: Oxford University Press.

Hartmann, H. (1976) Capitalism, Patriarchy and Sex Segregation. *Signs* 1: 137-70.

——(1980) The Unhappy Marriage of Marxism and Feminism: Towards a More Progressive Union. *Capital and Class* 7: 1-33.

Hartmann, H. and Markusen, A.R. (1980) Contemporary Marxist Theory and Practice. *Review of Radical and Political Economists*.

Hay, D. (1975) Property, Authority and Criminal Law. In D. Hay, P. Linebaugh, J.G. Rule, E.P. Thompson, and C. Winslow (eds) *Albion's Fatal Tree*. London: Allen Lane.

Heitlinger, A. (1979) *Women and State Socialism: Sex Inequality in the Soviet Union and Czechoslovakia*. London: Macmillan.

Home Office (1980) *Criminal Law Revision Committee Working Paper on Sexual Offences*. London: HMSO.

House of Commons (1974-75) *Select Committee on Violence in Marriage*. HC 553. London: HMSO.

Humphries, J. (1981) Protective Legislation, the Capitalist State and Working Class Men: The Case of the 1842 Mines Regulation Act. *Feminist Review* 7: 1-33.

Hunt, A. (1968) *A Survey of Women's Unemployment*. London: HMSO; Office of Population Censuses and Surveys.

Jowell, J. and McAuslan, J. (eds) (1984) *Lord Denning: The Judge and the Law*. London: Sweet & Maxwell.

Klare, K. (1979) Law-making as Praxis. *Telos* 40: 123-35.

Klein, D. (1979) Can This Marriage Be Saved? Battery and Sheltering. *Crime and Social Justice* 12: 19-33.

——(1981) Violence Against Women: Some Considerations Regarding Its Causes and Elimination. *Crime and Delinquency* 27: 64-80.

Land, H. (1976) Women: Supporters or Supported? In D.L. Barker and S. Allen (eds) *Sexual Divisions and Society*. London: Tavistock.

——(1980) Social Policies and the Family: Their Effect on Women's Paid Employment in Great Britain. In R.S. Ratner (ed.) *Equal Employment Policy for Women*. Philadelphia: Temple University Press.

Langley, R. and Levy, R.C. (1977) *Wife-beating – the Silent Crisis*. New York: Dutton.

Lasch, C. (1977) *Haven in a Heartless World*. New York: Basic Books.

Lister, R. (1970) *As Man and Wife*. London: London Child Poverty Action Group.

——(1980) Taxation, Women and the Family. In C.T. Sandford, C. Pond, and R. Walker (eds) *Taxation and Social Policy*. London: Heinemann.

McGrath, C. (1979) The Crisis of Domestic Order. *Socialist Review* 45: 11-30.

McIntosh, M. (1978) The State and the Oppression of Women. In A. Kuhn and A.-M. Wolpe (eds) *Feminism and Materialism*. London: Routledge & Kegan Paul.

——(1979) The Welfare State and the Needs of the Dependent Family. In S. Burman (ed). *Fit Work for Women*. London: Croom Helm.

Marris, P. and Rein, M. (1972) *Dilemmas of Social Reform*. 2nd edn. Harmondsworth: Penguin.

Martin, D. (1976) *Battered Wives*. San Francisco: Glide Publications.

May, M. (1978) Violence in the Family: An Historical Perspective. In J.P. Martin (ed.) *Violence and the Family*. Chichester: Wiley.

Mercer, J. (1974) A Policy Statement on Assessment Procedures and the Rights of Children. *Harvard Educational Review* (Reprint Series No. 9): 328-44.

Mill, J.S. (1869) *The Subjection of Women*. London: Longmans, Green.

Millett, K. (1969) *Sexual Politics*. London: Hart Davis.

Molyneux, M. (1979) Beyond the Domestic Labour Debate. *New Left Review* 116: 3-27

Moore, D. (1979) *Battered Women*. Beverly Hills: Sage.

Nichols, B. (1976) The Abused Wife Problem. *Social Casework* 57: 27-35

O'Donovan, K. (1979) The Male Appendage – Legal Definitions of

Women. In S. Burman (ed.) *Fit Work for Women*. London: Croom Helm.

Okin, S.M. (1979) *Women in Western Political Thought*. Princeton: Princeton University Press.

Pagelow, M.D. (1981) *Woman-Battering*. Beverly Hills: Sage.

Parker, R. and Land, H. (1978) Family Policy in the United Kingdom. In S.B. Kamerman and A.J. Kahn (eds) *Family Policy*. New York: Columbia University Press.

Peattie, L. and Rein, M. (1983) *Women's Claims – A Study in Political Economy*. London: Oxford University Press.

Pinchbeck, I. (1977) *Women Workers and the Industrial Revolution, 1750–1850*. London: Cass.

Pizzey, E. (1979) *Scream Quietly or the Neighbours Will Hear*. Revised edn. Harmondsworth: Penguin.

Pizzey, E. and Shapiro, J. (1982) *Prone to Violence*. London: Hamlyn.

Platt, A. (1969) *The Child Savers*. Chicago: University of Chicago Press.

Poster, M. (1979) *Critical Theory of the Family*. London: Pluto Press.

Rowbotham, S. (1981) The Trouble with 'Patriarchy'. In R. Samuel (ed.) *People's History and Socialist Theory*. London: Routledge & Kegan Paul.

Sachs, A. (1976) The Myth of Judicial Neutrality: The Male Monopoly Cases. In P. Carlen (ed.) *The Sociology of Law*. Keele: University of Keele.

Sachs, A. and Pearson, R. (1980) Barristers and Gentlemen: A Critical Look at Sexism in the Legal Profession. *Modern Law Review* 43: 400-14.

Sachs, A. and Wilson, J.H. (1978) *Sexism and the Law*. London: Martin Robertson.

Schechter, S. (1983) *Women and Male Violence*. London: Pluto Press.

Social Trends (1984) Vol. 14. London: HMSO, Central Statistical Office.

Spitzer, S. (1975) Toward a Marxian Theory of Deviance. *Social Problems* 22: 638-51.

Stang-Dahl, T. and Snare, A. (1978) The Coercion of Privacy: A Feminist Perspective. In C. Smart and B. Smart (eds) *Women, Sexuality and Social Control*. London: Routledge & Kegan Paul.

Stephen, Sir J.F. (1873) *Liberty, Equality, Fraternity*. London: Smith, Elder.

Straus, M., Gelles, R., and Steinmetz, S. (1980) *Behind Closed Doors – Violence in the American Family*. New York: Doubleday.

Supplementary Benefits Commission (1980) *Annual Report 1979*. Cmnd 8033, London: HMSO.

Thompson, E.P. (1975) *Whigs and Hunters*. London: Allen Lane.

Tilly, L.A. and Scott, J.W. (1978) *Women, Work and Family*. New York: Holt, Rinehart & Winston.

Walker, L. (1979) *The Battered Woman*. New York: Harper & Row.

Weitzman, L. (1974) Legal Regulation of Marriage; Tradition and Change. *California Law Review* 62: 1169-288.

Wilson, E. (1976) *The Existing Research Into Battered Women*. London: NWAF.

——(1977) *Women and the Welfare State*. London: Tavistock.

——(1983) *What Is to Be Done About Violence Against Women?* Harmondsworth: Penguin.

Zaretsky, E. (1976) *Capitalism, the Family and Personal Life*. London: Pluto Press.

Cases

Chorlton v. *Lings* (1869) 4 LRCP 398

Davis v. *Johnson* [1979] AC 264

Edward v. *Cheyne* (No 2) (1888) 13 App Cas 385

Edwards v. *Attorney-General for Canada* [1930] AC 124

Wachtel v. *Wachtel* [1973] Fam 72

Re Young (1913) 29 TLR 319

CHAPTER 5

Protection and paternalism

Katherine O'Donovan

> 'Even the disabilities which the wife lies under are for the most
> part intended for her protection and benefit: so great a favourite is
> the female sex of the laws of England.'
>
> (Blackstone 1765: I, 433)

It is generally assumed that Blackstone was attempting a little irony
in the above passage from his *Commentaries*, for he had just described a
system which denied a married woman's legal existence. Yet close
examination of the context in which he wrote reveals that the
common law of the eighteenth century did attempt to mitigate the
effects of a wife's legal loss of personality by protecting her from
some excesses of a husband's power. In effect what he describes is an
assumption by the law that a wife may have been compelled by her
husband to commit a felony or to perform some civil legal act such as
contract or conveyance. She can therefore be excused or protected.

A rational reaction to such a system would be to suggest that no
protection would be necessary were it not for the disabilities created
by law. Liberal political thought advocates the grant of equal rights to
women so as to put them on a par with men. Mill (1929) states the
position clearly. He believes in progress by human beings through the
ages and that the grant of formal equality of rights to women is part of
the continuing rationalization of society. This concept of equal rights
was the philosophical basis for legislation such as the Sex Discrimination
Act 1975 and the Equal Pay Act 1970.

Arguments based on formal equality are opposite to arguments
based on special rights or on the need for protection. Liberal arguments
are committed to creating similarities between women and men
where possible and to minimizing differences between them (Radcliffe

79

Richards 1982). This leads to the assimilation of women and men and to a denial of special rights. The claim for special rights is sometimes based on biology and sometimes based on gender roles. It is often said that the assimilationist argument ignores these differences between persons and offers a model based only on rights achieved by men and on a male life-style (Elshtain 1981: Chapter 5. Wolgast 1980: Chapter 1). It will be suggested below that this objection can be overcome by a plurality of rights which recognizes heterogeneity in life-styles and differences in biology and in roles.

A second objection to formal equality can be traced directly back to Mill's writing. For he confines himself to formal equality in the public sphere and sees women and men as having quite separate roles in domestic life. Thus he argues:

'When the support of the family depends, not on property but on earnings, the common arrangement, by which the wife superintends the domestic expenditure, seems to me in general the most suitable division of labour between the two persons'

(Mill 1929: 263)

Thus Mill accepts the split between private and public life and fails to see that it is precisely out of this division of labour that many of the problems concerning state policy arise. Mill's position is one of recognizing equality in the public sphere, and of saying that women and men are alike in all important respects. His analysis fails to uncover those sources of inequality between the sexes that lie outside public law.

This paper reviews arguments for and against special rules based on ideas about protection of women. These rules could be said to be contrary to the principle of formal equality. But, as the review reveals, the issues are complex. Protection is a concept which must be carefully analysed. Protection – for whom, why, from what, from whom? The paper does not tackle the even more difficult issue of differential treatment as compensation for lack of formal equality in the past. In analysing the notion of protection it should be separated from ideas about paternalism. Protection may imply a concern about the rights of others that could be labelled paternalistic. Examples can be found, however, where protective policies arise from inequalities, complexities, necessity, or a sense of justice. It is important to note that it is rights that are being protected.

The notion of protection implies inequality and weakness, a power imbalance which the law is to rectify by its intervention on behalf of the weaker party. This is accepted as unproblematic in relation to children, who are said to lack judgement as to where their own good and interests lie, and also to be unequal to and weaker than adults (Scarre 1980). In relation to children then, adults are the norm. Protection is necessary because children cannot conform to the adult norm. Full competency is adulthood. Childhood means less than full competency and therefore protection.

Consumers are protected by legislation because of the complexities of modern mass production. The rationale is that the individual lacks the knowledge or information to judge, for example, whether certain electrical goods are safe. But consumer protection goes further than that in allowing individuals to change their minds about agreements they have signed (Hire Purchase Acts 1938-65) and in recognizing inequality in contractual bargaining power (Unfair Contract Terms Act 1977). Again this is seen as unproblematic, perhaps because everyone falls into the consumer category, and there is no other norm from which consumers deviate.

In the case of employment contracts, however, there is an opposition between the category employer and the category employee. Yet the safeguarding of employees through employment protection legislation is not challenged as reducing them to the status of children, nor is it said to be against their best interests (Employment Protection (Consolidation) Act 1978). The policy is justified on grounds of inequality of bargaining power between the two categories. It is germane to note that the legal subordination of workers that existed until the nineteenth century was replaced by formal equality. Dissatisfaction with formal equality has led in the past twenty years to a policy of protection (Honoré 1982: 7). The analogy with wives is self-evident.

Examination of explanations for policies of protection of women reveals variety. Certain arguments take the same form as those made concerning children. Women, it is said, lack judgement about their own best interests. They need protection 'for their own good', even if they do not want it. Other arguments emphasize inequalities between women and men arising from the division of labour and disparities of power. Counter arguments insist that protection reinforces inequality and enables continuation of the conditions that necessitated it initially. Submission by, and control of, the protected is the outcome. Adult women, it is said, are equal to adult men and should have the same autonomy. Protection merely cushions and legitimates discrimination. In these arguments the opposing social categories are women and men. Rules concerning men are taken as the norm and where special treatment or protection is provided for women this is regarded as deviation, and often as a favour.

It is important to note that in the examples given of children, consumers, the employment contract, and women, clear opposition emerges between the category which is the norm, and the exception, except in the case of consumers. As suggested already, consumers' interests are everyone's interests.

'For her own good'

Legislation providing for differential treatment of women and men employed in factories is called 'protective'.[1] In *Muller* v. *Oregon* (208 US 412 (1908)) judicial approval for limiting days, times, and hours women could work was based on arguments about lack of physical strength, separate classification of women from men, and motherhood. Examination of motherhood gives a clue as to one major premise. Women's ability to give birth, their social role as mothers, and the health of future generations, are seen as requiring the control of women's working hours. What is revealed is that children are being protected, and for their sake women are being treated differently from men.

An illustration of how the argument based on maternity affects all women, and not just pregnant or hopeful mothers, is contained in *Page* v. *Freight Hire Ltd* ([1981] 1 All ER 394). A woman aged twenty-three brought an action against her employers for discrimination under the Sex Discrimination Act 1975 because she was prohibited from carrying out her job as a lorry driver under circumstances in which a man would have been permitted to work. The load the lorry was to have carried was DMF, a chemical that had risks for both men and women, but particularly of female sterility and for a foetus inside a pregnant woman. The lorry driver was willing to accept the risks of working with the chemical and to indemnify her employers against risk, but was prohibited from doing so. The Employment Appeals Tribunal held that there was a statutory duty on the employers to ensure the health, safety, and welfare of their employees and that therefore there was no discrimination. The distinction between the protection of any potential foetus and the lorry driver's own interest is not made in the judgement.

This case has two interesting aspects. The first is the point made above concerning the separation of the interests of a potential foetus from those of the mother, or of women generally. If all women are to be subjected to control for the sake of future generations, then surely this should give rise to compensation and not to disability. Furthermore, this classification of all women as having the same interests and needs in opposition to men overlooks the obvious fact that all individuals classed together do not share the characteristics that differentiate the average class representatives.

The second point is that the lorry driver had made her position very clear, she was divorced and did not want children. She knew the dangers and wished to accept them. The appeals tribunal said:

'We accept that the individual's wishes may be a factor to be looked at, although, in our judgement, where the risk is to the woman, of sterility, or to the foetus, whether actually in existence or likely to come into existence in the future, these wishes cannot be a conclusive factor.'

([1981] 1 All E.R. 394 at 398)

Thus, the employers' judgement of what is for the woman's good is substituted for her own. This 'for her own good' argument was rightly characterized by the Supreme Court of the United States as "romantic paternalism" which, in practical effect, put women not on a pedestal, but in a cage' (*Frontiero* v. *Richardson*, 411 US 677 at 684 (1973)).

In terms of freedom of contract women, controlled by protective legislation, are not free. It is true that employers can ask for an exemption from the legislation and that many do (Coyle 1980) but the necessity of so doing means that a refusal to employ women is permitted under the Sex Discrimination Act. This is because job working hours longer or other than those permitted under the Factories Act 1961 constitute a genuine occupational qualification. In *E.A. White* v. *British Sugar Corporation Ltd* ([1977] IRLR 121) the industrial tribunal held that sex was a genuine occupational qualification for a job that entailed Sunday work and that therefore the biologically female employee was not discriminated against since 'the job requires a man because of legal restrictions on the employment of women' (121).[2] This suggests that the state is paternalistic in claiming to know better than women where their interests lie. The evidence is that women factory workers wish to be free to negotiate their own hours of employment without the constraints of protective legislation (EOC 1979). The 'for your own good' form of argument denies women's capacity to make their own choices.

Yet the state does have a legitimate role as protector of children, born or unborn, as most discussions of paternalism agree. And it is because of their biological capacity to gestate and give birth that women have been controlled along with children. Complete separation of their interests may not always be possible. As a minimum, however, where the rationale is the protection of any foetus, this should be made explicit and all women should not be included. If the rationale is the assignation of a child care role to women, this should be articulated and women without such responsibilities should be excluded. If these policies were clarified then it might be possible for persons accepting the burdens and benefits of raising future generations to have their life-style recognized through some form of legal rights.

The Equal Opportunities Commission, with its liberal brief for formal equality, advocates the repeal of protective legislation because:

'the hours of work legislation constitutes a barrier – often an artificial one – to equal pay and job opportunities for women. So long as this legislation remains as it is at present, women as workers will be disadvantaged.'

(EOC 1979: 92)

The problem with this, as with all statements of formal equality, is that it presupposes a freely negotiated bargain between women and their employers without any constraints of existing inequalities of power, and trade union intervention. In any case, the contract of employment is no longer freely negotiated. Employers are bound by a system of legislative controls placing considerable limits on their autonomy. Yet state intervention on behalf of employees is seen as evening up the balance of power and preventing exploitation.

The debate over the repeal of protective legislation continues in Britain, but has been resolved in the USA after fifty years of argument. There social reformers opposed repeal in the hope that improved conditions would mean the extension to all workers of shorter working hours, and because of the needs of families of women workers. This is the position that has been adopted in Britain by the Trades Union Congress and by the National Council for Civil Liberties. Feminists in the American National Women's Party first introduced the Equal Rights Amendment in 1923, which, if passed, would obliterate sex as a functional classification in the law. This latter position has been adopted by the Equal Opportunities Commission. In the USA social reformers and trade unions have withdrawn their historic opposition to the Equal Rights Amendment. It is generally agreed that protective legislation reinforces women's lowly position in the labour market and at home. A society divided on sex or gender lines reinforces male hegemony and preserves the *status quo* (Babcock 1975: 247).

The language in which the Trades Union Congress has opposed the repeal of protective legislation deserves analysis:

'A large proportion of working women are married with not only a house to look after, they have in effect a multiplicity of jobs. Thus the pressures to which they are subject are likely to cause them to overwork against their better judgement. They may not only damage their health and increase the risk of accidents, but have serious effects on the well being of family. In the interests of society generally, . . . the state must intervene to protect women against the combined effect of social and economic pressure.'

(Department of Employment 1969: para. 20)

If paternalism is the substitution of another's judgement for that of the concerned individual on a 'I know what is best for you' basis, then this statement undoubtedly qualifies. Surely women must be the best judges of how to combine their multiplicity of roles. But there is a danger in raising individual autonomy in opposition to protective legislation in that this ignores the fact that family responsibilities, however voluntarily taken on, deprive individuals of autonomy.[3]

Protection means submission and control

Fitzjames Stephen, the Victorian judge, in an attack on Mill's *Subjection of Women* argued that 'submission and protection' were 'correlative'. 'Withdraw the one and the other is lost, and force will assert itself a hundred times more harshly through the law of contract than ever it did through the law of status' (Freeman and Lyon 1983; 35). If this is so and women are subordinating themselves in return for legal protection, then it may be that they are paying too high a price.

Marriage is presented in the conventional legal literature as an institution for the protection of women, who are said to have advanced, in the past century, from the status of servant to that of co-equal head of the household (Bromley 1981: 109). Yet others attack marriage as 'repressive benevolence' (Barker 1978). Freeman and

Lyon view the protection of marriage with scepticism. They argue that the cry of 'back to the kitchen, we have protected you' is likely to be used not only against independence for married women but also against cohabiting women whose status is being assimilated to that of the married (1983: 177). Marriage laws are a means of control in the guise of protection. This view of surrender of autonomy in return for protection identifies a serious cause for concern. It can be further illustrated by looking at Jeremy Bentham's ideal civil code.

In Bentham's good society the first principle of family law is that the wife is subject to the husband but has a right of appeal to the courts. In advocating a protective role for the courts Bentham rejects the views of those 'who of some vague notion of justice and generosity wish to give to the woman an absolute equality'. For he believes that 'man, assured of his prerogative, is not disturbed by the inquietudes of jealousy, and enjoys it while he yields it' (1931: 231). But if faced with a rivalry of powers, man would become a 'dangerous antagonist'. Whatever our view of Bentham's vision of domestic harmony, his idea of protection seems to be connected with his code's own preference for male authority and power. The protection of the wife comes from law, but the power against which she is to be protected is reinforced by law. Stripped to its essentials the argument is that law confers, woman defers, and law protects.

Bentham's vision has been defended on the grounds that he was a realist conscious of the inequality of women's condition in society and that his demand was for special protection. 'Today, minorities and women ask for the right to be different, arguing that formal equality brings a levelling which will always work in favour of the stronger, and against the weaker, the different, the oppressed' (Boralevi 1980: 43). If this is an argument for legal recognition of heterogeneity and plurality of rights then it is rather different from arguments about protection, and provides an indication of the direction the debate might profitably take.

Redressing the balance

A third form of argument about special treatment is that it results from the law's function as protector of the weak. Inequalities resulting from an imbalance of social and economic power justify consumer protection, so why not housewife protection? Legislation and case law giving non-owner spouses rights in the matrimonial home, or providing for their alimentary needs are a response to inequality.

Some of the problems with this are that it may be taken to imply that women lack full competency; it has to meet the submission and control objection; and it becomes structured in terms of opposition between the two gender categories. Some would deny the existence of inequality. Others say it is a matter for public rather than private law. Yet another suggested solution is that the debate be conducted in gender neutral terms.

Gender neutrality is the preferred American model under the proposed Equal Rights Amendment, and it clearly has an important place in public law. Since 'the very construction of men and women as separate and opposed categories takes place within, and in terms of, the family' (McIntosh 1969: 154) the imposition of neutrality may be an evasion of the issues. As Honoré points out it is misleading to talk 'as if wives supported husbands (financially) to the same extent as husbands support wives' (1982: 64). This raises again the point made at the opening of this paper, that a plurality of rights based on a variety of life patterns must be incorporated into models of equality. If formal equality means that any deviation from a model of rights based on a lifetime's employment in the public sphere is to be regarded as requiring special treatment, then it means very little. Gender neutral language enables the protection of rights based on a variety of factors, including choice of life patterns, and biology.

It has already been suggested that Mill's view of equality was limited by his failure to extend his analysis to private law and the private sphere. It is beyond the scope of this paper to provide an agenda as to how this might be achieved. But what is suggested is that the achievement of formal equality in the public sphere must be followed by material equality in private, or the integration of the two. For assimilation of women to men as required by current ideologies of equality will merely result in the perpetuation of inequality in the private sphere. It is a failure of liberal political thought that it ignores the private sphere and therefore cannot provide an answer to problems of inequality therein. But since the liberal tradition remains dominant in political philosophy and practical politics let us examine whether, within that tradition, special treatment of women is regarded as paternalism.

Paternalism

'The only purpose for which power can be rightfully exercised over any member of a civilised community, against his will, is to prevent harm to others' (Mill 1910: 73). Mill's definition of the boundaries between public control and the private sphere include an express rejection of paternalism, with an exception for children. If we apply this to the 'for your own good' argument we can concur with Mill in rejecting it. In the case of protective legislation, unless those others protected from harm are the families of women workers, control cannot be justified. It has been argued that protective legislation is not imposed on women against their wills and that the Equal Opportunities Commission survey is unreliable (Coyle 1980: 7). What seems likely is that not all women affected by the legislation share a common position on it, and this illustrates the fallacy of treating women together as a class in opposition to men as a class. If it is for the sake of their families that women factory workers are controlled, willingly or unwillingly, then this should be clarified by the policy-makers.

Mill does allow a weak paternalism where individuals are protected from harming themselves because their decisions are impaired through lack of knowledge, lack of control, or undue influence (Ten 1980: Chapter 7). This is why the rights of consumers are to be protected and why contracts tainted by inequality are unenforceable. An impaired decision is not freely made.

Mill's justification of interference to prevent harm to others will permit a plurality of rights that recognizes needs arising from a variety of life patterns. On this view those who are not to be harmed are being protected. What is being protected is their rights. From this we can conclude that it is possible within the dominant liberal tradition to justify what was earlier called 'special treatment'. In order to do so a model of rights which permits a plurality of rights based on different life choices is necessary. For instance, if pregnant mothers are to be controlled for the sake of their babies, this intervention is to protect children's rights. A corresponding duty is placed on the mother. Yet out of this relationship arise other rights stemming from child bearing and raising. Some of these are children's rights; others are the rights of the concerned adult.

We need a new language in which to elaborate claims that persons make upon one another in the private sphere and in which these can be translated into the public sphere. As yet the conclusion is limited to the observation that it is possible within the liberal tradition, and despite its acceptance of the public-private division, to project a model of rights which recognizes heterogeneity.

Notes

1 Under the Factories Act 1961, s.86, women's factory hours of work must not exceed nine a day, nor exceed forty-eight a week; the period of employment must not exceed eleven hours a day, nor begin earlier than seven o'clock in the morning, nor end later than eight o'clock in the evening, nor, on Saturday, later than one o'clock in the afternoon; no continuous period of work shall exceed four and a half hours without an interval of half an hour, or if there is a rest period of not less than ten minutes, then the period can be increased to five hours. Under s.89 a woman's overtime must not exceed one hundred hours in any calendar year nor six hours in any week, nor shall it take place in any factory for more than twenty-five weeks in any calendar year. Overtime worked in any one day shall not exceed ten hours, and the period of employment must not exceed twelve hours a day. The times worked are limited to 7 a.m. to 9 p.m. on weekdays. Sunday work is prohibited. It is possible to obtain an exemption order from the Health and Safety Executive and this is done by specific exemption to individual firms. General exemptions are available under s.117 by ministerial regulation for entire industries.

2 This case illustrates the injustice of classifying all women together on the basis of biology. The applicant was a transsexual who had moved from the social category female to the social category male. He was dismissed from his job as electrician's mate when his birth status was discovered. The applicant brought proceedings under the Sex Discrimination Act 1975 and the Industrial Tribunal held that the Act only envisages two sexes and the applicant belonged to the female sex. There was no discrimination of grounds of sex because the applicant was dismissed for deception. Furthermore if the applicant had disclosed that he was female the employers would have been entitled to refuse employment, since s.7(2)(f) of the Act permits an exception to be made on grounds of genuine occupational qualification where the protective legislation restricts the employment of women.

3 The National Council for Civil Liberties takes the view that the EOC proposals equalize 'down' and not 'up'. Women would simply be as vulnerable as men to economic pressure from employers. Their view is that men should have the same benefits as women in having their days, hours, and times of work restricted. In the meantime, because of their double shift, women need protective

laws. Jean Coussins (1979) *The Shift Work Swindle* (London: NCCL).

References

Babcock, B.A., Freedman, A.E., Norton, E.H., and Ross, S.C. (1975) *Sex Discrimination and the Law*. Boston: Little Brown.

Barker, D.L. (1978) The Regulation of Marriage: Repressive Benevolence. In G. Littlejohn, B. Smart, J. Wakeford, and N. Yuval-Davis (eds) *Power and the State*. London: Croom Helm.

Bentham, J. (1931) *The Theory of Legislation*. London: Routledge & Kegan Paul.

Blackstone, W. (1765) *Commentaries on the Laws of England*. Facsimile ed. (1979). Chicago: University of Chicago Press.

Boralevi, L.C. (1980) *The Bentham Newsletter* 4. London: Bentham Committee, University College.

Bromley, P.M. (1981) *Family Law*. 6th edn. London: Butterworths.

Coyle, A. (1980) The Protection Racket? *Feminist Review* 4: 1-12.

Department of Employment (1969) *Papers*, para. 20.

Elshtain, J.B. (1981) *Public Man, Private Woman*. Princeton: Princeton University Press.

Equal Opportunities Commission (1979) *Report: Health and Safety Legislation: Should We Distinguish Between Men and Women?* London: HMSO.

Freeman, M.D.A. and Lyon, C. (1983) *Cohabitation Without Marriage*. Aldershot: Gower.

Honoré, T. (1982) *The Quest for Security: Employees, Tenants, Wives*. London: Stevens.

McIntosh, M. (1979) The Welfare State and the Needs of the Dependent Family. In S. Burman (ed.) *Fit Work for Women*. London: Croom Helm.

Mill, J.S. (1910) *On Liberty*. London: Dent.

——(1929) *On the Subjection of Women*. London: Dent.

Radcliffe Richards, J. (1982) *The Sceptical Feminist*. Harmondsworth: Penguin.

Scarre, G. (1980) Children and Paternalism. *Philosophy* 55: 117-24.

Ten, C.L. (1980) *Mill on Liberty*. Oxford: Clarendon Press.

Wolgast, E.H. (1980) *Equality and the Rights of Women*. Cornell: Cornell University Press.

PART TWO
CHILDREN, THE STATE, AND THE LAW

CHAPTER 6

Rethinking child protection

Robert Dingwall and John Eekelaar

In the last ten years, the conventional wisdom among family lawyers appears to have turned full circle on the issue of local authorities' exercise of their powers and duties for the protection of children. From lamenting the way 'considerations of civil liberty [had] prevailed over children's welfare' (Freeman 1976: 139), concern now seems to focus on the 'dangers that parental civil liberties may be very easily infringed' (Freeman 1980a: 132). How has this shift in opinion come about and by what evidence is it justified? From the answers to these questions we can determine the status we should afford the policy recommendations that have been put forward.

This paper, then, is divided into three parts. The first reviews the evidential basis for the claims that social services are an increasing threat to family life. The second introduces some contradictory findings from recent research, including that conducted by the present authors in collaboration with Topsy Murray, which provided the first detailed and comprehensive examination of the child protection system as a whole. The third considers the competing principles by which the body of material presented in the previous sections may be translated into policy.

The existing evidence

Part of the difficulty in evaluating the change of direction is the way in which it confounds several different issues. Geach and Szwed (1983: 1) in their introduction to the most recent critical collection, *Providing Civil Justice for Children*, identify five: the philosophical underpinning of present policies; the way the law apparently favours the state rather than children or parents; the quality of state care; the extent of administrative discretion; and a global charge that 'the present system . . . is not functioning satisfactorily'.

Clearly most of these statements cannot be subjected to any empirical verification since they depend, essentially, on the adoption of an *a priori* normative position. The law, for instance, can only be said to 'favour the state' by reference to some alternative ideal standard. What is the bench-mark for judgements about the quality of state care? Is it comparison with the actual or prospective care these children would otherwise receive, the care typically given to children sharing their cultural and socio-economic background, or some higher ideal, whether derived from Tory paternalism or counter-cultural self-realization? We could equally propose that, given an apparent need for intervention, we should be trying to revive the generous philosophy of the Curtis Committee (1946: para. 435), 'that all deprived children have an upbringing likely to make them sound and happy citizens and that they have all the chances, educational and vocational, of making a good start in life that are open to children in normal homes'.

Geach and Szwed, however, trace these debates to what are clearly intended as empirical statements. 'This century has seen *a considerable increase* in the power of the state to intervene in the lives of children and their families . . . parents . . . have become *increasingly* "at risk" of state intervention including, as a final resort, the removal of their children into state care' (italics added) (1983: 1). The *fons et origo* of concern is a perceived growth in state intervention over a specifed time period, the present century, which is therefore held to require a critical reappraisal of the powers granted to the state and the manner of their exercise. If we are to accept this, we might reasonably look for some evidence of an increase in intervention, minimally a history of statutes and their scope, and of the current exercise of those powers, by reference to the relevant published statistics.

The volume under consideration (Geach and Szwed 1983) does not include any detailed historical account, although several of the papers do have some historical preamble. Contemporary practice is represented by two statistical references: Geach (p. 83) states that the number of children in England coming into care through court proceedings under s.1(2)(a) of the Children and Young Persons Act 1969 increased from 1,200 in the year ending 31 March, 1977 to 2,347 in the year ending 31 March, 1980. Maidment (p. 73) has compiled a useful table showing, between 1963 and 1980, the growing proportion of children in voluntary care in England and Wales over whom parental rights resolutions had been passed under procedures now to be found under s.3 of the Child Care Act 1980. A careful reading of an earlier contribution involving Geach and Szwed, *Justice for Children* (Morris *et al.* 1980), and the other major British critique, *In Whose Best Interests?* (Taylor, Lacey, and Bracken 1980), does not yield much additional evidence. Although frequent reference is made to the absolute number of children in care, there are no attempts to put this in perspective by showing how it relates to the size of the population under eighteen or to give time series which might allow trends to become apparent.

We have already discussed the legislative history elsewhere (Eekelaar, Dingwall, and Murray 1982; Dingwall, Eekelaar, and Murray (1984b) and do not intend to recount it in detail again. What can be said, however, is that the twentieth century has seen no fundamental innovations in the categories of children whose welfare may be thought to require some form of state intervention. The major statutes – the Children Act 1908, the Children and Young Persons Act 1933 and the Children Act 1948 – were essentially measures of consolidation and re-enactment which modernized powers and definitions first set out in nineteenth-century or earlier legislation. The net has not been cast ever wider: at most, a few holes have been patched.

The administrative changes the legislation has brought about make it hard to produce really long-term statistical series. We can, however, reasonably go back to 1951 when the first figures became available under the Children Act 1948 and look at a thirty-year period.[1] Over that time, there does appear to have been an increase in the number of children in care in England and Wales, from 62.7 thousand in 1951 to 96.9 thousand in 1981, with a peak of 101.2 thousand in 1977. Absolute numbers can, however, be very misleading given the changing size of the population at risk (all children under eighteen). The proportion of this population in care has increased from 5.5 per thousand in 1951 to 7.6 per thousand in 1981 with a peak of 7.8 per thousand in 1980. (We shall refer to this as the 'intervention rate'.)

Before attempting to draw any conclusions from these trends, however, two points should be noted about the statistical series. The first, and most important, is the effect of the Children and Young Persons Act 1969, the implementation of which in 1971 transferred several categories of children from criminal to care statistics by widening the range of circumstances in which care orders could be used as a disposition for juveniles convicted of criminal offences,

Table 9 **Children in care (England and Wales) 1970–81: gross numbers and as rates per thousand population under 18**

| | number in care | |
	gross (in thousands)	per thousand population under 18
1970	71.2	5.2
1971	87.4	6.4
1972	90.6	6.5
1973	93.1	6.7
1974	95.9	6.9
1975	99.1	7.3
1976	100.6	7.4
1977	101.2	7.5
1978	100.7	7.6
1979	100.1	7.7
1980	100.2	7.8
1981	96.9	7.6

compared with the antecedent fit person orders, and substituting remands to care for remands to remand homes. These are not children who are newly subject to state intervention but they are new to these statistics. In 1970 there were 71.2 thousand children in care, an intervention rate of 5.2 per thousand which had only been subject to minor fluctuations since 1951. In 1971 the number jumped to 87.4 thousand, an intervention rate of 6.4 per thousand. New admissions went up from 51.5 thousand to 71.0 thousand, an increase which is entirely attributable to these legislative changes. Because of the one-off impact of transitional provisions under the 1969 Act it seems more appropriate to take 1972 as the baseline for any calculation of recent trends. We are, then, really trying to explain an increase in the intervention rate of about 17 per cent in the last ten years.

The second point is that there was a major reform in the compilation of these statistics in 1976-77. The DHSS (1980: 5) specifically advise caution in comparing statistics from 1976 and before with those from 1977 and after. If we split the series around those dates, to compare figures collected on the same basis, we find a 14 per cent increase in the intervention rate over the five years 1972-76 and a 1 per cent increase over the five years 1977-81 (as shown in *Table 9*).

The picture, then, is one of a rapid increase in the number of children in care over the first half of the decade and an effective plateau in the second half. In order to explain this, we need to understand the basis on which the statistics are compiled. These figures represent the number of children in care on 31 March in a given year. As such, changes may indicate either or both of two different things: changes in the number of admissions or changes in the rate of discharge. An increasing number of children in care may be due either to more intervention or to more conservative policies on discharge damming the flow of children and backing up the level with longer stays in care.

While total admissions have fluctuated somewhat more than the numbers in care, they follow a rather different curve. There were 36.6 thousand admissions in 1951 rising to 51.5 thousand in 1970, an increase from a rate of 3.2 to one of 3.8 per thousand population under eighteen. This rise continued into the early seventies with a peak of 63.2 thousand in 1972 (disregarding 1971 for reasons discussed earlier) but then declining to 44.9 thousand in 1981. The rate follows the same pattern, falling from 4.6 per thousand in 1972 to 3.5 per thousand in 1981, the same level as the 1950s.[2]

Table 10 **Admissions to care (England and Wales) 1970–81: gross numbers as rates per thousand population under 18.**

	thousands	care periods per thousand population under 18	no. of children per thousand population under 18 thousands	under 18
1970	51.5	3.8	n.a.	n.a.
1971	71.0	5.2	n.a.	n.a.
1972	63.2	4.6	n.a.	n.a.
1973	53.6	3.9	n.a.	n.a.
1974	52.7	3.9	n.a.	n.a.
1975	51.6	3.8	n.a.	n.a.
1976	52.4	3.9	n.a.	n.a.
1977	52.1	3.9	46.6	3.5
1978	48.2	3.7	43.0	3.3
1979	44.4	3.5	39.7	3.1
1980	47.3	3.7	41.9	3.3
1981	44.9	3.5	40.0	3.1

Within this, voluntary admissions have become slightly less important. The earliest figures conveniently available, for 1959, show that 82 per cent of admissions were under s.1 of the Children Act 1948. By 1981, this had fallen to 75 per cent, under the equivalent provision of the Child Care Act 1980. (There is no change in the scope of the legislation between the two Acts.) This change is reflected in the composition of the population in care. In 1974, which seems to be the earliest year for which published figures are available, 52 per cent of children in care were not subject to a court order or parental rights resolution. By 1981, this had fallen to 43 per cent. A greater proportion of a declining number of children are coming into care and remaining there after some sort of legal review and court order. Once in care, they are clearly staying longer. Figures are only available for this since the 1977 statistics were compiled on the new system. In that year 41.5 per cent of children in care on 31 March had been there for three years or more, whereas in 1981 the proportion had risen to 48.1 percent.

It should not be assumed that care status necessarily implies the permanent removal of a child from his or her parents. Our study collected data on thirty-four children considered as possible candidates for care proceedings in one English county during 1977-78. In the event, fifteen of these became subject to care orders in that period. When we followed them up in May 1980, only seven children were still away from home. In two cases, this was clearly linked to organic brain damage caused by the original abuse, which had produced clinical problems that, in our judgement, would have led to institutionalization had the damage been congenital. A third was related to the irreversible decline of a child's only parent with Huntington's Chorea and the absence of any other potential caretaker, and a fourth to similar circumstances where the only parent was suffering a severe psychosis. Of the remaining cases, one was on a 'beyond control' application under pressure from parents whose marriage was breaking down and who were unable to cope with the behaviour problems presented by their disturbed and clinically mentally handicapped child. This leaves only two cases that could, in our view, properly be treated as 'failures', against eight 'successes', if restoring a mistreated child to his or her parent after appropriate intervention is taken as an outcome measure.[3]

The rising number of children in care during the 1970s seems more properly explicable by reference to growing conservatism about discharge, which probably reflects the reluctance of local authorities to ask for the determination of court-ordered committal to care. There is certainly no evidence in the figures of increasing readiness to remove children.

An attempt might be made to argue a contrary case by looking at the details of the statistics, to propose that the gross figures conceal shifts of emphasis between finer categories. This, in effect, is what Geach and Maidment (Geach and Szwed 1983) are attempting to do in the figures quoted earlier. Unfortunately, Geach's figures are based on a confusion between two different statistical series. His 1977 base is a figure for *care periods* while the 1980 figure relates to the most recent *care episode*. A care period is the total length of time in care, which may involve changes in legal status, each of which begins a new care episode. For example, a child who comes into care under an interim care order and is then made subject to a s.1(2)(a) care order will appear in the 'care period' series under the first order and in the 'most recent care episode' series under the second. *Table 11* compares like with like over the years ending 31 March, 1977 to 1981.

Table 11   **Children in care on 31 March whose legal status is defined by care orders under s.1(2)(a) of the Children and Young Persons Act 1969 (England only)**

	1977	1978	1979	1980	1981
most recent care episode	2,592	2,304	2,165	2,347	2,102
all continuous care periods	1,198	914	819	908	826

These actually show a *decline* of 19 per cent in care episodes and a 31 per cent *decline* in care periods, rather than the 100 per cent increase alleged by Geach. *Table 12* is taken from juvenile court returns of the number of care orders made relating to s.1(2)(a), which allows us to disregard the changes in the collection of local authority statistics and produce a ten-year series.

Table 12   **Care orders under s.1(2)(a) made in juvenile courts 1972–82 and as a rate per thousand population under 18 (England and Wales)**

	1972	1973	1974	1975	1976	1977	1978	1979	1980	1981	1982
care orders (thousands)	1.1	1.3	2.2	2.7	2.6	2.4	2.1	2.2	2.1	1.7	2.0
rate per thousand population under 18	0.1	0.1	0.2	0.2	0.2	0.2	0.2	0.2	0.2	0.1	0.2

The State, the Law, and the Family

This shows quite clearly that changes in the number of care orders
are almost entirely attributable to the changing size of the population
at risk. The intervention rate begins and ends the period at one order
per *ten* thousand and never rises above two per ten thousand. There
is no evidence here of a sinister trend.

Maidment's figures are more useful but do not prove her implicit
contention about the intervention rate. They are, indeed, remarkably
consistent with our thesis about the rising length of stays in care
which one would predict would lead to a higher proportion of
children being considered for the assumption of parental rights.
There is, however, another argument which could be made about
voluntary admissions. *Table 13* shows the distribution of reasons for
admission (beginning care periods) in England in 1972 and 1980.

Table 13 **Distribution of admissions to care (England) 1972 and 1980:
numbers and percentages**

	1972		1980	
	numbers	(%)	*numbers*	(%)
short-term illness of parent or guardian	15.2	36.4	8.6	28.1
deserted by parent, other unable to provide (includes child illegitimate, mother unable to provide)	6.7	16.0	3.4	11.1
other reasons	5.8	13.9	8.2	26.8
confinement of parent or guardian	4.3	10.3	1.4	4.6
unsatisfactory home conditions	3.4	8.1	5.4	17.6
homelessness	2.8	6.7	0.6	2.0
long-term illness of parent or guardian	1.0	2.4	0.6	2.0
imprisonment of parent or guardian	0.9	2.2	0.7	2.3
abandoned or lost	0.8	1.9	0.9	2.9
death of parent, other unable to provide	0.7	1.7	0.5	1.6
parent dead, no guardian	0.2	0.5	0.2	0.6
total	41.8		30.6	

'Natural causes' like confinement and illness have certainly declined
in importance while more subjective grounds like 'unsatisfactory
home conditions' have increased. On the other hand, both 'homelessness' and single parenthood have also declined as reasons for
admission. It is possible that there is some trade-off between these

categories. Where social services committees have adopted policies of not admitting to care by reason of homelessness, to ensure that housing authorities cannot evade the provisions of the Housing (Homeless Persons) Act 1977, departments faced with individual distress may be using the home conditions ground to relieve this without breaching council policy. Similarly, changing social and professional attitudes may be leading to a greater reluctance to use the single parent ground and a closer focus on the actual condition of the child. These explanations are, of course, speculative but combining these three 'subjective' groups still leaves us with a rare and apparently decreasing event – an admission rate for these groups of 0.9 per thousand under eighteen in 1972 and 0.7 per thousand in 1981. Indeed, what may be surprising is that rates have not risen despite the growth of poverty and unemployment during the worst recession since the present figures began to be compiled.

Some research findings

While these figures should be sufficient to dispel the proposition that care agencies have been running riot in the post-war period, they do not, of course, establish that the level of intervention established in the 1950s was the right one and is still appropriate. The difficulty lies in establishing the population of children who might fall within the definitions now to be found in the Children and Young Persons Act 1969 and the Child Care Act 1980. It is here that one comes to realize just how sweeping they are. If we were to add up all the children living in unsatisfactory physical environments, in disorganized families, or in conditions which adversely affected their physical, mental or moral development, we might end up with something like 20 per cent of all the children in England and Wales being candidates for care intervention. In reality, as we saw, less than 1 per cent of the child population experience this in any one year.

This picture, of intervention being minimized in relation to its possible scope, is confirmed by two recent studies of decision-making by state agencies.[4] Parker, Casburn, and Turnbull (1981) studied juvenile justice in two Merseyside districts during the 1970s. Their main focus was on 12-17-year-old delinquents but they also looked at the application of the 'care' elements of the 1969 Act to this group. They drew a sharp contrast between the management of delinquency, which they saw as tending to push cases into the criminal justice system, and the management of welfare cases:

'the local authority, the local state, through community health officials, social workers, education and "child guidance" workers is basically geared up to cope informally and voluntarily with family problems and "problem families". In short the goal to *prevent* children and adolescents or parents being taken to the care court is primary, the responsibility through law to take over parental rights, to remove the children, is only apparent when routine work fails or when a real crisis or emergency arises. This is borne out by the relatively small number of youngsters who are the subject of care proceedings, compared with the at risk population . . . we should be clear that the "push-in" is *not* a natural tendency in the professional ideology dominating social welfare, as with the police faced with alleged delinquency.
(Parker, Casburn, and Turnbull 1981: 165, original emphasis)

These findings were confirmed by our own study in three other local authority areas slightly later in the decade (Dingwall, Eekelaar, and Murray 1983). This study was exclusively concerned with care justice and the children included ranged from newborn infants to teenagers. It gave rather more attention to pre-court decision-making and the role of health workers than did Parker, Casburn, and Turnbull whose study focuses quite closely on the courts. As a result, it was possible to document in detail how agency staff preferred the least stigmatizing available interpretation of a child's presenting condition and the least coercive form of intervention possible at any point. This outcome was the product of the decision-making culture in which staff were socialized and the relations between the organizations in which they worked. The former incorporated assumptions about the natural love of parents for their children and the relative nature of all judgements of human behaviour which combined to produce what we called 'the rule of optimism', and resulted in constant attempts to think the best of parents and to explain away contrary evidence. The latter involved the division of information, skills, powers, and duties between independent agencies organized on different principles and with different modes of social accountability. This constitutes a structure of para-legal checks and balances often missed by a narrow focus on statutes and their administration by courts. Health and social services are not a monolith but riven by inter-professional tensions, rivalries, and conflicts. Both of these constraints were reinforced by a pervasive awareness of the limited and decreasing resources available to agencies and their qualitative inadequacies. The main counter-pressures are the need to maintain credibility in the face of persistent and blatant non-compliance and the risk of public scandal if a serious case of mistreatment becomes widely known.

It should, then, be clear that the liberationists' arguments fail *on the question of fact*. There is simply no solid evidence of dramatic expansion in the scope and aggressiveness of welfare intervention since the Second World War. We emphasize this strongly because of the way our own previous work has been represented as some sort of child-saving polemic (e.g. Freeman 1983a; King 1983). *The Protection of Children* deliberately refrains from making those sorts of normative judgements.

'Our first decision is to avoid transcendental criticism of the nature of Anglo-American society. This is not to deny the legitimacy of such contributions but rather to recognize the prevailing, more or less liberal, social order as a given fact for the purposes of this study . . . which may illuminate other arguments and may serve as a case study but which is designed to appraise the present order in its own terms.'

(Dingwall, Eekelaar, and Murray 1983: 232)

We took that decision in presenting a research monograph whose criticisms of the *Justice for Children* position were based on its inadequacies by social scientific criteria of evidence. Those inadequacies have been further revealed in the present paper.

What we are confronting is an ideological claim that can only be discussed at the level of the moral soundness of the arguments and the material interests they advance. (We do not have space to deal with the latter here, although no account of a movement with the effect of encouraging litigation can really be complete without reference to the market for legal services.) There is no ultimate court of appeal in which such claims can be resolved: they are, in the end, a matter of personal choice. The remainder of this paper will address the libertarian position on the basis that the intervention rate has not changed but the political climate has. An intervention rate that was socially acceptable in 1951 had lost its legitimacy by 1983.

The basic conflict

Thus far, in criticizing the empirical foundation of the libertarian position, we have not tried to distinguish within it. However, it does encompass two rather different claims, both of which are often formulated in the language of children's rights. The first of these might be represented as a 'self-determination' argument (e.g. Farson 1978; Holt 1975; Hoyles 1979). This proposes that children should be afforded the same civil status, with associated rights and duties, as adults. There should be no special privileges or obligations: state intervention should only be lawful in circumstances where it would be lawful in respect to adults, for example, where certain general wrongs had been committed and the child had requested the help of state agencies to apprehend and sanction the wrongdoer. The deficiencies of this position in its overestimation of the physical, moral, and psychological capacities of children are well crticized by Freeman (1980b) and we do not propose to reiterate his counter-arguments here.

More important by far is the 'family autonomy' ideology which appears in both 'left' (e.g. Morris *et al.* 1980; Taylor, Lacey, and Bracken 1980) and 'right' (e.g. Mount 1982; Goldstein, Freud, and Solnit 1980) versions. As Eekelaar (1984) points out, any attempt to accord children specified legal rights necessarily involves setting up enforcement agencies to supervise the care provided for them, since children lack the capacities to enforce rights on their own behalf. In most cases, this will involve constant intrusions into family autonomy. There is a central dilemma within western liberalism over the relative priority to be afforded to individual freedoms, social justice, and civil or moral order.

The 'family autonomy' position is an attempt to evade this dilemma by reformulating children's rights in terms of adult freedoms. Goldstein, Freud, and Solnit (1980: 9), in a discussion which has influenced most other exponents of this case, propose for example that children have a basic right to 'family integrity' that requires 'the privacy of family life under the guardianship of parents who are autonomous'. Morris *et al.* (1980: 127) put forward a similar 'principle of respect for family autonomy' that they immediately translate into the assertion that 'parental autonomy in child-rearing must be respected'. Children's rights are identified with a parental right to freedom from state supervision on the basis of an assertion that children have a right to develop and maintain unconstrained psychological ties with their parents.

In fact, this is not a theory of children's rights at all so much as a political theory about the proper relationship between families and the state. A theory of children's rights would actually need to express claims that enhanced their interests as a matter of principle rather than coincidence. An uninterrupted parent/child relationship can damage the child: it cannot, therefore, be said to be a right in itself. The relationship may be a vehicle for advancing the child's interests but this is a matter of empirical judgements about the validity of certain theories of child development and the desirability of state intervention. Goldstein, Freud, and Solnit (1980), and other writers, point to the inadequate resources available to the care system. This is a practical rather than a principled objection. The quality and quantity of resource input are the result of political decisions that could be changed by the democratic process.

Moreover, the implicit psychology is self-contradictory. Family autonomy writers, from Goldstein, Freud, and Solnit (1980) onwards, have sought to restrict intervention to the narrowest possible range of cases: parental death or abandonment; criminal conviction of a parent for sexual abuse; serious bodily injury inflicted by a parent; and refusal to authorize life saving medical care (Morris *et al.* (1980) would exclude the last). Emotional or psychological harms are specifically excluded on the grounds that they are too imprecise to give fair warning to parents, that they confer too much discretion on state agents, and that the knowledge of the causes and treatment of such harms is insufficient reliably to identify and remedy them. The first objection weighs adults' interests against children's and favours the former – a strange theory of children's rights! The second reflects an ideological suspicion of the state which, as we have shown earlier, is not justifiable on British data.

Most crucially, though, the same psychology that is used to justify strong statements about the indispensability of the parent/child bond is simultaneously said to be too weak to specify harms and therapies. Either the theory is too uncertain to warrant the case for non-intervention or emotional development is so important it ought properly to be guaranteed to children by the state, if their rights are to have any meaning. In fact this is an ideological use of psychology of a kind that goes back to the adoption of Bowlby's theories of attachment and maternal deprivation (see Clarke and Clarke 1976) and runs forward through the bonding literature (see Arney 1983: 155-74) to insist on a profoundly conservative view of parent/child relations in the face of more reliable contradictory evidence that it is the consistency, stability, and quality of care giving that are most important. There may be practical reasons why these conditions are more likely to be met by families than other institutions but the blood tie is not necessarily one of them.

The equation of children's rights with family autonomy rests on a political theory that actually denies the possibility of independent rights for children and on a series of contingent judgements about the present condition of developmental psychology that are inconsistent and self-contradictory. There can be no escape from the fact that the recognition of children's interests necessarily entails the abridgement of family autonomy. The trade-off between these objectives is a political decision.

We, therefore, oppose the family autonomy position with a different political philosophy. This is not discussed in detail in *The Protection of Children* because we, vainly as it proved, hoped that our data and findings could be judged on their own merits rather than in terms of the normative preferences of the research team. The result, unfortunately, has merely been that readers who had disliked the findings have imputed an ideology to attack rather than considering the shaky empirical foundations of their own. The remainder of this section will, then, set out our position in terms of what we have called the 'equality principle' and distinguished it from the 'child-saving' of which we have been accused (cf. Dingwall, Eekelaar, and Murray 1984a; King 1983).

The 'equality principle' states that, given the social and economic structure of our present society, all children should have an equal opportunity to maximize the resources available for them during their childhood (including their own inherent abilities) so as to minimize the extent to which they enter adult life affected by avoidable prejudices incurred during their childhood. This principle finds its earliest expression in nineteenth-century liberal writings, especially those of J.S. Mill, which argued that it was unjust to penalize children for the irresponsibility, poor judgement, or economic failure of their parents. Unlike the marriage contract, children were not free entrants into their relationship with parents and therefore required protection of their interests by the state until they were of an age to take responsibility for their own lives. The protection of their interests in childhood could involve supervision of their moral socialization to ensure that they were adequately equipped to make mature adult judgements when the time came. The principle seems also to be the basis for Freeman's (1983b) recently formulated concept of 'liberal paternalism'.

As we have shown elsewhere (Dingwall, Eekelaar, and Murray 1983: 217-21; Dingwall, Eekelaar, and Murray 1984b; Eekelaar 1984), the adoption of this principle was allied to what we called a 'national investment' view of children, which derived from perceived problems in the quality of social reproduction and a realization that child-rearing was too important for the future of the whole society to be left exclusively to parents. While such arguments may be necessary to move governing elites, it is, however, our belief that intervention is equally defensible by reference to egalitarian democratic ideals, the view that all citizens have rights to just shares in the national well-being. If unequal family relationships distort this distribution, they should be overcome. We can, then, talk of children's rights in the same way as we can talk of a homemaker's right to an equal share of the capital accumulated during a marriage. Our focus here, though, is on the duties that the equality principle imposes on parents and the state and the enforcement issues that arise.

Taking the social and economic structure as given has two particular consequences. First, it is clear that being raised outside a family-like environment is disadvantaging in various ways. There are, therefore, good reasons for preferring that children should remain in their families of origin or be found stable substitutes, not least because human diversity appears to require a kind of flexible and consistent relationship that is organizationally difficult to create in large-scale caring institutions. Second, though, if families are preferred child rearing environments, an unequal society would lead to children being unavoidably disadvantaged by their parents' lack of material or cognitive resources. From this we can argue for a collective duty to limit such inequalities by the provision either of redistributive economic support or of services like those for child health and education. We might observe at this point that much political argument concerning resource distribution, put, as it is, solely in terms of competition between *adults*, conceals the fact that distribution between adults is in practice distribution between children. The principles of such distribution have, therefore, important implications for any theory of children's rights.

Since children lack the capacity to gain access to these resources for themselves, the way we make redistribution work is by recognizing parents as agents for their children. By corollary this imposes a duty on the parent to exercise that agency for the child's benefit. Socially, if not legally, the parent is a trustee.

Two consequences follow from this. First, parents may be thought to be under some obligation to attempt to enforce collective duties, where for instance, redistribution is insufficient. Second, and much more importantly, we must pose the *quis custodiet?* question in relation to parents. If we are channelling resources through them as agents, how can we be sure they are really being used for the principals' benefit? To the extent that adults throughout the society give up resources, especially through taxation, to equalize opportunities for children, they acquire a collective right to monitor the extent to which the intended beneficiaries actually profit. Where this does not happen their trustees, parents, may properly be held to account. Family autonomy is not consistent with the public provision of child-directed income support or welfare services.

How does this differ from 'child-saving'? Platt in coining the term, describes nineteenth-century child-savers as

> 'a group of "disinterested" reformers who regarded their cause as a matter of conscience and morality, serving no particular class or political interests. The child savers viewed themselves as altruists and humanitarians dedicated to rescuing those who were less fortunately placed in the social order. Their concern for "purity", "salvation", "innocence", "corruption", and "protection" reflected a resolute belief in the righteousness of their mission.'
>
> (Platt 1969: 3)

As it is used in current debates 'child-saving' seems to have connotations of paternalism, do-gooding, and the promotion of class interests. It involves the imposition of an alien moral code on one section of a society by another.

We have no such evangelical ambitions. Our discussions (e.g. Dingwall, Eekelaar, and Murray 1983: 211-21; Dingwall, Eekelaar, and Murray 1984b) have stressed pragmatic motives for supporting and regulating child rearing. Of course, as parents, we cannot avoid feeling the contrast between the privileged existence of our own small children and the sad fate of many of those we saw in our research. Nevertheless we are not resting our arguments about social policy on bleeding hearts so much as a demonstration that the survival of the liberal social order we enjoy is integrally bound up with the conditions under which children are raised. That society has all sorts of problems, many of which result from its own internal contradictions, but it has brought shared wealth and liberty to an extent previously unknown on this planet. Its ability to accommodate contradictions, such as those between child protection and family autonomy, is part of its dynamic of change and evolution. The way that this will be preserved is not by forcing families into a moral strait-jacket but by recognizing the need to compromise between diversity and acceptability. The competition between family autonomy and children's rights should not be regarded as an antithesis between good and evil, but as a conflict between competing conceptions of the good. Just as we regard it as acceptable for a liberal state to ban certain forms of sexual or racial discrimination, trading freedom of speech, association, or contract against the rights of certain individuals or groups to enjoy access to the society on equal terms, so it is justifiable to prohibit certain forms of parental behaviour so that their children are not avoidably deprived of physical, moral, or emotional conditions to an extent that would have a permanent adverse effect on their life chances.

The 'national investment' argument for state regulation of family child care may now look like an expression of class interest. One can, however, reach the same conclusions from the principles of an egalitarian democracy and its political theory about the rights of all citizens – children as much as adults – against the state and the state's simultaneous role as the guardian of those rights. (Of course, democracy is an expression of class interest, as against aristocracy, for example, but we do not imagine that this is quite what our critics have in mind.) In so far as the state fails to transcend class interests it may, of course, properly be criticized but one cannot deny it is the right to define the limits of social, including parental, conduct acceptable to its controllers. To the extent that democratic control advances, that right is strengthened.

The practical problem is that of designing social institutions capable of enforcing children's rights under the equality principle without degenerating into a moral tyranny. The evidence presented in *The Protection of Children* and the first part of this paper suggests that the present system is reasonably successful in these terms. Designed in one normative climate, it has adapted to another. Enforcement workers are tied by a set of cultural and organizational checks and balances in such a way as to inhibit their intervention in the absence of strong counter-pressures. In a situation where a public allegation can be just as damaging as a successful prosecution, this is, surely, correct. The details of that system on the health and social service side do not need to be repeated here but we think it may be useful to develop our critique of legal formalism and our defence of magistrates' justice.

In doing so, we are strongly influenced by Silbey's (1981) attack on the critics of low-level courts. They are easy enough to challenge on the gap between ideal versions of due process or the rule of law and the realities of court practice. Silbey points out, though, that these complaints may be obscuring the courts' success in achieving other socially important goals. Specifically, she suggests that they are the arena where the formal justice encouraged by capitalist aspirations to reduce the legal uncertainty of economic activity beloved of academic lawyers, is reconciled with substantive justice. They are a safety valve against the oppressive effects of formalism. The justice of magistrates' courts is what Weber called Khadi justice, having its own order and rationality but dealing with localized troubles in a way that is consistent with community sentiments and individual circumstances. As such, it does not rest on literal-minded attempts to apply abstract rules so much as an attempt to solve practical social problems by the creative use of those rules.

Clearly, there are ways in which the present statutory framework could be improved and it must be said that magistrates' courts are not always a shining example of community justice. Nevertheless, this decentralized, lay element in the system is a critical safeguard against the potential for professional tyranny in a specialized, judge-led family court. While there are some areas of civil and criminal justice that require uniformity throughout the territory of a nation-state by means of explicit rules and a limited pool of judges, family intervention does not properly seem to be among these. Variations between one bench and another are less important grounds for criticism than is evidence that a bench is out of touch with local moral sentiment. In order to achieve this devolution, there must be what organization theorists call 'loose coupling' in the system, statutes, and procedures that set the limits within which local courts operate but which leave sufficient discretion for magistrates to perform their tasks with a common-sense view of the spirit of the law as much as its letter. In their demands for more stringent statutory regulation and pro-fessionalized justice, the legalistic critics of present arrangements are actually contributing to the movement towards a more centralized and unitary state apparatus which is a greater threat to social and moral pluralism than any aspect of the contemporary system.[5]

As our research showed, there are aspects of law and practice which are capable of creating a sense or an impression of injustice. The way forward, however, does not, in our view, lie in radical measures of change so much as in carefully calculated adjustments to a finely balanced system. We have shown that assertions about the growth of state intervention are unsupported by empirical evidence. If treated ideologically, we believe that they are equally misconceived.

We would argue that the equality principle, on which the present system is based, is morally justifiable and politically defensible. It produces a level of intervention that, in our view, is about right or, if anything, errs in the direction of conservatism, an understandable bias and one desirable for anyone who accepts our arguments about the virtues of diversity. Elements that may look unfair are, in practice, substantially mitigated. It is worth removing these grievances by reforming the law to reflect those widespread compromises, but fundamental change is, in our opinion, neither necessary nor desirable.

Acknowledgement

This paper develops many ideas originally evolved in collaboration with Topsy Murray. We are most grateful for the stimulation of her questions during our joint research. The research described in this paper was supported by funds from SSRC and DHSS. We would also like to acknowledge the advice of Branch SR6 of the DHSS Statistics and Research Division and S1 Division of the Home Office.

Notes

1 The statistics in this paper are derived from the series published in *Health and Personal Social Services Statistics for England and Wales*, the *Annual Reports on Children in Care in England and Wales*, the *Annual Abstract of Statistics*, and the *Annual Reports on Children in Care in England and Wales*, issued since 1979. There are also three triennial reports, *Social Services for Children in England and Wales 1973-5, 1976-8*, and *1979-81*. Figures on care orders made by juvenile courts 1971-73 are taken from the Home Office criminal statistics for those years. Unless otherwise indicated, all figures quoted relate to England and Wales.

2 The figures used in this paragraph relate to the beginning of care periods, following the view of DHSS statisticians (e.g. DHSS 1980: 14) that this is what pre-1977 returns actually collected. *Table 10* shows that the numbers of children have followed the same trends at a consistent lower level since 1977.

3 This is, of course, a very small number of cases and we would not wish to found great claims upon it. Nevertheless, we do believe it to be useful in illustrating the complexity of the reasons why children may not return home. We should also note our reservations about using 'return home' as a criterion for a successful outcome,

in the light of Tizard's (1977) work which suggests that this may be more damaging than remaining in care. See also Hensey, Williams, and Rosenbloom (1983).

4 The same may be said about the use of compulsory powers in respect of children in care. Adcock, White, and Rowlands concluded, from a study of four local authorities' use of parental rights resolutions, that

> 'in only four cases out of a total of 267 was there any evidence that the procedures had been abused. . . . Our view was that each one of these (267) children either needed protection from their parents or needed someone who would act as an effective parent.'
>
> (Adcock, White, and Rowlands 1983: 81, 83)

Although, like ourselves, they identified aspects of statutes and procedures that could create an appearance of injustice and needed improvement, their work provides further confirmation of local authorities' restraint in the use of the powers available to them.

5 These arguments are particularly important in the context of current glances toward the French model of the *juge des enfants* who combines the powers of British courts and local authorities in a single legal officer. This system has its own domestic critics (e.g. Donzelot 1979) for its lack of the internal checks and restraints the British system incorporates and the consequent oppressive potential of an intervention system centred on the office of a single, unaccountable judge, part of a centrally trained cadre of like-minded individuals. British advocates of this system claim that it is marked by a more conciliatory treatment of parents which has 'better' outcomes. It is at least as arguable that parents demonstrate greater compliance as a result of the intrinsically coercive nature of encounters with legal officers known to have such a wide range of powers at their personal disposal. The British system has less room for the possible abuse of judicial power to enforce decisions by the authority of office rather than on the basis of publicly tested evidence. The comparative impotence of social workers means that, when coercion is used, it is normally open and following a hearing at which parents have had a genuine chance to oppose it without the constraint of a prospective future relationship with the arbiter. On *juge des enfants* see Chapter 9. [Editor's note.]

References

Adcock, M., White, R., and Rowlands, O. (1983) *The Administrative Parent*. London: British Agencies for Adoption and Fostering.

Arney, W.R. (1983) *Power and the Profession of Obstetrics*. Chicago: University of Chicago Press.

Clarke, A.M. and Clarke, A.D.S. (eds) (1976) *Early Experience: Myth and Evidence*. London: Open Books.

Curtis Committee (1946) *Report of the Care of Children Committee*. Cmnd 6922. London: HMSO.

DHSS (1980) *Children in Care in England and Wales March 1978*. London: HMSO.

Dingwall, R., Eekelaar, J.M., and Murray, T. (1983) *The Protection of Children: State Intervention and Family Life*. Oxford: Basil Blackwell.

——(1984a) Reply to Michael King. *Legal Action,* January.

——(1984b) Childhood as a Social Problem: A Survey of the History of Legal Regulation. *Journal of Law and Society:* 207-32.

Donzelot, J. (1979) *The Policing of Families*. London: Hutchinson.

Eekelaar, J.M. (1984) *Family Law and Social Policy*. 2nd edn. London: Weidenfeld & Nicolson.

Eekelaar, J.M., Dingwall, R., and Murray T. (1982) Victims or Threats? Children in Care Proceedings. *Journal of Social Welfare Law*: 68-82.

Farson, R. (1978) *Birthrights*. Harmondsworth: Penguin.

Freeman, M.D.A. (1976) Children in Care: The Impact of the Children Act 1975: *Family Law* 6: 136-41.

——(1980a) Removing Babies at Birth: A Questionable Practice. *Family Law* 10: 131-34.

——(1980b) The Rights of Children in the International Year of the Child. In Lord Lloyd of Hampstead and R.W. Rideout (eds) *Current Legal Problems 1980*. London: Stevens.

——(1983a) Children's Rights – the Literature. *Childright* November: 19-21.

——(1983b) *The Rights and Wrongs of Children*. London: Frances Pinter.

Geach, H. and Szwed, E. (1983) *Providing Civil Justice for Children*. London: Edward Arnold.

Goldstein, J., Freud, A., and Solnit, A.J. (1980) *Before the Best Interests of the Child*. London: Burnett Books.

Hensey, O.J., Williams, J.K., and Rosenbloom, L. (1983) Intervention in Child Abuse: Experience in Liverpool. *Developmental*

Medicine and Child Neurology 25: 606-11.

Holt, J. (1975) *Escape from Childhood*. Harmondsworth: Penguin.

Hoyles, M. (ed.) (1979) *Changing Childhood*. London: Writers and Readers.

King, M. (1983) The New Child Savers. *LAG Bulletin* October: 10-11.

Morris, A., Giller, H., Szwed, E., and Geach, H. (1980) *Justice for Children*. London: Macmillan.

Mount, F. (1982) *The Subversive Family*. London: Jonathan Cape.

Parker, H., Casburn, M., and Turnbull, D. (1981) *Receiving Juvenile Justice*. Oxford: Basil Blackwell.

Platt, A.M. (1969) *The Child Savers*. Chicago: University of Chicago Press.

Silbey, S. (1981) Making Sense of the Lower Courts. *The Justice System Journal* 6 (1): 13-27.

Taylor, L., Lacey, R., and Bracken, D. (1980) *In Whose Best Interests?* London: Cobden Trust/Mind.

Tizard, B. (1977) *Adoption: A Second Chance*. London: Open Books.

CHAPTER 7

Children, care, and the local state

Madeleine Colvin

Whatever view one holds as to where the line should be drawn between intervention and non-intervention by the state, the state will certainly retain a power to intervene coercively and remove children from their natural families. However, at present, there are undoubtedly too many children in care and the increase in number over the past two decades (62,347 in 1959 to over 96,000 in 1981 (DHSS)) appears to reflect a complacent acceptance of the role of the 'benevolent' state in child care. Clearly this is now being challenged: when the state's benevolent intentions run counter to principles of natural justice, the call is – certainly from the consumers – for the protection of a 'due process' principle governing such intervention.

The legal framework governing the state's role in the child care system is an extraordinary patchwork of Acts and regulations (not noticeably improved by attempts at consolidation). Some statutes were enacted in alarmed reaction to public scandals, others came as a result of more systematic thinking by government committees – but their good intentions have often been undermined by partial implementation or imprecise drafting. Numerous inconsistencies, gaps, and contradictory provisions exist which not only profoundly frustrate everyone involved in child care but also diminish the principles of natural justice. The dozen or more different 'compulsory' routes into care present a multiplicity of different legal considerations and procedures.

It is not only the legal (and administrative) processes used by local authorities in taking a child into care that are being challenged: the apparent autonomy of local authorities to assess the 'best interests' of a child who is in their care has also caused profound dissatisfaction. In the confusing maze of child care law the rights of clients are barely

115

mentioned. The law is reprehensibly vague about parents' legal position when their children are in care. For example, there are no clear answers to questions about parental powers over children's property, medical treatment, nationality, or their rights over education, change of name, or consent to marriage. Even less is said about children's rights. Traditionally under the law children have been seen as passive objects in need of protective laws and not as individuals with enforceable rights.

Of course care has a great potential – as a social service, as a model of good parenting, and as a vanguard in changing society's attitudes to children. There are now many exciting models of 'good practice' to be found in local authorities and voluntary organizations but experience suggests that unfortunately these innovations are not adequately disseminated or encouraged by local government. There are too many children who do not develop or profit from life in care, indeed too many who acutely suffer.

This paper is necessarily only an outline of some of the current problems which cause particular conflicts of interest between local authorities, parents, and their children. It is generally acknowledged that a total overhaul of child care law and practice is urgently needed. Until then there are measures that could be adopted to bring greater coherence and justice to care, encourage good practice, and introduce necessary safeguards against abuse of power.

Going into care

Voluntary care (Child Care Act 1980, s.2) is a necessary form of local authority care for a significant number of children (over 33,000 voluntary care admissions during the year 1980-81 (DHSS)). Its use may well increase as social changes reduce the capacity of families to act independently and autonomously without help from the state. At the same time, the estimated £5 million a year spent by local authorities on 'section 1 money' (Child Care Act 1980) to prevent children being taken into care must be at risk with current policies on public spending.

However, many of these children in voluntary care are there unnecessarily. In the year 1980, 511 children came into care because of homelessness and 7,470 because of short-term illness of parents (DHSS). Although s.1 of the Child Care Act 1980 places a duty on local authorities to diminish 'the need to receive children into or keep them in care', it is a pale provision in comparison, for example, to the

Californian Family Protection Act 1977. Under this legislation, welfare departments must provide the following services to families in need: in-home caretakers, housekeepers, home makers, emergency housing, and respite and shelter care. All services must be available twenty-four hours a day, seven days a week. Vulnerable families are offered additional services on a voluntary basis after the initial crisis period which include family therapy, day care, and scheduled respite care. Children may not be received into voluntary care unless there are no appropriate services acceptable to the parents to keep the child at home. After three years of operation, the number of children taken into care was reduced by approximately 40 per cent (San Mateo County Children's Services).

Even where the placing of a child in voluntary care is a necessity in this country, it is far from being seen as a socially acceptable form of partnership care between the family and the state. It is often regarded with suspicion and fear by parents, as a 'last resort' and a surrender of family rights. There are, of course, many reasons for this, not least the fact that the law is unclear on whether parents retain significant control over what happens to their children in voluntary care. For example, do parents maintain their right of access as part of their parental right defined in s.85 of the Children Act 1975 and which cannot be informally transferred? (See s.6, sch.1 of the Health and Social Services and Social Security Adjudications Act 1983 which excludes children in voluntary care.)

The offer of this voluntary service to families, as presently legislated and practised, cannot therefore be viewed as truly voluntary. It can and increasingly does lead to a compulsory route into care (25.3 per cent of children in voluntary care in 1973 had parental rights assumed; by 1979 it had risen to 40.1 per cent: DHSS). The administrative mechanism by which parental rights are assumed by resolution has been widely debated following the National Council for One Parent Families Report *Against Natural Justice* (July 1982). Proponents for change argue that principles of natural justice require a judicial review of the removal of parental rights and that the procedures whereby the decision is taken by a local authority social services committee is in breach of the European Convention on Human Rights. The recent guidance from the DHSS (LAC (84)5), although suggesting ways in which parents are more involved in the decision-making process, falls far short of the substantial changes required. Opponents to such reform have pointed out that parents do have a court hearing if they object to the social services committee resolution. Children, in fact, do not have this right and have no voice in the decision. Moreover, because at present children are not parties to the action they cannot apply for a discharge and are entirely dependent on the support of either parent or social workers if they want to leave care, particularly if they want to leave and live independently. (The implementation of s.7 of Child Care Act 1980 on 27 May 1984 makes children parties to these proceedings in certain circumstances but does not, it appears, entitle them to initiate an application for discharge.)

Breach of the European Convention has also been alleged in the way the law governs local authority emergency powers to remove children under a Place of Safety Order (Children and Young Persons Act 1969, s.28.) Such an order, which is granted ex parte, and which does not allow for a right of appeal or review, commonly lasts for a period of twenty-eight days and is considered to be an unjustified draconian measure. The number of place of safety orders has increased thirty times since the Maria Colwell case in 1973: 6,212 orders were granted in the year 1980-81 (DHSS). According to the chairperson of the Juvenile Courts Committee of the Magistrates Association, when giving evidence to the parliamentary Social Services Select Committee (March 1983), only 10 per cent of these orders are being correctly obtained: in 90 per cent of cases place of safety orders are used as a routine way of commencing care proceedings. Although there is an obvious need for emergency powers, reforms should be introduced to provide safeguards, less secrecy, and greater accountability on the part of social services personnel and magistrates alike.

The grounds for taking compulsory measures under both s.3 of the Child Care Cat 1980 and s.1 of the Children and Young Persons Act 1969 need to be revised. Critics of these provisions believe that the focus of attention should be on specific harms to the child rather than on parental behaviour. It is not inconceivable that parental failings may not result in demonstrable harm to the child and yet being removed from from home can be both disruptive and traumatic.

The more specific criticisms concern the use of the 'criminal care order' (s.7 (7) of the 1969 Act) and the use of care proceedings for school truants.

The organization Justice for Children has long campaigned for the abolition of the 'criminal care order'. At present about 15 per cent of children in care are under such orders. Without wishing to dwell upon the 'welfare v. justice' debate on juvenile offenders or the relationship between residential care and re-offending rates, it appears that the use of care orders as part of the sentencing tariff has little beneficial effect. In one research study (Thorpe *et al.* 1980) it is argued that 85 per cent of the children on s.7 (7) care orders did not require residential care and could have been dealt with in the community. Although care as a sentence has been pushed up the tariff by the introduction of two new criteria introduced by the Criminal Justice Act 1982 (s.23) its use as a form of punishment is still open to abuse.

Approximately one in five children in care are there on orders made under the education ground (s.1 (2) (e) of the 1969 Act). There are many possible and acknowledged reasons for truancy, including poor or irrelevant education provision, and it would seem that care proceedings are an inappropriate way of dealing with a child who is a truant. It has been said that 'too ready use of legal sanction is counterproductive, frequently wrongly singling out the individual child as the focus for attention' and that research suggests that 'the most successful medium of intervention in the majority of cases is the mainstream school albeit with, in some cases, modifications to curriculum and internal management approaches' (Conn 1983). In any event the ability of care authorities to increase the educational input or level of attainment of truants in care is very questionable, as evidenced by HM Inspectorate of Schools Report, 'Community Homes with Education' (1980).

In the actual judicial process of taking a child into care, the manner in which the child is represented is a crucially important issue. There has for a long time been criticism of the unacceptably low standard of legal representation for children in care proceedings. (The Law Society is presently drawing up proposals for panels of solicitors with expertise in child care cases to be available in juvenile courts.) However the role of the child's lawyer is in need of urgent clarification: a lawyer is ethically bound to follow the instructions of a client who is capable of giving such instructions, but what is the position where the client is deemed to be too young to give instructions? The full implementation of the court's power to appoint a guardian *ad litem* for the child in care and related proceedings from 27 May, 1984 has widened the debate.

When the Government announced its intention in March 1983 to implement ss.64 and 65 of the Children Act 1975, there was a common belief that the appointment of a guardian could be nothing but beneficial. It was only on closer examination of the provisions that there appeared to be serious defects in the proposal. Many organizations, including the Children's Legal Centre, Family Rights Group, National Council for One Parent Families, Justice for Children, and the Law Society urged the Government to abandon implementing eight-year-old sections of the Children Act 1975 as they believed they would no longer safeguard the interests of children in care proceedings. In particular, the Children's Legal Centre pointed out that the court rules (Magistrates' Court (Children and Young Persons) Rules 1970 as amended) prescribed a role for the guardian which is an amalgam of advocate, expert witness, inquisitor, and adjudicator.

Despite this barrage of criticism, panels of guardians *ad litem* must be established under the auspices of local authorities from 27 May, 1984 (Children Act 1975 s.103; Guardians ad Litem and Reporting Officers (Panels) Regulations 1983). However the role of the guardian is substantially altered by amendments to the court rules (Magistrates' Courts (Children and Young Persons) (Amendment) Rules 1984). The guardian's role does not include advocacy in court: unless the court otherwise directs, the guardian must appoint a solicitor. The relationship between these two representatives is prescribed by a rule that states that the guardian must consider how the case is to be presented in conjunction with the solicitor. A significant amendment has been included that preserves the child or young person's right to give their own instructions to the solicitor, when of such an age and understanding to be able to do so, and even though this may be in conflict with the guardian's view.

Whilst in care

Local authorities have for many years resisted any challenge to their extensive discretionary powers to determine the lives of children in their care. The strongest opponents to any change have been the professional and local authority associations which have defended their powers on grounds that only social workers can properly assess what is in the 'best interests' of an individual child. This has been largely endorsed by a long line of High Court cases which culminated in the decision of the Lords in *A.* v. *Liverpool Corporation* 1981. The lobby for increased client's rights holds the view that, in the interests of natural justice, the way social workers exercise their powers must be subject to some form of independent review of appeal. Campaigns for legislative change solely based on principles of natural justice have not elicited sufficient support, whereas greater success has been achieved where the pressure for reform has been put in the context of allegations of breaches of the European Convention on Human Rights.

Certainly, in the case of the use of local authority secure accommodation for children in care, the Government introduced the judicial determination element (Child Care Act 1980 s.21A) into the procedure for admission as a pragmatic measure to ensure against any breach of the European Convention. Lord Trefgarne, for the Government, said during the debate: 'We certainly would not wish any situation which kept us in breach of the European Convention to be allowed to subsist for a moment longer than is necessary' (House of Lords Hansard, 28 June, 1982). The safeguards of the new legislation provide strict criteria to be applied before admission and a juvenile court hearing within seventy-two hours to authorize any further placement (s.21A Child Care Act 1980 as last inserted by the Health and Social Services and Social Security Adjudications Act 1983; Secure Accommodation (No.2) Regulations 1983). It was anticipated by many that the number of young people going into secure accommodation would significantly decrease. Certainly this appears to have been the result initially: the Children's Legal Centre, which was largely instrumental in bringing about the changes in the law, monitored the number of applications made in the seventy-two hours following implementation on 24 May, 1983. Of the 29 units responding, there were 203 operational places, but only 86 applications had been made to the juvenile court. However, from more recent monitoring both the Children's Legal Centre and others (for example, the London Boroughs Children Regional Planning Committee), it appears that over the months since implementation the figures have not substantially altered. The Children's Legal Centre makes the comment that from its monitoring it is apparent that the success rate for applications is running at nearly 100 per cent. This perhaps implies that juvenile court magistrates may not be fully aware of their unique role in these new proceedings: for example, decisions on granting the application are made on the basis of the best interests of the young person rather than on the strict criteria laid down in the Act.

Another new piece of legislation has also recognized the principle that the courts have a role and function to play whilst children are in care. There has been considerable controversy in recent years over the inability in law of parents (and children) to challenge access decisions taken by local authorities. Support for a change in the law led to amendments to the Health and Social Services and Social Security Adjudications Act 1983. The new laws (s.6 and sch.1) brought into effect on 31 January, 1984 allow parents to apply to a juvenile court when access is terminated or refused. At the same time the DHSS has issued a code of practice – the first code in child care law (HMSO 1984). Although these changes in law must be welcomed, critics point out that there is still no remedy for parents whose access is merely restricted (Atherton 1984).

The right of children in care to be involved in decisions affecting their lives was first given statutory recognition in the Children Act 1975 (s.59, now s.18, of the Child Care Act 1980). This 'welfare principle' is without doubt one of the most important duties affecting children in care, but its practical application is sadly limited. Too few social service departments have taken the duty seriously and children in care continue to have decisions such as placement, educational provision, access to family, and discharge from care, made about them without consultation. All these decisions can have a crucial effect on their lives. Mr Justice Latey however was persuaded in a recent case (*Liddle and Others* v. *Sunderland Borough Council*, 11–13 October, 1982) to decide that a local authority acted *ultra vires* in deciding to close a children's home before applying the s.18 principle. This was followed in the case of *R.* v. *Solihull Metropolitan Borough Council* ex parte *C, H, and Others (Minors)* 10 November, 1983, QBD, Mr Justice McCullough) where six young people in care sought an application through their Next Friend for judicial review to quash the local authority's decision to close their children's home.

If decisions are being made about a young person's future, it is crucial to ensure the child's co-operation and understanding. Hence the issue of giving children and young people the right (to exercise or not as they wish) to attend their review is an important one. This necessarily leads to the question of a young person's access to his or her file: it would appear somewhat meaningless to invite children to reviews for verbal discussion if there is another level of discussion being conducted on paper. A step in this direction has been promoted by a recent DHSS Circular (24 August, 1983) which sets out the principles governing the disclosure of information on files. It specifically refers to children and young people: 'requests from children or young people should be treated in the same way as adults'.

At present (1984) the DHSS is reviewing (and revising) the regulations required to protect children living in a variety of residential placements: local authority community homes, voluntary homes, and private homes. It seems an appropriate time to press for regulations that would provide consistent safeguards for the welfare of all children placed outside the family. These regulations should cover fundamental civil liberties provided for both in terms of general prescriptive rights and specific rights including prohibition of anti-welfare practices (for example, communication with parents and others should not be used as a form of punishment). Rules and regulations may not necessarily produce positive attitudes any more than additional resources or staff training will, but they can help. At the very least legal safeguards prevent an excessive abuse of power. Optimally they give children respect, and an understanding both of their rights and of the limits of choice which an individual within a community has.

References

Atherton, C. (1984): Access in Care. *Childright*, March.

Conn, W. (1983) Truancy: The Ball in Whose Court? In H. Geach and E. Szwed (eds) *Providing Civil Justice for Children*. London: Edward Arnold.

Department of Health and Social Security. *Children in Care in England and Wales* for each year ending March. Available from: DHSS Leaflets, PO Box 21, Stanmore, Middlesex HA7 1AY.

HMSO (1984) *Code of Practice: Access to Children in Care*. London: HMSO.

Thorpe, D.H., Smith, D., Green, C.J., and Paley, J.H. (1980) *Out of Care: The Community Support of Juvenile Offenders*. London: Allen & Unwin.

CHAPTER 8

State intervention in the family in the Netherlands

Madzy Rood-de Boer

Introduction

Last summer, an official ministerial advisory committee in the Nether-lands (Geelhoed 1983) produced a report entitled 'The Intervening State'. The report is mainly concerned with considerations of policy and practicality. Its themes are that official intervention costs money, that we must economize and so let there be as little intervention as possible. In this report not a word is said about either family law or youth protection. I mention the publication here merely to illustrate that 'state intervention' is a subject of investigation everywhere.[1]

In my paper I will concentrate on the subject of state intervention in matters relating to child protection. I look at some problems this has caused recently, some criticisms of current practices, some reforms. My article is illustrated by references to some noteworthy recent Dutch cases.

The system of state intervention in the family in the Netherlands

Although it will not be possible for me to speak for, or on behalf of, all western countries, it may be of interest, in connection with our subject, to mention that about the turn of the century most countries on the Continent adopted some system that made it possible to turn parental authority into a *contestable right* and to make those parents who exercised their parental authority badly – or, at any rate, in a socially unacceptable manner – *lose their parental authority*. In the abstract, this means the 'loss of parental rights'; in actual fact, it means that the children were placed in foster families or homes away from their parents (see Titles 14 and 15, book 1 of the Dutch Civil

Code, in particular articles 245/377). The starting point for this fundamental change in family law was the concept that parental authority was, not so much a competency of the parents with regard to their children, but a *social duty*. In the Netherlands, this view owed a lot to the writings of the influential French jurist, Léon Duguit (Duguit 1919).

Parents have the duty to educate their children in such a manner that they will become useful members of society. If the parents fail in this respect, if they do not comply with their social duty, or do it badly, the authorities must intervene. On the Continent, the term 'state intervention' is not entirely clear. What we would have in mind is that the competent *legislative body* should create a general legal framework, within which the *court*, basing itself on clear legal grounds, makes a decision in a special case with regard to parents and child, whereas the *administration* prepares the case and also assists in carrying out the decision after the intervention. State intervention in family law provides an example of team-work – in principle at any rate – between various official organs: the legislative, the judiciary, and the executive powers.

In the Netherlands, the child statutes were adopted by Parliament in 1901 and came into operation in 1905 (see Statute of 6 February, 1901, Statutes book 62). Thus the formal legal framework was created, within which the courts could make decisions with regard to parents and child. Since 1922 (Statute of 5 July, 1921, Statutes book 834), these cases have been referred to a special court: the juvenile court. Once the decision has been handed down, the child is cared for and educated by private institutions. Other European countries have systems under which these children are cared for and educated by state or local authorities. But in the Netherlands, this is always the task of private initiative. The fact that private institutions are essentially the ones who apply the child statutes does not make it any easier to deal with the subject of state intervention and the family. On the other hand, this fact must be kept in mind. If I am not mistaken, clear shifts in the direction of private initiative are also observed in countries that, for a long time and until recently, had almost exclusively systems of 'state education' of 'protection children'. This is the case in France, the Federal Republic of Germany, Austria, and in several other countries.

The only country in Europe that applies a system like that in the Netherlands is Switzerland. The Swiss even adopted the name of the oldest Dutch private institution for child protection, *Pro Juventute*.[2]

The fact that private initiative performs the work of carrying out the judicial decision after the court has intervened, does not prevent the authorities from subsidizing these private institutions, even totally subsidizing them. The intertwining of official and private initiatives is thus very marked in the Netherlands.

Although this may perhaps be considered to be superfluous, there is nevertheless a rule that judicial decisions must always be based on legal grounds, precisely laid down in the statutes. The decision to intervene is only taken if it is considered to be in the interest of the child. Many years before the books by Goldstein *et al.* (1973, 1979), the criterion for the Netherlands courts, whether they should, or should not, intervene in the family relationship, was: 'the best interests of the child'. The Dutch system of intervention has now been in existence for eighty years. It shows many cracks, many complaints are heard, and many changes have been, and are being, considered. It would, however, be incorrect to assume that the system of 1984 is still the same as that of 1905. The *legislature* has regularly made additions and amendments to the system, although no basic changes have been made in the eighty years. Present-day *judicial decisions* are very different from those of eighty years ago. So are the ways in which the decisions are implemented and operationalized. Naturally, they have been influenced by developments in the social sciences.

The growing discontent

Towards the end of the 1960s, serious criticism was voiced and great social discontent arose about the field of youth law. The discontent was, originally, voiced *mainly by those who worked in the institutions of youth protection: the social workers and group leaders in the homes*.

A number of tracts appeared (e.g. *The Pink Pamphlet* (1970); *The Field-Memorandum* (1971); *The Manifesto* (1971)), documents partly filled with self-criticism. Everything had to be changed, in particular and initially the institutions within which the authors of these publications worked. The result was that 'winds of change' began to blow through the ancient institutions. A start was made by democratizing the institutions, but the legal system itself was not altered. This required statutory amendments. Plans to do this accumulated, but, unfortunately, the Government did nothing to put these into effect.

Some criticisms of the Council for Child Protection

Since the child laws came into being, at the beginning of the century, there has existed an administrative semi-official body, the Council for Child Protection, which prepares the interventions in parental authority. In some cases, the Council acts as party in the lawsuit *and* as adviser to the juvenile court (as in cases of deprivation of, and exoneration from, parental authority, and placing under supervision of a child). In other cases, it acts only in an advisory function, as in the granting of parental authority after divorce and the settlement of visiting rights.

The Council for Child Protection has never been a popular body: it was always feared. Before 1956, when it was still called 'Custody Council', people in Amsterdam shouted at the representatives of the Council: 'Custody Council: child stealer'! But criticism during the last few years has not been directed *exclusively* against the Council in its function of carrying out judicial decisions. What is under fire now is the content of the advisory reports submitted to the court before it hands down its decision. On what grounds does the Council advise the court that, for instance, in the Council's view, a request for adoption should be granted, or that the father should not be granted visiting rights? The rule that the Council's reports can be read by the parties concerned (see below) has not, in my opinion, removed the suspicion against it. The advisory reports are prepared on the basis of information obtained from the police and third parties, but mostly on the basis of talks that the social workers of the Council have with the parents and/or foster-parents themselves.

Often, the parents do not know how they should answer a question from the Council's social worker; not understanding exactly what is meant by the question. They are afraid that a certain answer might create an unfavourable impression, be misunderstood, or misinterpreted. A couple of examples will be given to illustrate this problem.

Case 1: The family investigation

A fairly well-off childless family wanted to take foreign baby twins into its home with a view to adopting them. During the family investigation, the social worker of the Council for Child Protection is reported to have said to the future foster-mother: 'Surely you will never wash the babies' nappies by hand?' The foster-mother answered impulsively: 'Well, no. I have this lovely new washing machine' In the advisory report to the court, the social worker of the Council wondered whether the twins ought to be placed in this family, since she thought it questionable whether the foster-mother would be willing to do enough for the children, not being prepared to wash the babies' nappies by hand!

Since people have come to know more about their rights and the protection of their rights, the contents of the Council's advisory reports are less automatically accepted than they used to be. The consequences of this 'greater self-assertion' can be seen in the second illustrative case.

Case 2: The case of Merijn and Michiel

After divorce a father who did not have custody of his two sons tried to get access to them. The mother refused him access and the court did not grant him the right of access. With the help of friends and a special foundation, the father published a booklet, richly illustrated with pictures of his two children. The title of the widely distributed booklet is: *Report on a Judicial Crime*. It was, of course, reported in the Dutch media and had some not inconsiderable impact.

Some criticisms of the juvenile court

It is not surprising that the next institution to come under fire was the *juvenile courts*. The judges were personally attacked in the daily press and heavily criticized. Suddenly, the time of the sovereign judge, who could not be called to account by anyone, was past. When the institution of juvenile courts had been in existence for fifty years, in the autumn of 1972, the 'child protection children' stood outside the building where the festivities were organized demonstrating and distributing pamphlets. The discussion in the hall was thoroughly disturbed by a large group of banner carrying youngsters who wished to read out statements before the microphone. Since then no peace has reigned in the juvenile courts.

It must be said that it is not entirely clear what the juvenile courts are reproached with. Is it:
– Their treatment of parents and/or children, which is sometimes felt to be authoritarian?
– Their attitude of distance from, and lack of understanding for, the real problems of adolescents and their parents?
– The contents of the courts' decisions?

The following is a case in which a decision was made on appeal, which caused some commotion in professional circles.

Case 3: The case of the homosexual father

After a divorce in 1971, father X was granted custody of his two small daughters. Mother was, at the time, in an unstable condition, and she did not consider she could look after and bring up the children alone. The girls visited her once a fortnight and spent part of their holidays with her. In 1971, father entered into a homosexual relationship with another man who came to live with him after a year. This man carried out household duties; the girls were well looked after and did not appear to be deprived. In the meantime, the mother had recovered from her breakdown and had remarried. She asked the court in 1973 to be assigned custody of the children. The court rejected her application; the children were to remain with the father on the following grounds:

(a) that a disruption of the stabilized circumstances by changing custody could only be justified on the basis of compelling arguments;
(b) that at the present such an argument cannot rest alone on the fact of the father's homosexual relationship, which has not only proved durable but which would also be something with which the children would have come to terms, though less directly, if they were assigned to the mother.

The mother then lodged an appeal. The Court of Appeal granted the mother's application and the children were transferred from the father to the mother on the following grounds.

(a) that the father was a good father;
(b) that he paid a lot of attention to the children;
(c) that the homosexual relationship between the father and his friend was only relevant to this case in so far as it affected the upbringing and care for the children;
(d) that as a result of the friend's moving in to live with their father they were confronted daily with the relationship;
(e) that they were already aware that their father and his friend kissed one another and shared the same bedroom, and it might reasonably be expected that in the coming years, the girls (by then aged nine and seven) would become increasingly aware of the particular problems this relationship holds for them;

(f) that it considered the children's subsequent care and upbringing by the mother appropriate since, on the one hand, it was totally unsure how the girls would come to terms with their father's homosexual relationship as they grew older, and, on the other hand, the girls could live with their mother now that she had recovered and remarried, and

(g) that it was to be expected that these mentally and physically healthy children would be able to adjust well to moving to their mother.[3]

Case 4: The mother, Elisabeth, reincarnate

Johanna K, a teacher of nursing, was married to Bert D, a lung specialist. The couple had two children, now eight and six years old respectively. The divorce was granted in 1980; the children were assigned to the mother, after an intense legal battle. The mother was supported and comforted in her 'fight against male rationality, suppressive of feelings', by another woman. 'In our relationship we discovered the special centuries-old kinship of our souls and our absolute purity,' the mother wrote. The two women started treating people in distress and gradually they discovered that the one woman is the reincarnation of Mary, the mother of Jesus, and that Johanna K (the mother of the two children) is the reincarnation of Elisabeth, the mother of John the Baptist. When the two (reincarnate) women made a pilgrimage to Fatima in Portugal, in May, 1983, the children were placed by the court in a children's home. An application for withdrawal of custody from the mother has been introduced by the Council for Child Protection on the grounds of 'serious neglect of the education and care of the children as a result of her activities in a religious sect'. Provisionally, mother Johanna K has been suspended by the court from exercising custody. She is defending herself vehemently, sending stencils with her history to many people, calling it a 'witch hunt of 1983', and organizing religious displays.

In my view, both cases (3 and 4) concern parents who feel aggrieved by the judicial intervention because their 'being different' has caused courts to deprive them of their custody, although, in their view, they have not misbehaved towards their children at all. The intervening court, however, has held that the life-style of the parents concerned justifies the decision to intervene in the ways in which it has.

In itself, it is perhaps remarkable that the court intervened in these cases and placed the children elsewhere. In the Netherlands there are also some situations where there is no intervention but, in the view of many people, the court should have intervened. Before I give an example of such a situation, I must make it clear that the reason for this non-intervention cannot be attributed to the court alone. A court cannot make a decision on its own initiative. It can only do so where the Council for Child Protection seises the court of the case and applies for the court to intervene.

To give one example where there will not be intervention: since the establishment in the Netherlands, in 1971, of a system of 'confidential doctors' to deal with cases of child maltreatment (see Christopherson 1980; Freeman 1977), cases of child abuse are, as a rule, dealt with by means of assistance and social work. Only very rarely does a case of child maltreatment lead to criminal prosecution and intervention in parental authority. The public indignation and the cry for state intervention are loud, but rarely in such cases is there 'state intervention' of the kind just described in this paper.

The decline in state intervention

Fewer state interventions take place now than ten years ago. A number of reasons can be posited to explain this decline, in particular:

(a) the empirical evidence which proves the minimal positive effect of intervention and the harm such interventions may cause;

(b) the fear of stigmatizing parents that is so prevalent among judicial authorities in the Netherlands;

and

(c) the rise and development of a large number of extra-judicial assistance institutions that operate on a voluntary basis.

This decline of intervening has sometimes bizarre consequences.

Case 5: The case of the drug baby

Since 1980, a local working group of medical personnel and persons involved in judicial child protection has been active in Amsterdam. The fact that the number of babies of drug-addicted mothers has been growing during the last few years has attracted the attention of this group and has caused them concern, especially where the new-born child shows all the symptoms of addiction of his or her mother. It is essential that these babies be weaned off these symptoms of addiction speedily. The working group considers that measures of child protection should be applied to these 'addicted' neonates because the addicted mothers are (or will be) unable properly to care for their children and educate them. The judicial authorities (the Council for Child Protection and the juvenile courts) doubt, however, whether legal grounds for intervention can be found in cases where the mother's addiction is the real reason for concern.

Another reason for the decline in state intervention is the extraordinarily high level of cuts at present being applied to the entire youth assistance field, and new, unbelievable reductions are to be expected to continue for the foreseeable future. To what remarkable consequences this can lead is evidenced by the following case example.

Case 6: The angry mother and the unwanted child

This mother, three years ago when she was pregnant, wanted to have an abortion. For various reasons the abortion was not carried out. At the birth, her baby daughter proved to be seriously defective. The mother at once urged that child should be allowed to die. The doctors, however, refused to comply with her wishes. Thereupon, mother Y applied to the Council for Child Protection with the request that she should be allowed to give up her unwanted and unfit child. She felt that she was in no way able or fit to undertake the care and education of this child. At the request of the Council, mother Y was relieved (by the court) of authority of the child. The baby was placed in an institution and the costs were borne by the local authority. The medical directors of the institution have meanwhile come to consider that the little girl will be better off in a foster family and have placed her with such a family. Mother Y has received an order for payment of a contribution towards the cost of placement in the foster family. She is highly indignant. Her argument is that ever since the pregnancy she has not wanted the child; that when it was born in spite of her protests, she herself insisted on official intervention in her parental authority; and that never having had the care of the child, she considers it quite wrong that she should be burdened with its upkeep, when so far as she is concerned the child is a complete stranger.

Some criticisms of the makers of the rules

In some cases where a medical operation on a child has been deemed
to be necessary, and the parents have not wanted it to be performed,
the intervention of the court has been requested. But there is in the
Netherlands a body of juristic opinion that intervention, by means of
a measure of child protection, would be inappropriate in such cases.
Their argument is that a legal ground for intervention suitable to such
medical situations does not exist in Dutch law. Some examples may
be given to illustrate the debate and the problems. The first arises out
of the issue of inoculation.

In the Netherlands, there is no compulsory inoculation against
polio. When a polio epidemic occurs, as it did in 1978, the question of
whether or not the authorities should intervene and insist on the
compulsory inoculation of all children becomes a subject of heated
debate (Rood-de Boer 1984). Legislators are reproached with the
criticism that the packet of child protection measures is a typical
product of nineteenth-century thinking, which may have been progressive in 1901 but is out of touch with the social realities of 1984.
Fundamental changes have been proposed in legal writings (Van
Beugen and Rood-de Boer 1980), but Parliament has not taken any
steps to bring about a new, modern system in which the emphasis
would be less on incrimination of 'bad parents' than on their right to
assistance. At the moment no *ad hoc* interventions can be made by
the judge *fi* to order an inoculation of the child. And when the
makers of the rules do change the directives and adapt them (a kind
of state intervention via amended rules), this can also lead to results
that are not entirely satisfactory, as can be seen in the next illustration.

Case 7: The Jehovah's Witnesses and the second foreign foster-child

Family d V-V, Jehovah's Witnesses, having three children of their
own, aged sixteen, fourteen, and eight years respectively, obtained a
so-called 'permit in principle', from the Ministry of Justice in 1977, to
take in a foreign foster-child with a view, eventually, to adopting him.
A small Columbian boy was placed with this family. He is blind in
one eye and is also still very retarded. Further, the difference in age
between him and the foster-parents' own children is so great that the
foster-parents d V-V applied a second time in December 1978 for a
'permit in principle' to take a second foster-child into their family.
However, in the summer of 1978, the polio epidemic had taken place

and, in the spring of 1979, the Ministry of Justice amended its internal directives with regard to the taking in of foreign foster-children in such a way that parents can only be considered as prospective adopters if they intend to have the adopted child undergo 'those current medical treatments, of a preventive or curative nature, that are of vital importance to the child'. This implies that, if candidate foster-parents are unwilling to carry out this intention, for example with regard to inoculation or blood transfusion, they shall not be eligible for a 'permit in principle'. Without such a permit, one is not allowed to take in a foreign foster-child. The foster-parent couple of d V-V tried in vain to have the court annul the negative decision taken by the Under-Secretary of the Ministry of Justice to their application. The court held that, although, under the former rules, they were allowed to take in the first Columbian foster-child in 1977, they could not, under the new rules now obtaining, base their claims on the rules that were previously in force. This meant that, in 1979, they were not entitled to a 'permit in principle' and, consequently, could not take a second foreign foster-child into their family. As members of the Jehovah's Witnesses sect, they, for reasons of principle, objected to inoculations and blood transfusions.[4]

Modern safeguards against state intervention

Classical safeguards to state intervention have often been considered. I should like to mention, however, and deal with, some modern safeguards. These are intended to give better protection to the citizen against powerful authorities. At the same time, they are aimed at clarifying why state intervention is sometimes necessary.

Publicity of the reports: the question of open files

On 18 March, 1977 (nrs 356/377), the Under-Secretary of the Ministry of Justice sent a circular letter to the Council for Child Protection which contained the following directive rules:
(a) During the investigation, the Council's social worker should observe the greatest possible openness towards the client.
(b) Third parties consulted during the investigation should know that, in principle, the information they provide will be made known to the clients.
(c) The draft report should be discussed with the client, or read out to him, or be given to him to read.

(d) The final report shall, in principle, be deposited for the client's inspection in the office of the Council.

(e) The final report should mention whether the client took advantage of the opportunity to inspect files and, if so, how he reacted.

(f) If the Council is of the opinion that, for special reasons, inspection of the report by the client is not to be allowed, the client should be informed of this and the reasons.

(g) The client may apply to the court in order to obtain inspection of the file.

(h) Reports obtained from third parties should be treated with the same openness, unless these third parties object, for stated reasons.

(i) The client's lawyer is entitled, in principle, to inspect the report. As a rule, the reports should be sent to the lawyers by the Council.

In practice, there have been some hitches in these seemingly progressive rules on open files.[5] In particular, information obtained from third parties is not always made available for inspection by the client. Second, the risk of 'secret' or 'shadow' files, separate from the open file, exists. A third problem is caused by the fact that, although the client can inspect the report produced by him, this does not mean that he can amend, or add to, the report. Only once has a court rendered a decision on this subject up till now.

Rules of complaint

On 1 May, 1982, there entered into force the amended organization Decree concerning councils of child protection (KB 21 January, 1982, Official Gazette 16). Articles 35/43 deal with the completely new rules of complaint. Anyone who, as a party interested or as an informer, is concerned in a case of child protection pending before the Council may lodge a complaint. The complaint may concern only the behaviour or attitude towards the complainant by a worker employed by the Council. The complainant should first apply to the director of the Council; if that does not lead to an acceptable solution, he can submit his complaint to a 'complaints commission' (Delfos 1983). The rules only apply to 'complaints about treatment', lodged by those who are, or will be, the subject of state intervention. During the first six months of the rules, there were only eight complaints lodged. Five of these were declared non-receivable, and of the remaining three one was declared entirely unfounded and the other two partly unfounded.

We saw above (p.127) how prevalent and vehement criticism of the Council for Child Protection has become. It seems highly questionable whether the new rules of complaint, which deal only with discourteous or incorrect treatment of clients and others, will do much to undermine this current criticism. There are a number of reasons for this. The admissible grounds for complaint are restricted. Those who are discontented will want to complain, not so much about their treatment at the hands of the council's workers, as about the contents of the whole file that led to the court's intervention in family life. Thus, it seems to me that the existing 'rules of complaint about treatment' only partially allay the prevalent dissatisfaction. They form only at best partial protection against state intervention.

The hearing of minors

Recently, some legal protection was introduced for minors who are involved in some manner of state intervention concerning themselves or their family. On 5 July, 1982, there entered into force the statute of 2 June, 1982 (Official Gazette 315) concerning the hearing of minors in civil law matters that concern them. This statute amended the Code of Civil Procedure in the sense that the court is not allowed to make a decision concerning a child of twelve years or older, unless it has given this child the opportunity to inform the court of his thoughts on the matter. Even children of less than twelve years of age may be heard by the court. If the minor has not availed himself of this opportunity, the court may fix another date on which the child shall be brought before it. If, then, he again fails to appear, the case will be dealt with without him. With regard to this statute, which has now been in force for nearly two years, I am as yet unable to relate any evidence as to what has happened as a result of it. However, in my opinion, this compulsory hearing of the child is but a weak protection against state intervention.

The European Convention for the Protection of Human Rights and Fundamental Freedoms

In my view, the most important protection of citizens against national state intervention is at present located in Strasbourg, in the European Commission and Court of Human Rights. Because in the Dutch legal system there is direct applicability and overriding power of conventions binding on everyone (this includes the European Convention on Human Rights), the Netherlands authorities, whether the legislative bodies, or the courts, or the administration, are bound to interpret the clauses of the convention, not only from the point of view of Dutch law but also from that of the international legal order of which the Dutch legal system forms a part (Van Dijk 1983). The fact that this international public law approach is novel for many of our family and juvenile law experts and thus has caught them unaware does not imply that the highest court in the Netherlands overlooked it. This can be seen in my final illustration.

Case 8: Refusal of marriage consent

The refusal by the father-guardian of an under-age child of marriage-able age to consent to his child's marriage is based on article 35(1) and article 36(1) and (2) of the Dutch Civil Code. The father's refusal is however contrary to article 12 of the European Convention on Human Rights. This refusal cannot be interpreted as an absolute veto on the marriage. The Dutch Supreme Court held that the child is allowed to apply to a judge to give consent to the marriage instead of the father's consent (Hoge Raad, 14 June, 1982, NJ 1982, 118).

Notes

1 In the informal meeting of European Ministers of Justice in Rome on 12 May, 1983 they even discussed possibilities of non-state intervention, because of the financial problems of member states of the Council of Europe.
2 Established in Amsterdam in 1896 by Professor G.A. van Hamel, professor of penal law at the University of Amsterdam.
3 Decided by the Court of Appeal at Arnhem, 22 January, 1974, reported in NJ 1974, 492.
4 Jurisdictional Section of the Council of State, 22 June, 1981, reported in AB 1983, 210.
5 The law was amended in respect of the open files on 3 July, 1968, Stb 343; this led to a new text of WRv 908a and 909b. Practice however showed the necessity for official circulars, first one of 10 May, 1971 nr 270/771 and then the circular of 18 March, 1977 referred to above. Recently a new circular on this matter was published on 17 February, 1984 nr 126/784.

References

Christopherson, J. (1980) Child Abuse in Holland. *Community Care* 10 July: 22-3.

Delfos, G. (1983) The First Experiences with the Rules of Complaint for the Councils for Child Protection. *Tijdschrift voor Familie – en Jeugdrecht, pp. 99-106, (FJR)*.

Duguit, L. (1919) *Law in the Modern State*. Paris: Flammarion.

Freeman, M.D.A. (1977) Towards the Prevention of Child Battering – The Dutch Approach. *Family Law* 7: 53-6.

Geelhoed, G.A. (1983) *The Intervening State: Onset for a Doctrine of Means*. 'sGravenhage: State Publishing Office.

Goldstein, J., Freud, A., and Solnit, A. (1973) *Beyond the Best Interests of the Child*. New York: Free Press.

——(1979) *Before the Best Interests of the Child*. New York: Free Press.

Rood-de Boer, M. (1984) Decision-making About Health Care and Medical Treatment of Minors. In J. Eekelaar and S. Katz (eds) *The Resolution of Family Conflicts*. Toronto: Butterworths.

Van Beugen, M. and Rood-de Boer, M. (1980) *A House for Tomorrow*, FJR 1980, nrs 5 and 6 (Preliminary Report to Society for Family and Juvenile Law).

Van Dijk, P. (1983) To What Changes in Netherlands Law Should the Principles of Proper Protection, Laid Down in Article 6 of the European Convention of Human Rights and Fundamental Freedoms, Give Rise? Netherlands Assoc. of Jurists 'Tjeenk Willink, Zwolle.

CHAPTER 9

Child protection and the search for justice for parents and families in England and France[1]

Michael King

The picture that emerges from the recent parliamentary debate and press and television programmes on social workers' control of parental access to children in care is that of a powerful bureaucratic machine in the form of social service departments totally dominating the relationship between children and their families. According to the Family Rights Group (1983), the pressure group for parents of children in care, once a child is in care, this domination takes little account of the wishes of the child's parents or other relations, even to the point of cutting off any contact between the child and the family. It may be exercised in a manner which pays more regard to departmental policies and trends in social work practice than to the rights and feelings of those children and parents affected by the implementation of these policies or the pursuit of these trends. Yet until comparatively recently the power exercised by social workers not only reflected Parliament's view, as expressed repeatedly in child care legislation, as to the proper role of the local authority in relation to children and families with problems, but also a view expressed in a succession of court cases, culminating in *A.* v. *Liverpool City Council*, in which the Law Lords made it clear that parents could not use wardship jurisdiction to question the wisdom of local authority social workers' decisions. The inclusion in the recent HASSASSA[2] of a right for parents to apply to the juvenile court if access to their children is terminated and a procedure for social workers to apply to a magistrate before suspending parental access indicate, therefore, a significant move by the legislature away from the traditional doctrine of non-interference by the courts once a care order had been made or a parental rights resolution confirmed. It is a move advocated for some time by pressure groups such as the Family Rights Group and Justice for Children and even by some senior members of the judiciary (see e.g. Latey 1982). Yet what many who support these changes have failed to appreciate is that the juvenile courts, as presently constituted, are totally unsuitable institutions for the role of controllers of the social workers.

The juvenile court

One of the less welcome effects of the recent resurgence of support for justice, as opposed to welfare, for children is that it has tended to idealize the courts and legal decision-making[3] in much the same way as a previous generation of reformers idealized social work and the good that could be achieved through social work intervention. It has to be remembered, however, that juvenile courts are essentially extensions of the magistrates' courts. This is true not only in the sense that many juvenile courts take place physically in the same courthouse as magistrates' courts or even in the same courtroom, but also, and more importantly, in the sense that many, if not most, juvenile courts tend to adopt a criminal trial model when dealing with contested care cases. This is not particularly surprising when one considers it is common enough to find in the juvenile court the same magistrates assisted by the same clerks and addressed by the same lawyers as appear in the adult criminal court. Only the police and prosecutor are missing, their place being taken by the local authority's social workers and a solicitor from its legal department. What then are the features of this model?

1 Formality of procedures, including rigid turn taking in the presentation of each side's evidence, formalized cross-examination and re-examination and speech making before and after the presentation of evidence.[4]

2 Emphasis on oral evidence to the exclusion of any written statements during the 'fact finding' stage of the proceedings, including any reports by or files of the local authority. In addition to the oral tradition, which characterizes criminal trials in England and Wales, even statements permitted in criminal cases under s.9 of the Criminal Justice Act 1967 are not admitted in care cases. Neither have the provisions of the Civil Evidence Act 1968 allowing written statements and documents yet been extended to cover civil proceedings in the juvenile court.[5]

3 The imposition of strict rules of evidence in relation to hearsay and opinion with the important exception that social workers may and often do apply for the status of an expert witness which enables them to give opinions on what is and is not in the child's interests.
4 The adversarial nature of the proceedings. The bench as aloof arbitrator. Magistrates may not call for witnesses or documents to be available in court. They have no access, for example, to social workers' files. Although they may question witnesses, they often rely entirely on information given, as in criminal cases, through examination and cross-examination by the lawyers. In two cases in which I recently appeared the magistrates sat through over five hours of evidence without asking a single question of any of the witnesses. Hilgendorf *et al.* (1981) found that during their obser-vations of thirty-three full hearings in care and care discharge cases fifteen magistrates' benches asked no question at all, while another twelve asked only a few questions. Only in the remaining six cases did the bench 'ask a number of questions' (pp.115–16).
5 The absence of direct communication between the bench and the non-professional participants. Frequently the chairman will announce the court's decision in formal, statutory language without making any allowances for the emotional impact of such decisions. No attempt to conciliate is made as occurs nowadays in, for example, custody disputes (see e.g. Davis 1982).

To summarize, therefore, although there may be considerable vari-ations from court to court, the assumptions that tend to operate in contested care cases are those borrowed from criminal proceedings in magistrates' courts. The first stage in the proceedings, the attempt to prove the existence of the conditions specified under the 1969 Act, or the arguments for and against discharge of the care order, closely resemble the first, proof, stage in criminal trials. An opportunity is given to both sides to present their evidence to the bench in an orderly manner and to test the evidence of the other side through cross-examination. This, in theory, enables the magistrates, after hearing the closing speeches, to decide, on all the evidence before them, whether the condition has or has not been proved. In many juvenile courts the criminal model is even extended to allow the child or parent's advocate to submit a plea of 'no case to answer' and to have the final word before the magistrates retire to consider their verdict/decision. In applications for discharge of the care order the same model applies with parents or children having to prove to the court that there is no longer any need for the care order.

It could be argued that these formalities, far from being restrictive and inappropriate for care cases, in fact serve the interests of justice. There are good reasons, according to this view, as to why the court should stick as closely as possible to the rules of procedure and evidence that apply in criminal trials. It is the notion of 'welfare fettered by justice' that has inspired many of the proposals for reform coming from the 'justice' lobby. Unfortunately, it indicates a total misunderstanding of the nature of the evidence and decision-making in child protection cases.

To begin with, most criminal trials in magistrates' courts revolve around a single incident or a series of incidents of limited duration. In child protection care cases such neat, clean-cut cases, nicely defined in place and time, are rare. The issues covered in these proceedings, by comparison, are frequently highly complex. They may involve the relationship between parents and children over a period of months or even years. During this period several social workers and probably several different agencies, school, police, health visitor, social services, general practitioner, or hospital will have had contact with the family and will have relevant facts to present to the court. Even if the local authority wishes to confine the issues to particular incidents of, for example, abuse or neglect, the child or parents' advocate will often wish to extend the field of enquiry in order to put these incidents into the context of, for instance, the help or lack of help social services have offered to the family. All this necessarily involves much more complex and much longer presentation of evidence, cross-examination and re-examination than is normally the case in summary criminal trials.

A second difference concerns the role and status of the local authority social worker in court. It is far too simple to see his or her function as merely 'presenting the facts'. The social worker is the representative of the social services department, part of whose function is often to report to the court on decisions made collectively within the department at case conferences or child planning meetings and to present the court with the reasons for these decisions. In addition, the social worker frequently applies for and is granted the status of an expert in child care. As such the social worker is both a privileged and a protected witness. Privileged because, unlike other witnesses, he or she may present the court with opinions about the child's needs and the interests and nature of the parent/child relationship and about the effects both present and future of parental behaviour on the child. This makes cross-examination of social workers a much more difficult task than, say, cross-examination of a police officer about what he did and didn't see in a road traffic case, since the lawyer has to work with opinions based on child care policies and child development theories rather than light, distances, speed, etc. The social worker is protected because the status of expert carries with it an aura of objectivity and impartiality, implicit in the assumption that the social worker's only real concern is the child and its welfare. This means that cross-examination that attempts to probe the social worker's interpretation of events or opinions as to the child's welfare runs the serious risk of losing the sympathy of the bench, because the social worker is seen by the bench as being for the child and the child's best interests. If the magistrates are convinced of the risks to the child and have confidence in the expertise and goodwill of social services, there is very little the advocates for the child and parents can do. Cross-examination in these circumstances is often much more a question of trying to influence attitudes than one of establishing the truth. A bench impressed by social work expertise is not likely to allow its attitudes to be influenced by lawyers.

One can develop this issue further if one compares the tasks of the magistrates in child protection and criminal cases. The division of contested criminal trials into two parts, proving of the offence and (if proved) sentencing makes perfect sense when one is dealing in the first part with the establishment of facts and the application of firm principles of law to those facts, and in the second part with punishing the offender. It makes much less sense, however, if one is dealing in the first part with such value-laden notions as 'proper development', 'efficient education', 'moral danger', and the 'need of care and control'. Although the conditions set out in s.1 of the 1969 Act involve a factual element, they also involve a strong speculative factor in the court's judgement as to the risks and dangers involved in the alternative courses of action open to them. Nor is it correct to suggest that the element of prediction arises only after the condition has been proved and the need for care and control established. Each of the conditions, although expressed in the present tense, is future-directed, so that the magistrates are necessarily asked to speculate on the likely risks to the child if the present situation is allowed to continue without coercive intervention by the social services department. Moreover, in the overwhelming majority of cases parents and children would be reasonably happy to accept a supervision order. What they do not want is for the court to make a *care* order that would almost certainly involve the removal of the children against their will. If social services will not agree to supervision rather than care, the best way tactically for families to resist is to deny the need for any order of any kind. In contested care cases, therefore, the division between the two parts of the proceedings, far from assisting the process of justice, tends to bear little relation to the actual issues the court is being asked to decide. It often leads to confusion for everyone concerned and to the inevitable merging of the two stages, with social workers supporting the establishment of the condition by referring to the opinions and predictions contained in their social enquiry report and parents arguing right from the start that there is no need to take their children away. Conversely, it means that the really important issue so far as parents and children are concerned may be decided at the second stage in the proceedings, the stage at which formal safeguards against hearsay and opinion evidence no longer apply and at which social enquiry or school reports need not even be shown to parents, children, or their legal representatives.[6]

To conclude, the provision of lawyers for parents and children, the adherence to strict rules of evidence and procedure, the restriction of orders to cases involving a risk of serious harm or the imposition of a 'beyond reasonable doubt' standard in care cases – all reforms proposed by those who want to see justice for children and families[7] – are based on the myth that decisions in care cases depend for the most part on the formal applications of the law to a set of facts. Clearly facts are important to the concept of justice, particularly if they are distorted, omitted, or misrepresented in the evidence offered to the court, but, as I have attempted to show, much more depends on the credibility of social workers as experts in child care and on the attitudes and perceptions of the magistrates in assessing the child's needs and in predicting the risks and dangers for the child's future. These two factors interrelate in interesting and important ways, as we shall see in the following discussion on the role of the lay magistrate.

The lay magistrates

The latest proposals to emerge from the Lord Chancellor's Department make it clear that whatever else a family court may do, it will certainly stay well clear of care cases.[8] Not only will these remain for the foreseeable future in the hands of the juvenile court magistrates, but these magistrates are also to be responsible for deciding disputes between social services and parents over parental access to children in care. It is the magistrates who are, it appears, going to represent the judiciary in any future conflict with the administration over policies and practices concerning children in care. Since wardship is not and is not likely to be available for families wishing to challenge local authority decisions concerning their children, the only occasions when a professional judge will be involved in child care decisions is on appeals from juvenile courts. It is not a prospect that augurs particularly favourably for those who wish to see social workers more accountable for their decisions, since the lay magistrates, admirable as they may be, suffer from certain disadvantages and limitations which make it impossible for them to play the sort of controlling role the justice lobby seems to envisage for the courts.

In the first place, lay magistrates are part-timers, not merely in the sense that they do not work at being magistrates for five days a week, but also in that their role as magistrate in a particular case begins and ends with their involvement in the courtroom hearing. Most of them sit in the magistrates' court hearing criminal cases and are therefore in no way specialists in the peculiar problems of child care. One might add that their experience in the adult court has in most cases prepared them for an essentially passive judicial role appropriate to adversary proceedings. This is a very different judicial role from that, for example, of registrars in divorce cases, who often handle a particular matter all the way through from the interim to the final order and on to any variations of that order. A care case may start with a place of safety order which is then followed by an interim care order before it finally reaches the full hearing of the case. At each of these stages a different set of magistrates may hear the case and make the decision. If subsequently an application is made to discharge the care order, it is highly unlikely that this will be heard by the same magistrates who originally put the child into care. If this application fails, further applications are likely to come before still different magistrates. This lack of continuity has little to do with overcrowded court lists. It is rather a problem endemic to the use of part-time lay magistrates who are available only on certain days or half-days of the week.

In child protection cases the juvenile court's role is very much that envisaged by Lord Scarman when he argued against the introduction of welfare-orientated family courts:

'In respect of the children's jurisdiction the object of the court should be to get out of it as quickly as they can, confident that they have made the appropriate order . . . and confident that thereafter

145

the matter can be handled by the central or local adminstrative authority with their own social caseworker.'

(Sir Leslie Scarman 1973)

As already noted magistrates have no power to require the local authority to produce their files or to demand evidence from someone who has not been called as a witness by one of the parties to the proceedings, but must rely on summaries of assessments and the results of case conferences contained in the social enquiry report. This too may severely limit the court's effectiveness to play any sort of watchdog role.

Perhaps even more inhibiting and frustrating from the magistrates' point of view, however, is their lack of powers in any way to assist a family with financial problems, such as fuel bills or rent, even if they believe that these problems lie at the heart of the family's and the children's troubles. They cannot, for example, order the local authority to make *s.1 payments* to avoid the need to take children into care or order regular payments to be made to a relative who is willing and able to look after the child.

Anyone wishing to improve the quality of justice in juvenile courts is faced therefore with a judiciary that has serious inherent limitations. In part these limitations arise from restrictions imposed by the law on the magistrates' powers, but it is the very nature of the magistracy that makes these restrictions necessary. One could not seriously contemplate giving part-time lay justices the power to decide, for example, a foster family placement, the number of parental visits per month, or how much should be paid out of the social services' *s.1 fund* to help a family with their debts, when there are full-time, professionally trained social workers who are paid to make just these decisions. Any attempt to shift this decision-making responsibility is likely to create enormous problems both for the social workers and for the juvenile courts. However the weakness of the judiciary in the juvenile court is also a product of the manifestly ill-conceived attempt to apply to child care issues, with a few minor modifications, a process of justice designed for criminal cases. The episodic nature of the magistrates' involvement in the family's problems, the total dependence of the bench upon information selected and presented to them by others and the passive nature of their court-room role all contribute to creating a system of decision-making which in the majority of cases does little more than endorse the course of action previously decided upon by the child care professionals. Quite apart from the system's well-documented ineffectiveness in safeguarding the wishes and interests of children and their families against excessive social work intervention,[9] it represents an extremely expensive, time consuming way of achieving very little.

The limited role that a lay, part-time judiciary can realistically play in an adversary system and a court setting designed for criminal cases has meant that would-be reformers have been forced to introduce some bizarre measures with the objective of improving the quantity and quality of information and opinions presented to the magistrates. These include guardians *ad litem*, independent social workers and the provision of legal aid for parents (King 1983a and b) It is not that these reforms are wrong or misguided; it is rather that the assumptions on which they are based are almost entirely false. The belief that procedural changes will help make case hearings more 'just' for parents and families represents a total failure to understand how in practice decisions in child protection cases are made. The result is that fictions have been built upon fictions rather like a pyramid of playing cards. The system gives the appearance of solidity with all the formal trappings of justice, but everything collapses when the magistrates blow a puff of reality in its direction by following the social service recommendations in their decision to impose a care order or refusing a parent's application for care discharge. It is not that justice has failed, but that the nature of decisions in child protection cases do not for the most part depend upon justice in the sense of 'due process'. They have much more to do with the beliefs of the decision-makers and their advisers as to what is good or bad for children. Similar beliefs and value judgements lie behind the child protection decisions of French courts, but here the inquisitorial system and a disregard for the superficial trappings of procedural justice have allowed the development of a system much fairer for parents and families without detracting from the protection of the child.

The French *juge des enfants*

In case I should give the impression that I have fallen victim to the 'greener grass syndrome' that often claims academic researchers when they take subsidized trips abroad,[10] let me state from the outset that there are serious problems with the French system of judicial control of child care. Not least of these is the blurring of the dividing line between legal and administrative powers with the inevitable risk that the judge will become little more than a state functionary, or a mere extension of the social work machinery for controlling families and children.

Quite apart from these problems inherent in the French system, there are also fundamental differences between the child care and legal systems operating in France and this country, which, as well as making comparisons difficult, would make it quite impossible for us to import wholesale the French way of doing things, even assuming that this was what we wanted. These differences include a professionally trained, specialist judiciary, an inquisitorial tradition of justice, a state-employed social work profession divided between the Ministry of Justice and the *Direction departmental de l'Action Sanitaire et Sociale* (DDASS) and considerable numbers of private children's homes and private social work agencies. Nevertheless, even with these reservations, I believe it is worthwhile examining the French manner of dealing with the central relationship between the courts and the child care profession. Moreover, it is also useful to consider whether, despite the historical and cultural differences, it might be possible to adopt some of the French ideas for our own purposes and so to escape from the strait-jacket of legalism which seems to prevent any real progress in reforming the system in this country.

Although in France it is possible for children to be taken away on provisional orders *(ordannances de placement provisoire)* from their parents in emergencies without any prior opportunity for the parents to put their case to a judge, this is a rare occurrence. In those cases where the social services' written report indicates that urgent action is needed *ex parte* action is usually unnecessary for the judge has the power to call upon the *Brigade de mineurs*, a specialist department of the police to find the child and parents immediately, take the child and inform the parents of their rights to appear at once before the judge. Hearings before the judge, it must be emphasized, are not lengthy formal affairs – they can be over in ten minutes and usually last no longer than an hour – yet nor are they the mechanical rubber stamping of social workers' decisions. They take the form of informal discussions between judges, social worker, and parents with the judge controlling the sequence of such discussions. The child will be brought to the court and the judge will in the case of older children talk to the child, either to seek his or her views on possible solutions to the problem or to explain what has been decided. From the parents' or family's point of view, the hearing before the judge may provide real protection against arbitrary intervention by state agencies. Not only does it allow an opportunity for someone who has experience and knowledge in the field of child protection, but who has not been personally involved with the family, to take a perhaps more detached and less impassioned view of the dangers involved in allowing the child to remain in the family, but it also permits the judge to consider alternative solutions to that proposed by the social worker *before* any action is taken. The hearing before the judge also provides an opportunity for the parents to receive a full explanation from the figure of authority as to what is going to happen and why. In the French system it is the *juge des enfants* and not the social worker who plays this role of the authority figure. Since few parents are represented at this stage, it is also the judge who makes them aware of their legal rights.

The most important objective of the hearing in the judge's room, however, is to secure, wherever possible, the co-operation of the parents to the measures which the *juge des enfants* feels necessary to protect the child. I use the word 'co-operation' rather than 'consent', because it would be wrong to suggest that parents willingly allow their children to be taken away from home and placed with foster parents or in one of the many private children's homes that exist throughout France. Often the judge's only way to secure co-operation is by pointing out to the parents that the alternative is the forcible removal of the child. Yet one measure of the judge's success in involving the family in what happens to the child after the order has been made placing the child in a children's home is the fact that it is by no means unusual for the parents themselves to take the child from the court to a children's home chosen by the judge. What I wish to emphasize at this stage are not so much the details of the French system but rather the differences of approach to what are, after all, identical problems, whichever side of the Channel you happen to be. Two differences in particular seem to me to be important. First, the French system, unlike that operating in England and Wales, does not rely only on a social worker's individual assessment or on the collective view of a team of social workers as to what constitutes a dangerous situation for the child requiring emergency action. The second important difference concerns attitudes to the parents and wider family. In France, family rights involve much less the sort of procedural protection and legal representation that one finds in English courts and much more an ideological approach to child protection that sees the family, including the extended family, as central to the child's future welfare. As a result court hearings are not the alienating experiences of the juvenile courts in England and Wales, but are designed rather to secure wherever possible the involvement of the parents in what the judge considers to be the steps necessary to secure the child's future welfare.

In France the decision of the *juge des enfants* is never final. It may be reviewed at any time at the instance of anyone who believes he or she has good grounds for changing the judge's order. This includes social workers, parents, other relatives, or the child, who need simply to write to the judge to secure an appointment. Alternatively the judge, who has a continuing responsibility for the child once an order has been made, may take the initiative and require an up-to-date report on the child's situation. Appeals against judges' decisions may be made to a bench of three judges, but they are a comparative rarity, because lawyers usually advise the parent to bring the matter back before the judge responsible for the original order, for orders may always be changed without delay while appeals tend to be lengthy, impersonal affairs.

Another way in which the interests of families are protected lies in the power of the children's judges to carry out their own investigation independently of the social services department which brought the matter to their attention. All children's judges have a team of social workers to work with them, preparing social enquiry reports, undertaking the equivalent of supervision orders, running day centres, and so on. At first sight this may seem a similar arrangement to the recently implemented guardian *ad litem* system for care cases in juvenile courts. However, any attempt to equate the two would be misleading. These social workers, unlike guardians *ad litem*, take their instructions directly from the judge, who will specify the area and purpose of the enquiry. Moreover, in no way is the social worker's task to act as advocate for the child, but rather to seek out possible solutions to what are generally seen as problems in the functioning of the family. Even where the child is at risk according to the criteria set out in the *Code Civil*,[11] judges are still obliged, wherever possible, to allow the child to remain in his or her present environment. However, where this is not possible, they may place the child in a children's home of their choosing, place the child but delegate the choice of home to the social services department, regulate parental visits to and correspondence with the child, make the equivalent of a supervision order, or appoint someone responsible to take charge of the family's finances (*prestations sociales*).

Conclusion

What lessons then can be learnt from the French system to help bring about reforms in England and Wales that would really provide justice for parents and families? In the first place it is clear that the present relationship between the courts and social service agencies in England and Wales does not, as many commentators would have us believe, represent the end-product of the cumulative wisdom and experience acquired over the years in how to achieve a fair balance between justice and welfare, between the interests of the child and the rights of the parent. Our system has not evolved ever more sensitive, ever more compassionate, ever more efficient, ever more just ways of achieving that balance. It represents rather a motley collection of powers and procedures, reflecting the British adversarial, oral tradition in criminal trials, a now outdated interventionist social philosophy, the expansion of local government bureaucracy and the tradition of an amateur magistracy. The recent adjustments to the system represent not so much progress as the success or otherwise of different professional interest groups in securing reforms favourable to the interests of their members. In France different traditions, different social policies, and different professional groups have created a very different system to deal with what after all are very similar social problems. If providing protection to families against unjustified state intervention is really to become an important feature of social policy in the 1980s, then we must stop believing that providing people with ineffective lawyers and rights to apply to a weak, part-time judiciary will achieve anything more than the appearance of justice.

Parental involvement in place of safety orders

I have no doubt that there are occasions when a child is in such immediate danger and the parents are so far beyond the point where they will take advice from anyone that the only solution is to remove the child as quickly as possible. Such cases, I suspect, are comparatively rare and account for only a small number of successful place of safety applications. Furthermore, notorious cases of death or serious injury to children, such as Maria Colwell and Wayne Brewer, occurred not because the social workers did not act swiftly enough, but because they were not aware of what was going on or were mistaken in their judgements of the risks involved in leaving the child in the home. There are certainly occasions also when social workers are 'too fast on the draw', when the applications for a place of safety order reflect social workers' (or policemen's) frustration with the lack of parental response, when exaggerated anxiety for the child's safety, and concern over possible repercussions and recriminations should the child be harmed, rule the day rather than a balanced assessment of the risks to the child and the distress and disruption likely to be caused to child and family in removing the child from the home.

Once granted, the order carries with it a certain legitimacy, justifying the social workers' or police officers' fears and setting the tone for future proceedings. Magistrates, for example, are generally reluctant to refuse an interim care order in respect of a child whose situation was so serious that he or she had to be taken away to a place of safety. Moreover, the assumption that there must have been a real and pressing need for the order and that the parents represent a serious danger for the child are extremely difficult to overcome in the subsequent care proceedings.

My proposal is that at the very least, the parent(s) or person(s) from whose care the child is to be removed should have an opportunity of putting their case to the court *before* any action is taken. This precaution exists in almost all applications for matrimonial injunctions to remove violent husbands from the home and there is no reason why the principle should not be applied to the vast majority of place of safety applications. One would need to give social services departments the power to bring the child before the court, but, at the same time, one could impose an obligation upon them to inform the parents of the hearing and of their right to attend court. In those few cases where the situation is so urgent that any delay could result in serious injury or death to the child, I would want a judge rather than a single magistrate or a bench of magistrates to decide the application.

The objectives in securing the presence of the parents would be twofold. In the first place, it would, as I have already suggested, allow them an opportunity to put their version of events and their future intentions towards the child to the court, with, I hope, the help of legal representation from the duty solicitor. Second, it would present a chance to obtain the consent and co-operation of the parents, albeit under pressure, to any measures which the court felt necessary for the safety of the child.

Procedural reforms

The purpose of these reforms would be to give recognition to the special nature of care proceedings and the important differences that distinguish them from criminal proceedings, while at the same time providing parents and families with adequate protection against unwarranted state intervention.

1 The extension of the provisions of the Civil Evidence Act 1968 to care cases in order to allow both local authority and parents to bring hearsay evidence before the court with the agreement of the other party.
2 Regulations should be introduced to require the local authority seeking a care order or supervision order to file in court and serve upon the parents in advance of the hearing a statement setting out the events and evidence on which they will rely in seeking the order together with their plans for the child should the order be made. The parents should then have the opportunity of filing and serving a counter-notice indicating the points of contention and setting out their own proposals for the child's future.
3 Clarification of the status of social workers as witnesses. Unlike Dingwell, Eekelaar, and Murray (1983), I see no reason why social workers should be treated any differently than other witnesses, unless they have some specialist knowledge, not available to the magistrates, which enables them to draw inferences from the evidence.
4 Limitating the role of the guardian *ad litem* to that of carrying out investigations on behalf of the court into the child's situation. Whether or not the child should be separately represented should be the court's decision and not that of the guardian *ad litem*. Similarly the child's lawyer should play a limited role, testing the evidence presented by the local authority and by the parents and bringing any other evidence he or she considers relevant to the court's decision.

Extending the 'family'

The law should be changed to give recognition to extended relation-ships between members of a family and to the fact that relations, particularly grandparents, may play an important part in the upbringing of children.

These proposals are based on the assumptions that the juvenile courts do not provide a suitable forum and that magistrates are not the appropriate decision-makers for resolving disputes between families and child protection agencies. Yet it must be stressed from the start that reforms in child care cases should not merely be a matter of moving the hearings to a family court to be heard by specialist judges in a more congenial environment. A complete shift of emphasis is needed away from the accusatorial legalistic approach towards a child care system that attempts to involve parents and other members of the family in planning for the future well-being of their children, even at the stage of legal proceedings when 'voluntary measures' appear to have failed or where the parents have been guilty of serious abuse. These reforms should take their lead from the movement towards conciliation in custody and access disputes in divorce proceedings, where efforts are made within the court setting to resolve disputes by agreement before resorting to adversary procedures and imposed decisions. While there are of course differences in child care cases arising from the alleged failure of the family to provide adequate care and control for the child, the demands made on the court would be very similar to those applicable to divorce proceedings. They are:

(a) an environment and procedures conducive to the promotion of co-operation between parents and social workers;
(b) the intervention of an independent, impartial authority figure who would encourage such co-operation, but where it failed to materialize, to take such measures as necessary for the protection of the child;
(c) the assistance of lawyers, not in the first instance to fight cases, but to ensure that both parents and social workers were aware of the law and of their rights under the law, to assist in the conciliation process and to make sure that any agreement reached was fully understood by all concerned;
(d) a court welfare service, independent of the police or social services, which could be called upon by the court to assess the situation of the child and family and report back to the court;
(e) considerable flexibility in the powers available to the court.

This would involve the abolition of the stark choice available at present between care orders, which transfer virtually all parental rights to the local authority, and supervision orders, which give social workers very little formal authority to impose measures necessary for the child's welfare. Instead, there should be a continuum of powers ranging from regular visits to the home to the removal of the child and including powers to regulate the financial arrangements within families and between families and state agencies. If parents failed to respect the agreement they had made in court with the social workers, or to obey the court's order, then the matter would be brought back immediately before the court, and

(f) a system of appeals against the court's decision, whereby parents who are aggrieved by the solution imposed would be able to demand a full adversary hearing.

The scheme's success would depend upon the existence of members of the judiciary sufficiently knowledgeable in the field of child care to be able to take an independent view of child care to be able to take an independent view of the measures necessary to protect the child's interests and not rely upon the assessment of the child protection agency that had brought the matter before the court. Ideally what is needed is a *Children's Registrar* whose jurisdiction would include, as well as care and care discharge cases, custody and access disputes between parents, custodianship applications, parental rights resolutions, and adoption.

It would not be necessary to go as far as the French in making the registrar personally responsible for the welfare of each child in respect of whom he or she had made an order. One could still retain the English concept of the courts as essentially institutions for the resolution of conflicts, so that judicial intervention would only take place where there were disputes between families and social workers. If a lay element was considered desirable, and there are strong arguments for retaining lay participation in all areas of the administration of justice, it could be brought in at the appeal stage with a judge and two lay magistrates constituting the appeal court.

I realize that the sort of long-term reforms I am suggesting represent a move in the opposite direction to that taken by pressure groups seeking rights and 'justice' for parents, children, and families, and by the Government, if one can assume that government policy is reflected in the recent changes in legal aid and access applications for parents whose children are in care. Nor are these reforms likely to be popular with lawyers, for they represent a rejection of legalism and traditional adversary justice as being entirely inappropriate for child care decisions. They offer also a very different way forward from those suggested by those non-lawyer, academic researchers, such as Dingwall, Eekelaar, and Murray (1983), Hilgendorf (1981), and Parker, Casburn, and

Turnbull (1981). Dingwall, Eekelaar, and Murray, for example, wish to see protective care proceedings become even more of a dispute between parents and agencies than at present, the dispute to be 'over the appropriate care of the child' (p. 241). Their solution lies in making parents respondent parties with 'full participation' in the adversary hearing and access to legal aid. What these and other academic researchers seem not to appreciate, however, is that, even with the trappings of adversary justice, the contest between parents and the state cannot, for the reasons we have examined in this article, be an equal one. The moral indignation, the moral righteousness, the power to interpret behaviour and define risks and dangers are all in the hands of the social workers and other state agencies involved in care cases. Lay magistrates sitting in juvenile courts do not have the force or the specialist knowledge to redress this imbalance. If present trends continue protective care proceedings will become not so much adversary as accusatorial in nature, with parents being put in the position of criminals defending themselves and their right to keep their children.

There is therefore a clear choice for policy-makers: either they continue in the present direction, preoccupied with legal representation and due process ideals, while ignoring the real inequalities of power between families and state agencies and discounting the negative effects of acrimonious court battles on all concerned children, parents, and social workers, or they decide to take a very different path. This alternative is to continue to use the courts as institutions for conflict resolution and child protection, but wherever possible, through a process of conciliation and co-operation, bringing parents, social workers, and other members of the family together to try to find a solution acceptable to everyone concerned. It is an alternative that emphasizes, not the punishment of parents nor the evangelical saving of children, but the reinforcement of the family unit to enable it to operate in a way that does not threaten the children's safety and well-being. Only with such a change in direction in the use of courts and the judiciary is there any chance of justice for parents and families becoming a reality.

Notes

1 A longer version of this chapter appears as Warwick Law Working Paper, vol. 6, no.3 (1983). It contains references to the author's

experiences while acting for parents in child protection proceedings in London and the Home Counties.
2 Health and Social Services and Social Security Adjudication Act 1983
3 See, for example, the description of magistrates' justice as 'a common sense justice which seeks to resolve the tension between formal legal rationality and individual human troubles' (Dingwall, Eekelaar, and Murray 1983: 139).
4 For details of these procedures see Magistrates' Courts (Children and Young Persons) Rules 1970.
5 See *Humberside County Council* v. *D.P.R.* [1977] 3 All ER 964, *Shropshire County Council* v. *P.J.S.* (a child) [1975] 141 JPN 394, and *re S & W (minors) The Times, 23 April, 1982.*
6 Rule 20, Magistrates' Courts (Children and Young Persons) Rules 1970.
7 See Taylor, Lacey, and Bracken (1980) pp. 85–93; and Morris *et al.* (1980) pp. 96–105.
8 See 'A Family Court', consultation paper issued by the Lord Chancellor's Department, February, 1983.
9 See e.g. Family Rights Group (1983); Freeman (1982).
10 My research was made possible by a SSRC/CNRS Travel Fellowship.
11 *The Law of 4th June 1970.*

Acknowledgement

I should like to thank Jenny Levin, Stewart Asquith, and Michael Freeman for their helpful comments on the longer version of this paper.

References

Davis, G. (1982) Conciliators and the Profession. *Family Law* 13: 6.
Dingwall, R., Eekelaar, J., and Murray, T. (1983) *The Protection of Children.* Oxford: Basil Blackwell.
Donzelot, J. (1977) *La Police des Familles.* Paris: Editions de minuit.
Family Rights Group (1983) *Problems over Access.* London: Family Rights Group.
Floud, J. and Young, W. (1981) *Dangerousness and Criminal Justice.* London: Heinemann Educational.

Freeman, M. (1982) Controlling Local Authorities in Care Cases. In *Accountability in Child Care*. London: Family Rights Group.

Hayes, M. (1978) Separate Representation of Children in Care Proceedings. *Family Law* 9: 91-6.

Hilgendorf, L., Holland, D., Irving, B., and Schlaefi, D. (1981) *Social Workers and Solicitors in Child Care Cases*. London: HMSO.

King, M. (1983a) Experts in the Child's Best Interests? *Legal Action Group Bulletin* June: 11–12.

——(1983b) Children's Justice – French Style. *Social Work Today* 15: 22–3.

Latey, Mr Justice (1982) Postscript to *Accountability in Child Care*. London: Family Rights Group.

Morris, A., Giller, H., Szwed, E., and Geach, H. (1980) *Justice for Children*. London: Macmillan.

Parker, H., Casburn, M., and Turnbull, D. (1981) *Receiving Juvenile Justice*. Oxford: Basil Blackwell.

Scarman, Sir L. (1973) A System of Family Courts. Transcript of Conference on *The Domestic and Matrimonial Jurisdiction of Magistrates' Courts and County Courts,* Institute of Judicial Administration, Birmingham University, 56–63.

Syndicat de la magistrature (1980) Special Justice des mineurs. *Justice* Oct./Nov.: 80–1.

Taylor, L., Lacey, R., and Bracken, R. (1980) *In Whose Best Interests?* London: CobdenTrust/Mind.

CHAPTER 10

The Matrimonial Causes Act, s.41 and the children of divorce: theoretical and empirical considerations

Susan Maidment

Theoretical considerations

The current philosophical interest in the balance between family or parental autonomy or privacy, and state or legal (*parens patriae*) intervention on behalf of children has in this country mainly concerned local authority intervention in respect of children 'in need of care'. But the *parens patriae* principle also has an important place in the law of divorce, since the welfare of the child is central to the modern divorce process. First, in questions of custody, whatever the practice, the law places the child protection or nurturance philosophy at the centre of the decision-making process, and whatever interpretations are given to the welfare principle, nowadays the pre-eminence of the child-centred approach receives universal support (Maidment 1984).

But the very divorce itself is also dependent on the arrangements that the parents have made for their children's welfare. According to the Matrimonial Causes Act 1973, s.41, a decree of divorce cannot be made absolute unless the court has declared its satisfaction with the arrangments for the children. The child's welfare as a pre-condition to the granting of a divorce reflects a modern belief that while parents may choose divorce for themselves and must face the consequences of their own decisions, children need legal protection against their parents' actions. The legal justification for this fundamental intrusion into parental autonomy in the interests of the children is based on the premise that children may be damaged by their parents' divorce and that it is the responsibility of the courts to protect them against such damage. It is not clear in practice whether this responsibility is

159

meaningfully executed, and indeed the very premise requires elaboration. The *parens patriae* role has been thus described:

> 'The modern function of parental rights [autonomy] is to permit parents to discharge their duties to their children. . . . The issue to be critically addressed is the point at which an exercise of parental choice over the child's management and future is so potentially harmful to the welfare or interests of the child as to require state intervention and possibly a countermanding of parental choice. . . . This indicates another means of expressing the modern function of parental rights. They exist to preserve and to prepare children for adulthood and emerging autonomy.'
>
> (Dickens 1981: 463)

On this view current legal intervention on behalf of the children of divorce must be justified by the premise that the children may be denied by their parents the opportunity of optimal development to prepare them for adulthood. The law therefore reflects modern society's concern for the protection of future generations, for their socialization, development, education, and training. Society places responsibility upon parents not only to provide physical upbringing, but also 'to recognise the child's emotional and egotistical needs as valid while still giving him a moral framework of principle' (Newson and Newson 1978: 436). Despite the feelings of inadequacy that this responsibility may engender, 'society requires [parents] to see the job through, and judges them acccordingly' (Newson and Newson 1978: 437). The law plays a part in making this judgement, for example in laws against child abuse. But in the context of marriage breakdown also, the law at least in theory expects parents to judge and be judged according to the implications of their behaviour for their children. The law thus justifies state intervention in private family life on the grounds of the interests of the children because the parents have chosen to end their marriage. But, since upholding the sanctity of marriage is no longer an official purpose of the law it is difficult to construct an argument for state intervention on behalf of children merely by reason of the parents' divorce, for it is not clear what distinguishes this from any other family circumstance that does not present itself to a court for decision but which in the privacy of its home creates emotional conflict and disharmony, but without attracting child care intervention.

The child protection philosophy of s.41 has rarely been explicitly dealt with in the context of divorce; and when it has, only in *a priori* terms. The purpose of this paper is to explore the justification for the centrality of the *parens patriae* principle and the proper limits of state intervention in respect of the children of divorce in the light of current social science evidence and understandings of the divorce process. The premise that children's development is at risk by reason of divorce will be elucidated empirically through a current review of literature of the effects of divorce on children.

Are children 'at risk' by reason of divorce?

There is extensive literature indicating that children brought up in one-parent families resulting from divorce are disadvantaged and more likely to have behavioural or delinquency problems (Finer 1974; Rutter 1975), and that probably the most important variable affecting these children is poverty. There is also extensive evidence of the psychological disruption caused to children by the 'family discord and disharmony' (Rutter 1973) accompanying marriage breakdown.

Clinicians (e.g. McDermott 1970) also have reported the feelings and problems that children of divorce experience, including 'denial, guilt, depression, fears of abandonment, loss of self-esteem, feelings of blame, guilt, shame, anger, sexual and oedipal difficulties, acting out and withdrawal, immaturity and hyper-activity, and other pathological sequelae' (Levitin 1979: 3). These outcomes are no doubt related to the parents' divorce, but those children who present for clinical treatment may be the worst, and most highly distressed. These findings cannot be generalized to all children of divorce.

Children of divorce studies

Researchers in the USA have recently begun to study the impact of divorce on ordinary, rather than atypical or clinical, samples of children, and to provide wider understandings of the effects on children of the divorce process. The two major studies (Hetherington, Cox, and Cox 1982; Wallerstein and Kelly 1980) are of children in mother-custody families, since, as here, most children of divorce live with their mothers. These studies have exposed certain effects of divorce that are probably not gender-specific, that is they would apply whichever parent has custody; other effects seem to be specific to mother-headed one-parent families. Father-custody studies to the contrary have sought to identify the particular problems of motherless families.

MOTHER-CUSTODY

The first gender specific effect of mother-custody is associated with the downward economic mobility of divorced mothers. Hetherington, Cox, and Cox (1982) in Virginia, USA, compared a sample of white, middle-class pre-school children and their divorced parents where the mother had custody with a similar number of non-divorced families, over a period of two years from divorce. They noted that mothers with custody confront particular changes in their life experiences that create stress in the one-parent family. Divorce causes a drop in income for women but not for men (Finer 1974), so that 'children in homes in which the father has gained custody are exposed to less actual financial duress' (Hetherington 1981: 45). The employment of mothers is also problematic:

> 'The economic problems of divorced mothers and their children are compounded by the fact that many divorced women do not have the education, job skills, or experience to permit them to obtain a well-paying position or to pay for high-quality child care. Divorced mothers are more likely to have low-paying, part-time jobs or positions of short duration. For the child this results in temporary, erratic, sometimes inadequate provisions for childcare, and if the mother feels forced to work, in a dissatisfied, resentful mother. . . . If the divorced mother wishes to work and if adequate provisions are made for child care and maintenance of childhood continues, maternal employment may have no adverse effects on children and positive effects on the mother such as increased self-esteem, less social isolation, and greater financial resources. However . . . if the mother begins to work at the time of divorce or shortly thereafter, the pre-school child seems to experience the double loss of both parents, which is reflected in a higher rate of behaviour disorders. . . . Great task overload is experienced by working divorced mothers with young children.'
>
> (Hetherington 1981: 45)

In addition to 'downward economic mobility', 'increased task overload', and maternal employment, the mother-custody family may also move home, bringing further personal losses, disruption, and social isolation, at a time when 'continuity of support systems and the environment can play an ameliorative role' (Hetherington 1981: 46). Indeed the British judicial practice of allowing the custodian parent to remain in

the matrimonial home with the children is well supported by obser-
vations of the effect of relocation of the child's home.

Secondly Hetherington, Cox, and Cox (1978) noted the negative
behaviour, harassment of, and aggression to divorced mothers by
their (pre-school) sons which persisted at two years after divorce. A
differential response to divorce according to sex has often been found
(Hetherington 1981), with higher rates for boys of behaviour disorders
and problems in interpersonal relations at home and in school.
Hetherington suggests that both mothers of sons and sons themselves
find divorce more stressful compared with daughters:

'After divorce mothers of boys report feeling more stress and
depression than do mothers of girls . . . After divorce, boys confront
more inconsistency, negative sanctions, and opposition from parents,
particularly from mothers. Divorced mothers are less sensitive to
the needs of their sons, and are more likely to identify sons in a
negative way as being similar to their fathers. In addition boys
receive less positive support, solicitude, and nurturance and are
viewed more negatively by mothers, teachers and peers in the
period immediately following divorce than are girls.'
(Hetherington 1981: 42-3)

Finally there is evidence that fathers are more important than mothers
for children's sex-role modelling.

'When the mother is hostile and critical of the father, the child
begins to view the father in a more ambivalent or negative manner
and as a less acceptable role model. For young boys [under 5] this
is associated with disruption in sex typing. For girls it may be
associated with disruptions in heterosexual relations at adolescence.'
(Hetherington 1981: 47)

The explanation offered is that:

'fathers usually are much more concerned than mothers about the
maintenance of stereotype sex-role behaviour in their children and
more likely to vary their role as they relate to male and female
offspring. . . . By 2 years following divorce the only paternal
variable related to sex typing in sons and daughters was paternal
availability. If fathers maintained frequent contact with their
children the children were more stereo-typically sex-typed.'
(Hetherington, Cox, and Cox 1982: 276-77)

FATHER-CUSTODY

The father-custody studies now emerging recognize that the families they are studying are a more unusual product of divorce, although they may be increasing. In 1978 12 per cent of one-parent families were headed by men, and this was increasing at a rate of 6 per cent a year (Leete 1978). Just over half of the 100,000 one-parent families headed by men were the result of marital breakdown (OPCS 1978). The first major finding from the studies suggests that the reasons why the father has custody may be an important indicator of the success of the arrangement. Gersick (1979), comparing twenty custodial fathers with twenty non-custodial fathers in America, found that eighteen of the twenty father-custody cases (90 per cent) were with the mother's pre-trial consent, either because the mother did not want custody, or it was agreed that the husband could offer the children a more secure home, or the husband's determination to fight for custody scared the wife out of a contest, or in seven cases (35 per cent) the child was allowed to choose. Santrock, Warshak, and Elliot (1982) (USA) also found 'no difference between the father- and mother-custody groups in the number of custody decisions that had been reached by a court in a contested case' (1982: 291). Luepnitz's study (1982) (USA) of sixteen mother-custody, sixteen father-custody, and eighteen joint custody parents, however, found

> 'twice as many legal contests over custody among paternal as among maternal families (25% v 12%). In an additional 19% of paternal cases, there was a bitter struggle over custody, which was settled out of court. In nearly half of the paternal families, the children had been initially in the custody of the mother. Most of these children were turned over to their fathers explicitly because their mothers felt incompetent to care for them.'
>
> (Luepnitz 1982: 24)

Santrock, Warshak, and Elliott (1982) suggest that ex-spouses relinquish custody either because they actively do not want it, or they do not care, or believe that the child is better off with the other parent. They also indicate why men seek custody: some genuinely want it, some feel wronged or sufficiently vindictive to use custody to intimidate or harass ex-wives, some believe they are the better parent, some mothers do not want custody, and some fathers 'may seek custody as a means of economic gain if they believe their ex-wives would be willing to take less property or support in the divorce settlement' (Santrock and Warshak 1979: 113). Gersick (1979) also noted that nearly all the fathers with custody remained in the marital residence; and he found no greater interest in custody of sons.

A British study of fifty-nine fathers with custody suggests that the success of the father's transition from joint to lone parenthood depends not only on choice but also on 'whether there was any discussion; the extent of hostility involved; the degree of abruptness in the transition; and whether the needs of the child were put before or after the needs of self' (O'Brien 1982: 186-88). Fathers who were conciliatory negotiators (one-third of the group) more often made joint decisions, were more concerned with what was the most suitable solution for the children, had more egalitarian marriages and participated extensively in child care, had mutually agreed separation, and were committed to and involved in parenthood. The 'hostile seekers' (one-third) made, intentionally or by default, the children 'pawns' in the marital conflict, were 'morally outraged' by their wife's conduct, and seeking custody was a symbolic way of punishing her. This group fought for custody, despite relatively lower levels of pre-separation child involvement. The third group were 'passive acceptors' who involuntarily became lone fathers after their wives' desertion; the absence of choice resulted in feelings of conflict about their new role and negative feelings about their own parenting abilities despite substantial child care responsibility prior to the wife's desertion (O'Brien 1982). Gersick found four variables affecting fathers with custody: relationships in their family of origin ('men with custody showed more closeness towards their mothers and less towards their fathers; they were more likely to be later-born children with both male and female siblings . . . men from traditional families are more likely to make the extremely non-traditional decisions to seek custody' (Gersick 1979: 319)); feelings about the departing wife ('The more wronged, betrayed or victimised that a man felt, the more likely he was to have sought custody. . . . Anger and revenge seemed to be components of many decisions to seek custody' (Gersick 1979: 320)); the wife's intentions about custody; and the attitudes of lawyers. There were however no differences between the custody or non-custody fathers on measures of participation in child care prior to the divorce; all of the fathers were described as 'active'.

Each variable may produce different outcomes for both custodial parent and child, in particular concerning male satisfaction with the new life-style and status, and motivation to succeed in parenting.

'The child's adjustment is intimately connected with that of the father and the nature of the father's feelings towards his wife, his present role, and how the community view him' (Hipgrave 1981: 163). Hipgrave (1982) identifies a number of 'risk factors' both institutional (such as material disadvantage, downward mobility associated with single parenthood, community responses) and interpersonal ('time, money and feelings' difficulties) which affect father-custody families.

The second major aspect of father-custody studies concerns the effects on children. Santrock, Warshak, and Elliot (1982) studied sixty American white, middle-class families with children aged six to eleven; in one-third the father had custody, one-third the mother, and one-third were intact families. Parents had been separated for two and three-quarter years on average. Comparing divorced and intact families (Santrock and Warshak 1979), father-custody boys were found to be *more* socially competent with their fathers (measured by warmth, self-esteem, demanding behaviour, maturity, sociability, independent behaviour) than intact family boys; father-custody girls were *less* socially competent than intact family girls; mother-custody boys showed higher self-esteem than intact family boys, and were 'not faring poorly' (contrast Hetherington, Cox, and Cox 1982); mother-custody girls showed lower self-esteem; mother-custody children generally were more demanding of their mothers than in intact families. Boys in father-custody homes were therefore more competent than boys in intact homes; father-custody girls were less competent.

Comparing father-custody with mother-custody, the findings were that father-custody boys were more socially competent than father-custody girls, but mother-custody girls were more competent than mother-custody boys. Significant differences in measure of social competence were found for demanding behaviour, maturity, sociability, and independence. Mother-custody boys were also more demanding and less mature with their mothers than father-custody boys with their fathers. Hetherington, Cox, and Cox (1982) made a similar finding. Santrock *et al.* conclude that 'competent social behaviour is more characteristic of children whose custodial parent is the same sex as they are . . . on the whole children living with the same-sex parent seem to cope better with divorce' (Santrock, Warshak, and Elliot 1982: 301).

The findings of Hetherington, Cox, and Cox (1982) concerning mother-custody boys and of Santrock, Warshak, and Elliot (1982) favouring a 'same-sex child-custodial-parent family structure' could indicate same-sex custody dispositions. But Santrock, Warshak, and

Elliott are concerned to point out that the effects of father- or mother-custody are mediated by factors other than the child's sex. In particular they claim that quality of parenting and child rearing practices are linked to social competence in children. Authoritative parenting (Baumrind 1971) (warmth, clear setting of rules and regulations, extensive verbal give and take) is significantly correlated to higher levels of competence, regardless of custodial arrangement. Mother-custody boys may not display disruption in sex-typing (Hetherington, Cox, and Cox 1982) when mothers 'encourage masculine and exploratory behaviour and do not have a negative attitude toward the absent father' (Santrock, Warshak, and Elliot 1982: 301).

Availability of support systems and additional caretakers were also positively related to the child's social competence, regardless of custodial arrangements. Fathers however made more use of these than mothers, and of particular significance, fathers enlisted the aid of the non-custodial parent. Father-custody children therefore had more frequent contact with the non-custodial parent than mother-custody children; and fathers with custody reported an improvement after the divorce in the mother-child relationship, whereas mothers reported a deterioration in the father-child relationship (Santrock, Warshak, and Elliott 1982: 294-95).

The third major area in the father-custody studies considers the custody arrangement from the parents' point of view. Fathers report problems of too little free social time if continuing employment with home making and parenting: financial problems, due to decreased family income, or difficulties in managing a household budget; and emotional difficulties related to the expression of community attitudes, feelings of isolation or loneliness, feelings connected with sexual identity, parental competence and household tasks. Many of these concerns reported by fathers are however also reported by mothers in one-parent families (Gersick 1979; Hetherington 1981: 50). Some men report few problems running their households or in raising children (Gasser and Taylor 1976; O'Brien 1982). Luepnitz (1982) found that the major problem for fathers with custody was loneliness; for mothers with custody it was low income, overwork, exhaustion, anxiety, limit-testing in children. The advantages for fathers with custody were less discrimination in housing and credit; the advantages for mothers with custody were fewer custody fights than with father- or joint-custody; both father and mother sole custodians had the advantage of being free to take the children and leave town. The disadvantages for fathers with custody were the need for substitute care; for mothers the disadvantages were being overwhelmed by total responsibility for the children, no break from parenting, being less likely to receive maintenance from her ex-husband, needing more substitute care but barely affording it. Both sole mothers and fathers missed the perspective of a second adult in disciplining.

The father-custody studies all agree that 'there is nothing inherently pathological in the motherless family unit' (Orthner and Lewis 1979); 'on all measures of children's psychological adjustment, there were no differences by custody type. The emotional climate was as positive in families headed by a father as in those headed by a mother' (Luepnitz 1982: 149); 'regardless of the custodial arrangement, we believe the quality of the ongoing relationship with the custodial parent is a critical factor in both the boy's and girl's social development' (Santrock and Warshak 1979: 115); 'type of custody was not linked in any way with any of the children's acute reactions to the divorce' (Santrock, Warshak, and Elliot 1982: 295).

NON-GENDER SPECIFIC EFFECTS OF DIVORCE

Apart from the particular effects of mother-custody, the much wider noted effects of divorce on children and parents in the mother-custody studies are probably not gender specific to the custodian. These studies show that in the first year after divorce both parents may display some deterioration in parenting (Wallerstein and Kelly 1980: 34-41):

> 'Parents in the first year following divorce often are preoccupied with their own depression, anger, or emotional needs and are unable to respond sensitively to the wants of the child. The parenting practices of both mothers and fathers tend to deteriorate in the first year following divorce and recover markedly in the second year after divorce. In the immediate aftermath of divorce both parents tend to be inconsistent, less affectionate, and lacking in control over their children.'

(Hetherington 1981: 49)

The second year after divorce showed great improvement however although less so for boys than for girls (Hetherington, Cox, and Cox 1982: 252-58). As regards social development, in the first year, children from divorced families 'were more oppositional, aggressive, lacking in self-control, distractible, and demanding of help and attention

168

in both the home and school than were children of non-divorced families with high rates of marital discord' (Hetherington, Cox, and Cox 1982: 261); but at two years, the adverse factor was not whether the family was divorced, but whether there was still a high degree of conflict in the family whether divorced or not. Nevertheless boys from high conflict divorced families showed more problems than any other group (Hetherington, Cox, and Cox 1982: 261). Wallerstein and Kelly (1980) and Rutter (1973) also found that children are affected by the marital discord accompanying divorce.

Hetherington, Cox, and Cox (1982) also observed children at school; by two years after divorce differences in free play behaviour between girls from divorced and intact families had disappeared, but boys still differed. Similarly as regards social interactions in school with adults and peers; boys in particular seemed to be less helpful, played less with others and were becoming more socially isolated. At two years, children in non-divorced families scored higher on some IQ tests, but not on verbal IQ.

Children of many divorced parents receive less adult attention and are more likely to have erratic mealtimes and bedtimes and to be late for school (Hetherington, Cox, and Cox 1978); the parent's 'chaotic life-style' and 'task overload' (childcare, work, and household responsibilities) make coping difficult for custodians, whether mother or father (Hetherington 1981: 46). Changes in the parent-child relationship also affect the child (Hetherington 1981): family conflict may lead to hostile alliances with one parent against the other; to 'dissonance, questioning and revision and deidealisation of children's perceptions of their parents'; to an increased awareness in adolescents of their parents' sexuality, when parents begin new relationships or remarry. The contribution of a second parent to the family and the child's development is lost, both as indirect support, as an agent of socialization and as a protective buffer between the child and one of the parents.

The custodian parent becomes an increasingly salient figure in the child's life, thus influencing the child's personality, social, and cognitive development. Poor parenting in the first year dramatically improves in the second year, but 'problems in parent-child relationships continue to be found more often with divorced mothers and children than with mothers and children in [intact] families' (Hetherington 1981: 51).

Three major findings emerge from Hetherington, Cox, and Cox's (1982) study; first, the significance of continuing marital conflict:

'In the first year following divorce, children in the divorced families

169

were functioning less well . . . than were children in non-divorced families with high rates of marital discord. By two years following divorce the pattern of differences between children from stressed non-divorced and low-conflict divorced families were reversed.'

(Hetherington, Cox, and Cox 1982: 261)

Second is the greater suffering of boys. The impact of both discord and divorce seems more pervasive and long lasting for boys than for girls. The third concerns divorce as a 'process'. By the end of the second year of divorce

'a process of re-equilibration in the divorced families seemed to be taking place . . . particularly in mother/child relationships. However . . . on many dimensions parent-child relations in divorced and intact families still differed. . . . In this study, we found that families in which the parents had divorced encountered many more stresses and difficulties in coping, which were reflected in disturbances in personal and social adjustments and family relations, than did non-divorced families. [In the families we studied] we did not encounter a victimless divorce, that is, a divorce in which at least one family member did not report distress or exhibit disrupted behaviour. However, if these effects were not compounded by continued severe stress and adversity, most parents and children adapted to their new family situation within 2 years and certainly within 6 years.'

(Hetherington, Cox, and Cox 1982: 285)

Hetherington, Cox, and Cox do not generalize their findings: 'There is already considerable evidence that such factors as age of the child, sex of the custodial parent, socio-economic status, culture, and ethnicity shape the response to and outcomes of divorce' (Hetherington, Cox, and Cox 1982: 285). But, despite the different methodological and professional background the findings of Wallerstein and Kelly (1980) are remarkably similar. They studied sixty divorced Californian families headed by a custodial mother (in all except one case), with 131 children aged initially between three and eighteen years, who were referred to a clinic for the purposes of the research as well as for the offer of divorce counselling, and they followed the families over a five year period from separation. Wallerstein and Kelly also found acute distress in the first year after separation, but by two to three years later 'many children recovered their usual functioning [although] girls recovered faster than boys'.

Particularly useful findings relate to the different impact of divorce according to the age or developmental level of the child. In the first year after separation pre-school children were not psychologically disturbed but responding to a severe stress in their lives which left them unprepared and bewildered. They made extensive use of fantasy to deny the separation and loss, and continued to believe that some day their family would be reunited. The most striking response of six to eight year-olds was 'their pervasive sadness' and difficulty in obtaining relief from it. The nine to twelve year-olds however showed great perception of the realities of the divorce and actively struggled to give coherence and continuity to the disorder in their lives. The distinguishing feature of this group was 'a fully conscious, intense anger' rather than sadness or helplessness. The thirteen to eighteen year-olds experienced anguish and fear at parents leaving them at a time when as adolescents they needed a stable family structure from which they could make their own springboard into adulthood. At three years after separation almost half of all the children had resumed expectable developmental progress, but a quarter had suffered a moderate or severe developmental inhibition or regression, with the main psychopathological finding being depression which manifested itself in sadness, poor self-esteem, impaired school performance, social withdrawal, petty stealing, obesity, or sexual promiscuity. Another quarter (mainly with psychiatrically disturbed fathers) experienced a significant developmental spurt after the divorce. At five years, one-third of the children were well adjusted, but one-third were still unhappy, angry, yearning for the absent parent, feeling deprived and rejected.

Wallerstein and Kelly's conclusion largely accords with Hetherington, Cox, and Cox:

'Although the initial breakup of the family is profoundly stressful, the eventual outcome depends, in large measure, not only on what has been lost, but on what has been created to take the place of the failed marriage. . . . A major conclusion . . . is that the relationships with the post divorce family are likely to govern long range outcomes for children. [If these relationships are successful] children are not likely to suffer developmental interference or enduring psychological distress as a consequence of the divorce.'

(Wallerstein and Kelly 1980: 316)

Nevertheless it appears that the effects of divorce on children are mediated by two major factors: first, the continuance of marital discord. Luepnitz's study of custody arrangements after divorce found that only eight out of ninety-one children were psychologically impaired and all eight had a history of problems preceding the divorce. There were no differences in the children's psychological adjustment according to whether the father or mother had custody. 'The only variable that predicted poorer adjustment in children was parental conflict' (Luepnitz 1982: 149). 'It is the current conflict rather than the past conflict that is associated with most emotional and behavioural problems in children. Children who find themselves in a stable, conflict-free situation recovered within a two year period from the hostility and dissension associated with the separation and divorce' (Hetherington, Cox, and Cox 1982: 263). The second mediating factor concerns upbringing in a one-parent family: 'The longer term adjustment of the child is related to more sustained or concurrent conditions associated with growing up in a one-parent household' (Hetherington 1981: 36).

The most important finding from a policy orientation is that the effects of divorce on children *need not* be damaging. The weight of opinion (see also Benedek and Benedek 1979; Hess and Camara 1979; Santrock and Warshak 1979; Weiss 1979) now emphasizes the quality of the post-divorce experience for the successful adjustment of children to divorce, and that all noted consequences of divorce for children are moderated or mediated by other factors. Factors considered particularly significant are the quality of the child's relationships with both parents, custodial and non-custodial (Wallerstein and Kelly 1980), the child rearing practices of the custodial parent (Santrock, Warshak, and Elliott 1982), and the availability of support systems to the custodial parent (Hetherington, Cox, and Cox 1982; Santrock, Warshak, and Elliot 1982).

INTERGENERATIONAL EFFECTS OF DIVORCE

While researchers are now investigating the short-term and longer-term responses of children to divorce, in some cases seeking to measure the impact of different custodians (Luepnitz 1982; Santrock and Warshak 1979), less is understood about the intergenerational effects of divorce. Clinical impressions are that childhood experiences such as institutional care or cold relationships with parents can influence parenting skills in later life, and experimental studies have shown that monkeys isolated during infancy become incompetent parents (Rutter 1975). Women whose parents had divorced or separated during their childhood may be particularly likely to have illegitimate children or pre-marital conception (Illsley and Thompson 1961) and such women may be more likely to marry young and give birth young (Rutter and Madge 1976). Children from homes broken by divorce or separation may be more likely to show marital instability when adult (Gurin, Veroff, and Feld 1960; Langner and Michael 1963; Rutter and Madge 1976) and to get divorced themselves (Mueller and Pope 1977). In the most recently reported English study of seventy-eight working-class women and their first-born babies, it is suggested that early life experiences influence later mothering behaviour. No distinction however is made between parental death or divorce and separation when considering the effect of a 'disrupted family of origin' on later mother-baby interaction, and to that extent the findings are unsatisfactory. Nevertheless the study concludes that

'[20 week old babies] of women from a disrupted family of origin received significantly less physical and social stimulation at the hands of their mothers in their early months . . . [and] at 27 months [these] children were less advanced than other children in their language development.'

(Hall, Pawlby, and Wolkind 1979)

On the other hand, there is evidence that a parent's own experiences of child rearing do not influence his or her parenting behaviour (McGlaughlin 1981). American research suggests that, after controlling for contemporary life circumstances and social background factors such as class, geographical location or religion, there is little evidence for the existence of *any* long-term effects of coming from a home broken by parental divorce or separation (Kulka and Weingarten 1979). Kulka and Weingarten did note that adults from divorced homes still identify childhood as the most unhappy time of their lives (unless they themselves have been divorced), that men from broken homes report higher psychological anxiety when marital problems arise, and that married women from broken homes may consider the marital role as less important to them than women from intact homes. Nevertheless none of these findings are statistically large, and they conclude that 'early experiences have at most a modest effect on adult adjustment' (Kulka and Weingarten 1979; see also Ferri 1976; Willmott and Willmott 1982). An English review of the literature suggests that although there are important and statistically significant continuities in terms of marital behaviour, intergenerational *dis*continuity is more common (Rutter and Madge 1976). These findings seem consistent with other research. Psychological research on the long-term effects of early experiences, such as maternal and social deprivation or institutionalization, now suggests that the effects of early misfortune and deprivation can be reversed by subsequent environmental changes during the whole period of a child's development (Clarke and Clarke 1976), for example by the adoption of older children who have been brought up in an institution.

This belief that the child's 'resiliency and capacity for adaptation very often enable him to struggle effectively and successfully with the tragic circumstances of his life' (Kadushin 1976) has been noted also the context of divorce. In a study of 120 children from 82 one-parent families, 80 per cent of which were the result of divorce or separation, attending a Gingerbread Playschool for working lone parents, between one-quarter and one-half of the children showed 'no sign of stress apparent to the staff' (Willmott and Willmott 1982). The study concluded

> 'that children can indeed come through such changes wholly or relatively unscathed . . . although research suggests that there is probably a somewhat greater propensity to difficulties among people whose childhood was affected by parental separation, most children are probably more resilient [and adaptable] than it has been fashionable to admit.'
>
> (Willmott and Willmott 1982: 345)

CONCLUSIONS

There are two major implications from current empirical research: first, that divorce is a process and the effects of divorce will vary over a period of time, and according to the individuals involved, and that effects are and can be mediated: divorce is 'a sequence of events involving a transition in the lives of children', a 'process' of 'reorganisation to an eventual attainment of a new equilibrium' (Hetherington 1981: 34-5).

Second, 'the eventual outcome depends, in large measure, not only on what has been lost, but on what has been created to take the place of the failed marriage' (Wallerstein and Kelly 1980: 316). One of Wallerstein and Kelly's most important findings is 'the significance of the relationships within the present in determining outcome at the time. . . . The parent-child relationship of previous years appeared not to be sufficient to maintain good functioning within the present' (Wallerstein and Kelly 1980: 208). They suggest that while pre-divorce relationships between parent and child are significant (indeed the stronger the relationship, the greater will be the child's difficulty in adjusting to the divorce (Wallerstein and Kelly 1980: 208)), the post-divorce relationship is a more important consideration. Relationships change, and pre-divorce relationships are unreliable indications of post-divorce relationships. Wallerstein and Kelly (1980: 315, 258) found no correlation between the non-custodian father's post-divorce contact with the child and the pre-divorce relationship. Hetherington (1981: 49) also noted the discontinuity between the quality of pre- and post-separation parent-child interaction, particularly for fathers: 'A substantial number of fathers report that their relationship with their children improves following divorce, and many previously relatively uninvolved fathers become competent and concerned parents when confronted with becoming a custodial parent'. There is indeed unanimous support for Wallerstein and Kelly's 'major conclusion . . . that the relationships within the post-divorce family are likely to govern long-range outcomes for children and adolescents' (Wallerstein and Kelly 1980: 316), and for the view that the risks of divorce and of one-parent family upbringing can be mediated and moderated by factors not related to which parent is custodian, nor necessarily to pre-divorce parent-child relationships. Identifiable risks normally associated with one-parent family upbringing, or with particular custodian and access arrangements, may not necessarily be consequent therefore on the quality of pre-divorce or even trial-date parent-child relationships. Nevertheless despite recent increases in knowledge of the effects of divorce on children, both short-term and longer term, 'we know nothing about the long-term effects of children growing up in mother-custody compared to father-custody families' (Santrock, Warshak, and Elliot 1982: 303); and the full-term effects of divorce for children as adults or the intergenerational effects are barely beginning to be understood. The long-term effects of early experience, and the influence of childhood experiences on parenting behaviour remain uncertain (Rutter 1981).

Conclusion

The centrality of the child's welfare in s.41 as a pre-condition to his parents' divorce is based on the premise that children of divorce are necessarily 'at risk'. There are however dangers implicit in the premise, for intervention may occur on grounds that do not otherwise justify child care intervention under other legislation. Another danger lies in the absolute nature of the assumption which hides the relative basis of comparison: are children of divorce 'at risk' as compared with children of some ideal model happy family, or as compared with children in pre-divorce unhappy families? The third danger concerns the empirical evidence for the premise.

There is no simple answer to whether and how divorce affects children. There is some evidence that growing up in a broken home, or a one-parent family resulting from divorce or separation, can cause educational retardation, anti-social behaviour such as delinquency, or impair later parenting. But most of these effects may be associated with other factors, such as poverty, class, occupational status, and so on; much research does not take a longitudinal approach, but relies upon evidence at one point in time, rather than considering the family breakdown as a process over many years; it also fails to make comparisons with intact families in which there is parental disharmony; and much earlier research fails to consider possible mitigating factors. The American research studies by Hetherington, Cox, and Cox and Wallerstein and Kelly are likely to be much more reliable, and need to be replicated in this country.

It is possible that the damage to children caused by parental divorce has been overstated. With the increased rate of divorce, marriage breakdown is less likely to be treated as deviant, so that the social stigmatic effects of divorce on children will diminish. Short-term effects of divorce may also have been over-emphasized over longer-term resilience and adaptation by children to new family circumstances. One must also distinguish between the general pattern and individual differences, particularly by sex and age. Most important, mitigating factors in the post-divorce arrangements may be the most significant variables in the success of the family to restructure their relationships. In other words, children of divorce *need* not be 'at risk'; there is a potential danger of it, although the nature of that danger is not at all clear. After controlling for factors such as social and economic disadvantages, there is very little direct evidence that family breakdown itself is linked with any longer-term consequences (although this could be a result of lack of evidence rather than lack of effects), and certainly none that cannot be reversed by a satisfactory change in environment.

The issue here is the justification for making the welfare of the child central to the granting of divorce; it is now becoming apparent that it is not the divorce itself, but the circumstances to which the divorce gives rise that have deleterious consequences for children.

It is clear from the research cited above that in our present state of knowledge the ill effects for children of divorce may not be as widespread as have been believed, not as serious, and are probably reversible, able to be mitigated, or even avoided altogether by satisfactory post-divorce arrangements. The justification for present legal intervention in the divorce process on behalf of children then is to identify those cases where children may be 'at risk' and to provide for the introduction of mitigating circumstances. And it may be that the 'welfare of the family' rather than the 'welfare of the child' is a more appropriate criterion for intervention in the light of psychological understandings of parent-child interaction and family processes.

There remains the issue whether the law should provide that the divorce itself cannot be granted until the judge has declared his satisfaction for the arrangements for the children. The issues which are addressed in the Children's Appointment, that is the facts as stated in the petitioner's proposed Arrangements for the Children (relating to the child's residence, education, financial provision, and access) may only indirectly or partially bear on the circumstances now understood to conduce to the success or failure of the divorce process for the child. Nevertheless the Children's Appointment is the one stage in the present process when any potential difficulties can be detected. As the mechanisms of post-divorce problems are becoming better understood new methods may be able to be devised to screen out those families where children are likely to be 'at risk' from their parents' divorce. Suggestions of this type have been made but the proposed criterion for assessment has usually been whether there are any contests between the parents over the children. Thus it has been suggested that welfare reports should not be used in uncontested custody cases (Eekelaar et al. 1977), and that judicial Children's Appointments should not take place where there is no 'issue' between the parents (Davis, McLeod, and Murch 1983). Certainly parental conflict is understood to result in post-divorce problems of children, but it is questionable whether the presence of a formal issue or contest is an indication of whether parental conflict exists. Many conflicts, in particular over access, may not present themselves to the court at this stage or at any later stage, and indeed the present law which makes the granting of a divorce conditional on the judge being satisfied about the arrangements for the children may actually conduce to the parents hiding any conflicts that may exist.

The purpose of s.41 must be as a screening procedure to identify cases (formally contested or not) in which there is the potentiality of damage to children. Criteria for consideration must include less the pre-divorce relationships, but more importantly prognostications of post-divorce relationships and arrangements. But the ability of courts to operate an effective screening procedure is severely limited in practical terms (Dodds 1983). The policing of arrangements once made is also both impractical and objectionable (such as where supervision orders are made on grounds not otherwise justifying child care intervention (Southwell 1982)). If the concern of the legal system is to minimize the known potential risks of divorce, then this concern and knowledge on which it is based ought to be embodied in the provision of facilities for advice and counselling on the material and psychological factors that can mediate and mitigate the effects of divorce. This is a task going beyond present proposals for conciliation services which seeks to address only one of the known mediating factors, that is, family discord.

Many children of divorce probably emerge nowadays unscathed in any deeper or longer lasting sense. Legal procedures must therefore be devised that can identify that minority of cases of potential damage to children. There can be no other justification for making the welfare of the child the linchpin of the legal process of divorce.

Acknowledgement

I acknowledge with thanks the financial assistance of the Nuffield Foundation which made this work possible.

References

Baumrind, D. (1971) Current Patterns of Parental Authority. *Developmental Psychology Monographs* 4(2).

Benedek, R.S. and Benedek, E.P. (1979) Children of Divorce: Can We Meet Their Needs? *Journal of Social Issues* 35: 155-69.

Clarke, A.M. and Clarke, A.D.B. (1976) *Early Experience: Myth and Evidence*. London: Open Books.

Davis, G. and Murch, M. (1977) Implications of the Special Procedure in Divorce. *Family Law* 7: 71-8.

Davis, G., McLeod, A., and Murch, M. (1983) Undefended Divorce: Should s.41 of the Matrimonial Causes Act 1973 be Repealed? *Modern Law Review* 46: 121-46.

Dickens, B. (1981) The Modern Function and Limits of Parental Rights. *Law Quarterly Review* 97: 462.

Dodds, M. (1983) Children and Divorce. *Journal of Social Welfare Law* pp. 228-37.

Eekelaar, J., Clive, E. with Clarke, K. and Raikes, S. (1977) *Custody After Divorce*. Oxford: Centre for Socio-Legal Studies.

Ferri, E. (1976) *Growing up in a One-Parent Family*. Slough: NFER Publishing.

Finer Report (1974) *Report of the Committee on One-Parent Families*. Cmnd 5629. London: HMSO.

Gasser, R.D. and Taylor, C.M. (1976) Role Adjustment of Single Parent Fathers with Dependent Children. *Family Co-ordinator* 25: 397-401.

Gersick, K. (1979) Fathers by Choice: Divorced Men Who Receive Custody of Their Children. In G. Levinger and O. Moles (eds) *Divorce and Separation*. New York: Basic Books.

Gurin, G., Veroff, J., and Feld, S. (1960) *Americans and Their Mental Health*. New York: Basic Books.

Hall, F., Pawlby, S.J., and Wolkind, S. (1979) Early Life Experiences and Later Mothering Behaviour: A Study of Mothers and Their 20 Week Old Babies. In D. Shaffer and J. Dunn (eds) *The First Years of Life: Psychological and Medical Implications of Early Experience*. New York: Wiley.

Hess, R.D. and Camara, K.A. (1979) Post-divorce Family Relationships as Predicting Factors in the Consequences of Divorce for Children. *Journal of Social Issues* 35: 76-96.

Hetherington, E.M. (1981) Children and Divorce. In R.W. Henderson (ed.) *Parent-Child Interaction: Theory, Research and Prospects*. New York: Academic Press.

Hetherington, E.M., Cox, M., and Cox, R. (1978) The Aftermath of Divorce. In J.H. Stevens and M. Matthews (eds) *Mother-Child Father-Child Relationships*. Washington DC: National Association for Education of Young Children.

——(1979) Play and Social Interaction in Children Following Divorce. *Journal of Social Issues* 32: 26-49.

——(1982) Effects of Divorce on Parents and Children. In M.E. Lamb (ed.) *Non-Traditional Families: Parenting and Child Development*. New Jersey: Lawrence Erlbaum Associates.

Hipgrave, T. (1981) Child-Rearing by Lone Fathers. In R. Chester, P. Diggory, and M.B. Sutherland (eds) *Changing Patterns of Child Bearing and Rearing*. London: Academic Press.

——(1982) Lone Fatherhood: A Problematic Status. In L. McKee and M. O'Brien (eds) *The Father Figure*. London: Tavistock.

Illsley, R. and Thompson, B. (1961) Women from Broken Homes. *Sociological Review* 9: 27-54.

Kadushin, A. (1976) Adopting Older Children: Summary and Implications. In A.M. Clarke and A.D.B. Clarke (eds) *Early Experience: Myth and Evidence*. London: Open Books.

Kulka, R.A. and Weingarten, H. (1979) The Long Term Effects of Parental Divorce in Childhood on Adult Adjustment. *Journal of Social Issues* 35: 50-78.

Langner, T.S. and Michael, S.T. (1963) *Life Stress and Mental Health*. New York: Collier Macmillan.

Leete, R. (1978) One Parent Families. Numbers and Characteristics. *Population Trends* 13: 1-25.

Levitin, T.E. (1979) Children of Divorce: An Introduction. *Journal of Social Issues* 35: 1-25.

Luepnitz, D. (1982) *Child Custody: A Study of Families After Divorce*. Lexington: D.C. Heath.

McDermott, J. (1970) Divorce and Its Psychiatric Sequelae in Children. *Archives of General Psychiatry* 23: 421-28.

McGlaughlin A. (1981) Generational Continuities in Child-Rearing Practices. In R. Chester, P. Diggory, and M. Sutherland (eds) *Changing Patterns of Child-Bearing and Child-Rearing*. London: Academic Press.

Maidment, S. (1984) *Child Custody and Divorce: The Law in Social Context*. London: Croom Helm.

Mueller, C.W. and Pope, H. (1977) Marital Instability: A Study of Its Transmission Between Generations. *Journal of Marriage and the Family* 39(1): 88-93.

Newson, J. and Newson, E. (1978) *Seven Years Old in the Home Environment*. Harmondsworth: Penguin.

O'Brien, M. (1982) Becoming a Lone Father: Differential Patterns and Experiences. In L. McKee and M. O'Brien (eds) *The Father Figure*. London: Tavistock.

OPCS (1978) Office of Population Census and Survey Monitor. Reference FM2 78/2. *One Parent Families* 1971-1976. London: HMSO.

Orthner, D.K. and Lewis, K. (1979) Evidence of Single Father Competence. *Family Law Quarterly* 13(1): 27-47.

Rutter, M. (1973) *Maternal Deprivation Reassessed*. Harmondsworth: Penguin.

——(1975) *Helping Troubled Children*. Harmondsworth: Penguin.

——(1981) *Maternal Deprivation Reassessed*. 2nd edn. Harmondsworth: Penguin.

Rutter, M. and Madge, N. (1976) *Cycles of Disadvantage: A Review of Research*. London: Heinemann.

Santrock, J.W. and Warshak, R.A. (1979) Father Custody and Social Development in Boys and Girls. *Journal of Social Issues* 35: 112-25.

Santrock, J.W., Warshak, R.A., and Elliott, G.L. (1982) Social Development and Parent-Child Interaction in Father-Custody and Stepmother Families. In M.E. Lamb (ed.) *Non-Traditional Families: Parenting and Child Development*. New Jersey: Lawrence Erlbaum Associates.

Southwell, M. (1982) Arrangements for Children on Marriage Breakdown with Special Reference to Access. Unpublished PhD thesis, University of Keele.

Wallerstein, J. and Kelly, J.B. (1980) *Surviving the Break-up: How Children and Parents Cope with Divorce*. London: Grant McIntyre.

Weiss, R.S. (1979) Growing up a Little Faster: The Experience of Growing up in a Single Parent Household. *Journal of Social Issues* 35: 97-111.

Willmott, P. and Willmott, P. (1982) Children and Family Diversity. In R.N. Rapoport, M.P. Fogarty, and R. Rapoport (eds) *Families in Britain*. London: Routledge & Kegan Paul.

PART THREE
AFTER DIVORCE: PICKING UP THE PIECES

CHAPTER 11

Maintenance: problems and priorities

Jennifer Levin

The Matrimonial and Family Proceedings Bill was introduced into the House of Lords by the Lord Chancellor in November, 1983. Its provisions on financial relief are almost identical to those contained in a private member's Bill which failed to achieve a second reading in February, 1983. This paper is a response to the Bill's provisions, put forward not as an academic critique, nor as a blueprint for the future. It reflects the author's current role as campaigner on behalf of one-parent families and of the Legal Action Group which is concerned with the effect that the Bill may have on the conduct of matrimonial litigation, especially from the point of view of legally aided parties.

The problems

The last legislative changes relating to financial provision on marriage breakdown were introduced just over a decade ago, in 1971.[1] They were not based on any particularly systematic or fundamental examination of the topic[2] – and certainly not on any research on the social significance of maintenance payments or property adjustments after divorce, or their relationships with the tax or social security laws. The 1970 Act was, in fact, introduced rather hastily because the Government had been forced by various interested organizations to promise that the new 'easier' divorce laws embodied in the 1969 Act would not be brought into force without corresponding reforms in the law on maintenance. At the time these laws operated unfairly on the wife who stayed at home to housekeep and look after children.

The current attempt to change the law on financial provision is similarly lacking in comprehensiveness, nor is it based on any research evidence on the way the current law operates. It is a response to pressure, largely from middle-class men and their second wives, who object to the amounts of maintenance they are ordered to pay to the first wife. Their complaints have been well orchestrated and have received a ready response from the media and MPs who, for rather obvious reasons, identify with the problems of middle-class men. It is openly acknowledged by both the Lord Chancellor and the Law Commission that it was these complaints that led the former to refer the issue to the latter for report[3]. The Bill contains some of the Law Commission Report's recommendations.

The Report was concerned primarily with one issue. Should a wife expect to be maintained after divorce and, if so, for how long? How far should a wife be expected to become financially independent after divorce? This is a very limited issue upon which to concentrate.

In England therefore, we still have not taken a fundamental look at the general principles that should determine property adjustment and maintenance after divorce. The Law Commission recommended the abolition of the principle that the parties should, as far as is practicable and subject to conduct, be placed in the position they would have been in had the marriage not broken down – and this is provided for in the Bill. But no alternative criteria were suggested. The Matrimonial Causes Act 1973, s.25, lists the various factors that the court should take into account – age, contributions, length of marriage, needs, resources, etc. – but it does not indicate *how* they should be taken into account, nor their order of priority. The Law Commission did no empirical research and had none at its disposal so it did not know how the present law was being applied in the courts, how long orders lasted, whether they were in arrears, and so on. Nor did it seek to look at maintenance in the wider context, in particular its relationship with the tax and social security laws. It did not even consider the question of compensating a divorced wife for loss of rights under her husband's occupational pension scheme, a problem it has allegedly been concerned with for at least fourteen years.

This presents a contrast with the position in Scotland. The Scottish Law Commission took over five years to complete its review and produced a reasonably comprehensive report on all aspects of financial provision.[4] It was also able to commission research into the actual practice of the courts.[5] Details of their proposals can be seen in the paper by Professor Clive in this volume.

The provisions of the English Bill

As already noted, one of the Bill's main provisions is the abolition of the principle that the court should seek to place the parties in the financial position that they would have been in had the marriage not broken down. The Bill also provides that the interests of the children should be given first consideration when maintenance is being ordered (for a discussion of this see later in this paper).

In making financial orders the court is required to assess how far the earning capacity of the spouses could be increased if steps were taken to do so. This is aimed at wives and is intended to encourage them to undergo training or retraining. Connected with this are the 'clean break' provisions. A duty is imposed upon the court to consider whether or not to terminate all liability for periodic maintenance, either immediately or at some specified date in the future. Orders could be made for a definite period, for example three years, to allow a wife to 'adjust without undue hardship to the termination of . . . her financial dependence on the other party'. Clean break orders will be available without the need to get the consent of the other party (thus reversing the effect of *Dipper* v. *Dipper*).[6] How these provisions will be interpreted in practice is impossible to predict. That they will produce a crop of problems to be litigated is highly likely. Some of these problems are noted later in this paper.

Finally the Bill adopts a new basis upon which to consider the relevance of conduct in assessing financial provision. It should be taken into account if the court considers that it would be 'inequitable to disregard it'. The precise effect of this formula is doubtful. To some conduct is made more important than hitherto. To others it gives statutory form to the decision in *Robinson* v. *Robinson*,[7] a case which, however, modified the decision in *Wachtel* v. *Wachtel*[8] so as to increase the relevance of conduct. In his most recent statement the Lord Chancellor has actually suggested that the relevance of conduct is decreased by this formula.[9]

The need for the Bill

The Bill is obviously based on the premise that wives are receiving too much maintenance, or for too long a period, under the present law. There is however little evidence of this from the available research.[10] The study done for the Scottish Law Commission found that in only two-thirds of cases where it was claimed was maintenance ordered for a wife, the average amount being £18 per week.[4] Main-tenance was more frequently ordered for children, where claimed, but the amounts were low, on average £7 per week. The study made in 1981 by Maclean and Eekelaar[11] found that the total maintenance paid to wives with dependent children was below £10 per week in half the cases, between £10 and £20 in a quarter, and over £20 in one quarter. These sums obviously do not cover the cost of maintaining the children alone in the vast majority of cases.

Even where ex-wives are looking after dependent children they seem to need little urging from the legislature to go out to work. The decision is influenced far more by the availability of state benefits and child minding facilities than by the availability of maintenance.[12] Indeed, women receiving maintenance were *more* likely to be working than those who were not. The reason was that those not in work were likely to be getting supplementary benefit and therefore would get no benefit from maintenance if it were to be paid. Working women get the maximum advantage from the payment of maintenance, including tax advantages.

It seems that the proposals in the Bill are aimed at solving a virtually non-existent social problem. It may be, therefore, that they will have little practical effect. On the other hand, by upsetting the basis on which *all* orders in favour of spouses are now made or agreed, the chief effect of the Bill, as already indicated, may be to provoke a considerable amount of litigation, generally legally aided, in which the courts will either confirm old approaches or forge new ones.

Children

All agree that the children should be given priority when financial arrangements are being considered, but little effort is expended in translating this rhetoric into reality.

It is unlikely, of course, that the economic position of children on divorce can be significantly improved by changes in the private law on maintenance. The Law Commission recognized this: 'We do not think there is any real dispute that the most serious problems faced by the majority of single parent families are caused by economic factors and that changes in the private law can do little, if anything, to alleviate the hardship and deprivation which they experience.'[13] Measures which would alleviate this hardship, for example more jobs, better day care, a guaranteed maintenance allowance as proposed by Finer, would all cost money that the present government is unwilling to find. There are, however, some public measures that would cost little or nothing to introduce. One of these would be to abolish the married man's tax allowance – a clearly anomalous relic – and recycle the resources into child benefit. Benefit could thus be raised to about £13 or £14 per week. Another beneficial change would be the rationalization of the laws on taxation after divorce so as to maximize the benefit to the children and minimize the complexity, delay, and trouble caused by the present system.

Reform of the private law on maintenance could produce some benefits, however, and it seems clear from the available research that there are many fathers who could afford to pay more than they now contribute towards the maintenance of their children. Moreover maintenance can make an important contribution to the standard of living of one-parent families where the custodial parent is working, as has been demonstrated by the research of Davis, MacLeod, and Murch (1983).[12] It is important therefore that any changes in the private law should, at the very least, not further erode the provision that is now made and attempt to improve it.

There are also important non-financial reasons for encouraging the non-custodial parent to support his or her children after divorce. First, it is generally thought to be 'right' that they should do so and accept an equal responsibility for the children's welfare. Second, this is generally in the best interests of the children. Research indicates that children fare best if they retain contact with both parents, and contributing financially towards the upkeep of children is an essential part of such contact.

What changes in the private law could improve the present system? One basic change would be to separate child support from spouse support so that financial provision for children is not seen simply as another 'ancillary' to the divorce and therefore another weapon with which to fight the other side. A Child Support Act that dealt comprehensively with all maintenance for children, whether in the context of matrimonial, guardianship or other proceedings, would serve to concentrate the minds of the parties and their advisers on the real issue – the needs of the children to be adequately supported. Most existing orders for financial provision, though expressed as being support for both spouse and children, rarely provide enough money to support the children alone. Orders of, say, £20 per week for a wife and £8 for a child do not make any contribution in reality towards the maintenance of the wife. All of that sum is needed to support the child.

It is of course not possible to separate entirely the maintenance of the child from that of the parent in reality. As the paper in this volume by Maclean and Eekelaar demonstrates, the two are inter-mingled, the child taking its standard of living from the custodial parent. However, it seems that divorced parents often do take the view that the two can be separated. 'I don't mind paying for the kids but I'm damned if I'll give her anything' is a statement that solicitors and advisers must have heard on many occasions. As few maintenance orders actually cover the cost of the children, it would seem to be desirable in these cases to make it clear that no contribution is being made towards maintenance of the wife by ordering that all the available money be paid for the children, preferably in distinct proceedings that are not part and parcel of or 'ancillary' to matrimonial proceedings.

A Child Support Act should also lay down, with as much particu-larity as is sensible, how the court should approach the question of the assessment of child support. It should obviously be dealt with first, before any question of spousal support is considered. The court should look at the resources of the paying spouse and calculate what he needs to support himself and any new family. It is suggested that the liable relative formula used by the DHSS in assessing the contri-butions due from liable relatives towards the upkeep of dependents on supplementary benefit is the appropriate level. This entitles the payer to retain his supplementary benefit entitlement, housing costs, plus one quarter of his income, whichever is the larger. However, it would seem to be desirable to fix an upper limit on this latter sum of, say, £20. Income above this level should be regarded as available for child support. The needs of the child should then be assessed in the light of up-to-date information on what it actually costs to keep a child of the relevant age. This information has for years been available in the form of figures produced annually by the National Foster Care Association. Using official data (such as the Family Expenditure Survey) the NFCA have calculated what is actually spent on the maintenance of children by the average household and these figures are accepted by local authorities as a basis for the calculation of foster-ing allowances. These are intended to cover costs only and not to pro-vide any 'profit' element. The figures for April 1984 are given in *Table14*.

Using these figures a court can ascertain a child's basic needs. If the family had, or have, a higher than average standard of living, the court should then consider what additional expenses should be added, for example school fees or other extra education.

Table 14 **Average household weekly expenditure on maintenance of children**

child aged (years)	average weekly expenditure (£s)	
0–4 years	25.66	(amounts for London are higher)
5–7	29.94	
8–10	32.79	
11–12	35.64	
13–15	38.49	
16–18	51.32	

The next step is to ascertain the resources of both the child and of the parent. The basic principle to be followed should be that parents are equally liable for the maintenance of their children. However where a parent is engaged in the physical day-to-day care of the child this liability should be regarded as wholly or partly discharged. Of course, a normal child over eleven or so does not require the full-time care of an adult and the court would be able to take this factor into account. If the custodial parent goes out to work and is not therefore engaged in full-time care, then he or she will incur expense in the form of substitute care – baby-sitters, nursery fees, and the like. This expense should be added to the other basic costs of child maintenance and split between the parents in an appropriate proportion.

The next step is to fix the amount of child support bearing these factors in mind. In the vast majority of cases the resources available from the non-custodial parent will be insufficient to cover the actual cost of maintaining the child, at least where that parent is liable for the full cost because the other parent has to provide full-time care. In such a case a smaller amount will have to be ordered. But the advantage of first calculating the sum for which the parent *would* be liable if he or she had the necessary resources is that it brings home to both parents how much is needed to maintain a child adequately and how far each of them is discharging his or her responsibilities. It will therefore be less easy for absent fathers, in particular, to delude themselves that the sum they pay over contributes towards the maintenance of their ex-wives. This method also provides parents, legal advisers, and the courts with a clear and reasonably detailed method of arriving at appropriate orders.

There are many other issues that could be dealt with in a Child Support Act. First, it should apply to all children, not just those whose parents are involved in a matrimonial dispute. In particular it should cover the illegitimate child. Second, the child himself should have the right to bring proceedings for maintenance. This right could, of course, be exercised only through a next friend or guardian *ad litem*, though a child over sixteen should be given an independent right to sue. If the right to sue belonged to the child then it could be exercised on the child's behalf by persons other than parents who might be caring for the child, such as grandparents, foster parents or step-parents. Finally, there are a number of issues relating to tax, child benefits, and social security that could usefully be sorted out in a Child Support Act.

Spouse maintenance

Once the maintenance of the children has been sorted out there will in most cases be little left over for the maintenance of wives (or husbands in appropriate cases). Their maintenance will be a problem only for the comparatively wealthy. But it is still necessary to consider on what basis continuing spouse support after divorce can be justified.

The criterion contained in s.25 of the Matrimonial Causes Act 1973, that the parties should be placed in the economic position that they would have enjoyed had the marriage continued, subject to conduct, is clearly unattainable in the vast majority of cases. But this is not, by itself, a sufficient reason for rejecting it. It does at least provide some criteria by which a claim for maintenance can be evaluated. For example, a wife on divorce may claim that she should be compensated for loss of pension rights under her husband's occupational scheme. This entitlement may well be more valuable, in the long run, than a right to the matrimonial home. At present the basis upon which the ex-wife is compensated (though inadequately in most cases) for this loss is that she would have enjoyed the fruits of the scheme had the marriage continued. If this criterion is abolished, on what basis will she be able to claim compensation in the future? No criteria are provided in the Bill, though, as already noted, a basis is provided in the proposals of the Scottish Law Commission.

It is often maintained that the provisions in s.25 discourage divorced women from working. It is assumed that to put a wife in the financial position that she would have enjoyed had the marriage not broken down, inevitably involves a claim to life-long maintenance. This is incorrect. If the wife worked during the marriage, or would have been expected to resume work once the children no longer needed her full-time attention, then this should and will be taken into account in making financial orders on divorce. The wife in such a case did not expect to be maintained for life even if the marriage continued and would not therefore expect it on divorce. (For an example of such a case under the present law see *Mitchell* v. *Mitchell*.)[14] Therefore, if marriage were a genuinely economically egalitarian institution – with both spouses sharing equally the economic burdens, child care, household tasks, loss of job prospects, etc., as well as the economic advantages such as the opportunity to build up savings, pension rights, and work experience, there would be little scope for continuing maintenance after divorce for either spouse. Marriages are not in fact conducted in this manner and nor do the state or other social institutions expect that they will be, or make appropriate provision for such equality.

There is therefore little need for the changes in the law on spouse maintenance proposed in the Bill. The law does not discriminate unfairly against husbands. It merely reflects the fact that in economic terms men benefit more from marriage, in general, than do women.

The actual proposals in the Bill could, however, have some unfortunate consequences, though how far these are intended by the Government is unclear. First, if conduct is to be more significant in assessing maintenance this could inhibit progress towards conciliated settlements. It also makes it essential that the maintenance of wives is clearly separated from the maintenance of children and that a realistic amount is awarded for the latter. Children will be unable to participate in the amount awarded to their mother if it is cut down because of her conduct.

Second, the Bill requires the court to make final decisions on the basis of speculation about future earning power. The court must assess a wife's future earnings on the assumption that she not only succeeds in finding appropriate training but also completes it and finds a job commensurate with her new skills. On this basis the court can make a final order cutting off all maintenance either immediately or at some specified date in the future. How final will such orders be? Suppose the wife's earning capacity has been overestimated, or a husband fails to discharge some of his obligations under the order, or the children unexpectedly require full-time care because of illness? Is the order nevertheless unalterable? It seems so, under the provisions of the Bill. This leads to a consideration of the whole question of the role of the court, both in settling the terms of orders, consenting to agreements reached by the parties, and in varying them later. English family law has no consistent theory on this. Some orders are unalterable, such as lump sum or property adjustment orders, others are alterable. Consent orders and agreements are reopenable on a variety of rather ill-defined grounds and under a confusion of procedural rules (see e.g. *Dean*,[15] *Thwaite*,[16] *Tommey*,[17] *Edgar*[18]). When making consent orders courts adopt different criteria. Some simply rubber stamp the agreement reached by the parties; others make some effort to ascertain that the agreement has been freely and fairly arrived at. None of these issues has been examined in any depth by the Law Commission despite the fact that the majority of financial orders are in fact consent orders.[19] If final 'clean break' orders and agreements are to become fashionable it is urgently necessary to look at the basis upon which the court makes or consents to them, and at whether and how they can be subsequently varied or upset.[20]

Notes

1 In the Matrimonial Proceedings and Property Act 1970.
2 The Law Commission's Report on Financial Provision in Matrimonial Proceedings, issued in 1969, Law Com. No. 25 was not a profound examination of the basic principles – it was concerned more with the particular practical issues of the time. In particular it did not examine the topic in the light of either property division in marriage or of taxation, or social security provision.
3 The Financial Consequences of Divorce, 1981, Law Com. No. 112 (following the discussion paper issued in 1980, Law Com. No. 103). No draft legislation was included in the Report, contrary to the usual practice of the Law Commission. Possibly this reflects their unease at the task they had been instructed to undertake by the Lord Chancellor.
4 Scottish Law Commission, Report on Aliment and Financial Provision, 1981, Scot. Law Com. No. 67.
5 Scottish Law Commission, Report on Aliment and Financial Provision, 1981, Scot. Law Com. No. 67, para. 31, p. 158.
6 *Dipper* v. *Dipper* [1981] Fam. 31.
7 *Robinson* v. *Robinson* [1982] 2 All ER 699.
8 *Wachtel* v. *Wachtel* [1973] Fam. 72.
9 *The Guardian* 2 January, 1984.
10 The results of which are now conveniently summarized in the Family Policy Studies Centre Briefing Paper on the Bill, available from 3 Park Road, London NW1 6XN.

11 Children and Divorce: Economic Factors. Oxford: Centre for Socio-Legal Studies.
12 Davis, G., MacLeod, A., and Murch, M. (1983) Divorce: Who Supports the Family? *Family Law*. 13(7): 217-24.
13 Law Com. No. 112, para. 5.
14 *The Times*, 6 December, 1983.
15 [1978] 3 All ER 758.
16 [1981] 2 All ER 789.
17 [1982] 3 All ER 385.
18 [1980] 3 All ER 887. See also Levin, J. (1983) The Finality of Financial Agreements and Orders. *LAG Bulletin* 76, June.
19 There are no official figures on this though a study of legal aid statistics cited in the Consultative Paper issued by the Booth Committee on Matrimonial Procedure (1983) indicates that the proportion of consent orders in the divorce courts could be as high as 80 per cent of all financial orders.
20 The Matrimonial and Family Proceedings Bill 1983 got the Royal Assent on 12 July 1984 as this book was going to press. All the provisions referred to as clauses in this paper were enacted in the same terms in the Act; all the gaps pointed out in this paper remain. [Editor's note.]

CHAPTER 12

The financial consequences of divorce: reform from the Scottish perspective

Eric Clive

Introduction

Any attempt at a rational debate on this subject must take place in an emotional minefield. No one who has had any communication with people caught up in the financial aftermath of divorce can have any doubt about the strong and often bitter feelings that can be aroused. Nevertheless, an attempt at rational debate is essential if we are going to do anything to reduce the bitterness and feelings of injustice and the consequential harm to both adults and children caused by the present law. We have to be aware of the strong emotions aroused. We have to make allowances for the stridency and apparent unreasonableness to which strong emotions often give rise. We have to look for the underlying justified complaints about the present law on the financial consequences of divorce and try to do something about them in a way that will improve the position rather than make it worse.

No simple approach

There can be no simple solution to these problems. It can easily be demonstrated that such solutions as complete abolition of all periodical payments after divorce or a three-year cut-off on such payments, or, at the opposite extreme, a life-long obligation of support between former spouses are all equally liable to produce unacceptable results in a whole range of cases. The difficulty, of course, is that the law has to apply to many different kinds of dissolved marriage – from the short childless two career marriage at one extreme to the long and traditional housewife and mother marriage at the other.

The limited impact of private law

Moreover it has to be recognized that even a carefully balanced solution that tries to take into account the legitimate claims of divorced people of both sexes in different situations can have only a very limited impact on the whole question of the financial situation of divorced people and their children. Two of the research projects carried out for the Scottish Law Commission show that in Scotland in a substantial proportion of divorce cases there is virtually no property and very little income to divide.[1] This is reflected in the awards made. In 1980 in Scotland only 6 per cent of divorces granted were accompanied by an award of a capital sum and only 22 per cent were accompanied by an award of periodical allowance to the ex-wife. The average capital sum awarded was £4,500. The average periodical allowance awarded to an ex-wife was £18 per week. It seems only realistic to recognize that in a large proportion of cases the law of financial provision on divorce is irrelevant to the actual financial position of divorced people. Any hope of improving the general condition of one-parent families cannot to any material extent depend on improvements in the law on financial provision on divorce.

Employment situation of women

It would clearly be unwise to base any reform of the law on financial provision on divorce on the assumption that an unemployed divorced person could easily obtain a job. This is particularly true of divorced women. It would also be unwise, however, to draw the conclusion that because women as a whole are at a disadvantage in the employment market this justifies an award in any particular marriage even although it would otherwise be regarded as unjust. The fact that a person belongs to a section of the population at a disadvantage in the labour market is not by itself a reason to impose a financial obligation on someone to whom he or she was formerly married.

Maintenance of children a separate and prior matter

There is a difference in approach between English and Scottish law on this point which may help to explain some of the misconceptions which have grown up on the extent to which the recent reports of the English and Scottish Law Commissions are 'child centred'.[2] In Scotland, we have always taken the view that the claim of the child for

197

maintenance is the child's own claim and that it does not depend on the parents' decision about whether or not to divorce. Divorce terminates the legal link between husband and wife but it does not terminate the legal link between parent and child. Parents remain liable to support their child after divorce as before and the succession rights and other legal rights of the child against the parents are not affected in any way by the divorce. In fact, the first half of the Scottish Law Commission's report dealt at some length with improvements to the law on the support of children. We took it for granted that the question of support for children would be determined first before any question of periodical allowance for the parent looking after the children was considered. This is implicit in clause 11(3) of the draft Bill attached to our Report. So far as the maintenance of children is concerned, I do not think there is any difference in the policy of the two commissions although the Scottish Commission could certainly have done a better public relations job if it had placed greater emphasis on the children's claims in its press releases. I am not sure whether there is a difference in policy between the commissions with regard to capital sums or awards of property to children when their parents divorce. In Scotland, we took the view that there was no justification for what are in effect accelerated succession rights for some children merely because their parents choose to divorce.

The need for reform

Although the law relating to the court's powers to award financial provision on divorce is of marginal importance, statistically speaking, to the welfare of families after divorce, it is nonetheless extremely important to those people who are affected by it. What then is wrong with the present law? Here again, the Scottish perspective is rather different from the English. In Scotland the courts are not under any obligation to try to put the parties into the position in which they would have been had the marriage continued. We do not, therefore, have the problem in Scotland of trying to get rid of a simplistic, inappropriate, and unrealistic objective. Our problem is that the law gives the court no guidance at all as to the objective or objectives of an award of financial provision. It simply says that the court shall make such order, if any, as it thinks fit. This has the advantage of flexibility. It also, however, has serious disadvantages. It leads to unpredictability and variability in awards.

These defects are only imperfectly remedied by arbitrary and unsatisfactory rules of thumb such as the so called one-third to one-half rule. Different judges have different views on various questions concerning the financial consequences of divorce. The parties do not know which judge is going to decide their case until the day it comes up. The whole system is designed to encourage bickering and wars of nerves and to discourage amicable settlements on agreed principles. We are talking, of course, only of a small range of cases but within this range it is clear that the results of the present system are often very questionable from the point of view of both husbands and wives. Husbands find it hard to understand why a wife should have a claim to a third to a half of property owned by them before marriage or acquired by inheritance, or acquired after separation. They also object strongly to the fact that even after a short marriage they are potentially liable for the support of the ex-wife for life. Wives object to the fact that they have no legally recognized claim to property built up during the marriage but must go to the court and appeal to the court's discretion. This is a risky business because there is no doubt that the Scottish courts can and do take matrimonial misconduct into account in awarding financial provision on divorce. What is needed in Scotland and what, I venture to suggest, may well be needed in England if the tailpiece to s.25(1) of the Matrimonial Causes Act 1973 is repealed without anything firm being put in its place, is a clear statement in a statute of the principles governing awards of financial provision on divorce.

There is another defect in the present Scots law on this subject but it is uncontroversial and I will merely refer to it briefly. At present the courts have only very limited powers to redistribute property on divorce. They can award a periodical allowance or a capital sum and they can order the transfer of a tenancy but they have no power to order the transfer of other property or to make various potentially useful incidental orders such as orders for the provision of security. They do not have anything like the range of powers enjoyed by the English courts. The Scottish Law Commission has recommended that the courts should have a wide range of powers to order property transfers and to make incidental orders. These recommendations are, I think, uncontroversial and I shall say no more about them. The difficult and controversial question is what principles should govern the award of financial provision on divorce. Here and elsewhere in the paper I include the distribution of property within the term financial provision.

The Scottish Law Commission's recommendations

Having considered various objectives of the law on financial provision, the Scottish Law Commission concluded, for reasons set out fully in our Report, that no one objective could be found which was sufficiently wide to cover all possible cases that might arise and yet was sufficiently precise to be helpful. We concluded, therefore, that what was necessary was to provide a combination of principles. These would be more than mere guidelines to be taken into account, they would be principles or objectives to be achieved, but they would be so framed as to leave adequate room for judicial discretion in the actual application of them. We had no doubt that any acceptable system had to leave adequate room for judicial discretion. The circumstances of individual cases vary so greatly that no rigid rules could hope to achieve justice across the board. There would still, therefore, be discretion under the Commission's recommendations but it would be discretion within a framework of principles. The principles which we recommended are five in number. They are set out in clause 9(1) of the draft Bill attached to our Report. I would like to comment briefly on them.

A norm of equal sharing of matrimonial property

The first principle is that the net value of the matrimonial property should be shared fairly between the parties to the marriage. There are two questions here. What is meant by matrimonial property? And what is meant by fair sharing?

Matrimonial property is defined in the draft Bill as the property belonging to the spouses at the date of their final separation that was acquired (otherwise than by gift or succession from a third party) during the marriage. Under the present law the starting point is the property owned by the spouse at the date of the divorce and it does not matter when it was acquired. Under our proposals the starting point for a fair division of property on divorce would be the property built up by the spouses during the marriage. Inherited property would be excluded. Property acquired after the final separation would be excluded. Property acquired before the marriage would be excluded. There would be one exception to this last rule. Property bought before the marriage for use by the couple as a family home or as furniture or equipment for that home would be included within the definition of matrimonial property – for fairly obvious reasons. There is one other very important point – the proportion of the parties' rights under a life policy or occupational pension scheme that is referable to the period of the going marriage would be taken to be matrimonial property. Such rights in fact represent a very important and widespread form of saving and it would be unfair to exclude them.

It will not escape your notice that this approach to matrimonial property, unlike the present law, caters automatically for the problem of the short or long marriage. After a short marriage there will normally be little accumulated property to split. After a long marriage there may be very much more. The solution also caters automatically for the case of inherited property and property acquired before the marriage or after the separation.

What is meant by fair sharing?

The Bill says that matrimonial property will be taken to be shared fairly if it is shared equally or in such other proportions as are justified by special circumstances. There is therefore a norm of equal sharing but this can be departed from in special cases. Special circumstances may include – the terms of any agreement between the parties; the source of any funds or assets used to acquire property when those funds or assets were not derived from the income or efforts of the parties during the marriage (e.g. property acquired during the marriage with funds owned before the marriage or with funds provided by the wife's father); destruction, dissipation, or alienation of property; the nature of the property, the use made of it, and the extent to which it would be reasonable to expect it to be realized or divided or used as security; and the actual or prospective liability for the expenses of the valuation or transfer of the property.

Due recognition of contributions and disadvantages

The second principle is that there should be due recognition of contributions made by either party for the economic benefit of the other party, and of economic disadvantages sustained by either party in the interests of the other party or of the family. Contributions would include contributions before or during the marriage and would also include indirect and non-financial contributions. The most obvious example of a claim under this principle would be a claim by a wife who has given up her career to promote her husband's interests or to look after the children of the marriage. Other examples would be cases where a wife has worked unpaid in her husband's business and has helped to build it up or where a husband has worked unpaid improving and extending property owned by his wife before her marriage. A point to note in this connection is that it is not contributions as such that are taken into account. A wife who has suffered no economic disadvantages in the interests of her husband or children, and who has not contributed to the economic benefit of the husband, will not have a claim under this head. Neither will a husband in similar circumstances. The thinking behind this proposal is that the law on financial provision on divorce is concerned with economic adjustments and not with the reward of good conduct that has had no economic effect or the penalization of bad conduct that similarly has had no economic effect.

Fair sharing of economic burden of child care

The third principle is that the economic burden of caring after divorce for a child of the marriage should be shared fairly between the parties. This is a very important principle. There can be no question of a clean break where there are still children of the marriage in dependency. There is one point which I must emphasize and that is that any periodical allowance under this head would be for the spouse and would be in addition to support for the child. Child in this context would be limited to a child under sixteen but would include a child accepted by both parties as a child of the family. The factors to be taken into account by the court would include the amount of aliment being paid for the child, any expenditure or loss of earning capacity caused by the need to care for the child, the age and health of the child, and the availability and cost of suitable child care facilites.

Fair provision for adjustment to independence

The fourth principle is that a party who has been financially dependent to a substantial extent on the other party should be awarded such financial provision as is reasonable in the circumstances to enable him or her the more easily to adjust over a period of not more than three years from the date of decree of divorce to the cessation on divorce of such dependence. This is designed largely for short childless marriages where there is no property and no claim based on contributions but where one spouse has been dependent on the other and will take some time to adjust to independence. Under the draft Bill the dependent spouse could be awarded a short-term financial provision to enable him or her to adjust.

Relief of grave financial hardship

The fifth and last principle is that a party who at the time of divorce seems likely to suffer grave financial hardship as a result of the divorce should be awarded such financial provision as is reasonable in the circumstances to relieve him or her over such period as is reasonable of such hardship. The reason for this provision, which at first sight seems slightly out of step with the others, is quite simply that consultation[3] made it clear that a long stop of this type was necessary. Many people would clearly be unwilling to accept a package of proposals that made no provision for the innocent spouse who is abandoned in old age or illness and left to suffer grave financial hardship. The Commission was anxious, however, that this principle should not be used as a gateway to life-long support after divorce just as if the divorce had never taken place and it is for this reason that the emphasis is on grave financial hardship that seems likely at the time of the divorce. After the divorce the parties bear their own risks. Supervening hardship is not the concern of a former spouse. Under the present law for example a man divorced at the age of twenty-five could claim a periodical allowance from his former wife if he became unemployed at the age of forty-five. This seems wrong and would not be possible under the principle recommended by the Commission.

Some significant features of this scheme

The scheme we have proposed is strictly sex-neutral. Each of the principles could apply equally to men or women.

The scheme also caters for various types of marriage from the short childless marriage to the long traditional housewife marriage. We did not see it as any part of our function to try to influence patterns of married life. We thought that it would be wrong to ignore the fact that the law on financial provision on divorce has to cater for many marriages entered into many years ago when expectations may have been different. Nor did we think it safe to assume that all marriages entered into today were necessarily entered into with expectations very different from those prevailing in the past.

The scheme also makes no assumptions about employment patterns or levels of social security. It is not based on the assumption that a divorced woman (or a divorced man for that matter) can readily find suitable employment.

A very significant feature of the scheme is that it takes a major step towards a system of deferred community property. It is concerned only with the situation on divorce and it does leave a discretion to the court to depart from the norm of equal sharing of matrimonial property in special circumstances. Nevertheless, it goes a long way in the direction of recognizing the idea of marriage as an equal partnership. There are, of course, various ways of defining the property which should be subject to a norm of equal division for this purpose. One way would be to confine the division to particular types of assets such as the home and furniture or other assets labelled as 'family assets'. It seemed to us, however, that a technique of this nature was liable to give rise to arbitrary results as between one couple and another depending on how they chose to invest their property.

Techniques available to the court

In general, the court would under the Commission's proposals have a whole range of techniques available to it to give effect to these principles – including orders for the transfer of property, for the payment of lump sums, for the payment of capital sums by instalments, and for the payment of a variable periodical allowance either for a definite or for an indefinite period. The Commission received much evidence, however, to the effect that the use of potentially lifelong, constantly variable periodical allowances after divorce was regarded as objectionable. Men who had no objection to a reasonable financial settlement on divorce objected strongly to the open-ended commitment implied in this type of allowance. It was seen as a Sword of Damoclēs hanging over them and their second wives and families for the rest of their lives. The Commission felt that there was force in these objections and that something should be done to restrict the use of open-ended life-long periodical allowances in cases where they were inappropriate. The Commission, therefore, proposed two restrictions. The first was that the court should not make an order for payment of a periodical allowance unless satisfied that an order for payment of a capital sum, or for transfer of property, would be inappropriate or insufficient to give effect to the five principles I have mentioned. This, of course, has nothing to do with maintenance for children which is a continuing obligation. The Commission also recommended, and this has been the most controversial and misunderstood part of our proposals, that an order for periodical allowance should not be made so as to subsist for a period of more than three years from the date of the divorce, except where the court thinks that a longer period would be proper for the purposes of the child care principle, or the relief of grave financial hardship principle. This, however, would be without prejudice to the court's power to award a capital sum payable by instalments.

It is worth stressing the three important qualifications on this three-year rule. First, a spouse with young children could obtain a periodical allowance for more than three years. Second, a spouse making a claim under the grave financial hardship principle could be awarded a periodical allowance that might in appropriate cases be life-long. This exception would be particularly important in the case of an older spouse. Thirdly, the three-year rule would not affect the court's power to award a capital sum payable by instalments. This technique could be used, for example, to ensure that a wife who had contributed to the economic benefit of her husband, or who had sacrificed her career over a period of many years of marriage, could be awarded instalments of so much per month until a certain substantial capital limit was reached.

The Commission's intention in proposing this limitation on the court's powers to award periodical allowances was to shift the courts, in appropriate cases, from the use of one technique (involving an open-ended potentially life-long commitment) to another technique (instalment payments until a predetermined limit was reached). This is made perfectly clear by the terms of Recommendation 39(b), which is as follows:

'Without prejudice to the court's power to order a capital sum to be paid by instalments, a periodical allowance should not be awarded for a longer period than 3 years from the date of the divorce, unless the payments are required in accordance with [the child-care principle or the relief of grave financial hardship principle] in which case the award should be for such period as the court may determine in the application of those principles.'

Although this recommendation has given rise to misconceptions and controversy, I still think that, seen in its context, it is justifiable. We are not talking about maintenance for children. That can continue, under the Commission's proposals, until the child is eighteen or even twenty-five if there is continuing education or training. We are not talking about a child care allowance for a divorced parent. That is additional to maintenance for the child, can continue until the youngest child is sixteen and is not affected by any three-year limit. We are not talking about relief of grave financial hardship caused by the divorce of an elderly or incapacitated spouse. Provided the hardship seems likely at the time of the divorce an allowance for this purpose can continue indefinitely. What we are talking about (given that any transitional allowance for adjustment to independence has a built-in limit of three years) is the appropriate form of a financial award designed to give effect to the principles of fair sharing of property and fair recognition of past contributions and sacrifices. It seems arguable that any award for these purposes should be fixed once and for all at the time of divorce (even if, for practical reasons, it has to be paid by instalments over many years). The amount of the award depends on past events, not future needs or means.

The effect of conduct

One of the great advantages of an approach based on different governing principles is that it is possible to resolve the vexed question of conduct in a reasonably satisfactory manner. It becomes possible to distinguish between those principles based on accrued rights or earned rights on the one hand and those principles based on the relief of hardship on the other. In relation to the first, conduct can be regarded as irrelevant unless it has affected the economic basis of the claim. In relation to the second, conduct can be regarded as relevant if it is sufficiently weighty. This is the solution adopted by the Scottish Law Commission. Conduct that does not affect the economic basis of the claim is irrelevant except in relation to claims based on the transitional principle or the relief of grave financial hardship principle. In these cases, conduct can be taken into account if it would be manifestly inequitable to leave it out of account.

Conclusion

I would like, in conclusion, to return to what seems to me to be the important question from the Scottish perspective. What objectives should the courts be trying to achieve in making orders for financial provision and property distribution on divorce? This in my view is a nettle that has to be grasped. There is no point in telling the court to give first consideration to this and to have regard to that if there is absolutely no indication of the objectives to be achieved. We have tried in the Scottish Law Commission to provide a framework of principles that would be regarded as acceptable by reasonable spouses of both sexes and would provide a more satisfactory basis for amicable settlements than the present law. Whether or not we have succeeded is for others to judge.

Notes

1 A.J. Manners and I. Rauta, *Family Property in Scotland* (OPCS, Social Survey Division, 1981); B. Doig, *The Nature and Scale of Aliment and Financial Provision on Divorce in Scotland* (Scottish Office, Central Research Unit, 1982).
2 Scottish Law Commission, *Report on Aliment and Financial Provision* (Scot. Law Com. No. 67, 1981); Law Commission, *The Financial Consequences of Divorce* (Law Com. No. 112, 1981).
3 The Commission, in accordance with its usual practice, published a consultative memorandum with provisional proposals for reform and invited comments. See Scottish Law Commission *Aliment and Financial Provision* (Memo No. 22, March 1976).

CHAPTER 13

Financial provision on divorce: a re-appraisal

John Eekelaar and Mavis Maclean

Divorce is becoming a significant life event for a rapidly expanding proportion of the population, who are likely to experience it either as adults or indirectly as children.[1] But, although a divorce decree is granted, and later made absolute, at specific points in time, it is but one of a series of events whose longer-term consequences on individuals depend on a variety of factors whose implications are little known. In the case of children, for example, the data on the impact of member-ship of a family broken by divorce is very tentative.[2] As far as the adults are concerned, the data is similarly imprecise. There is a good deal of evidence about the economic implications of single parenthood following divorce[3] and increasing attention is paid to the incidence and durability of remarriage (Leete and Anthony 1979). But the relationship between the circumstances and duration of single parent-hood, the nature and effectiveness of financial arrangements made on divorce and remarriage, have not been fully explored. In brief, we lack detailed knowledge of the consequences of divorce over time.

This lack of knowledge makes it difficult to evaluate arrangements made, or imposed, at the time of divorce. Those arrangements may partly represent the 'settling of accounts' between the parties at the end of their relationship, but it is well established that what is also at issue at this stage is how the parties' lives will be ordered *in the future*. This is clearly so in the case of arrangements for the children. But the alleged role of the law at this stage in feather bedding a former wife to the longer-term detriment of the former husband and (possibly) his new family has also been the subject of much criticism.[4] So what is done at, or around, the time of divorce can have, or is believed to have, important longer-term effects. But if we know little about the post-divorce financial history of individuals and families, it is very hard to make an informed evaluation of the impact of the principles or practices employed at this time. The Law Commission was very conscious of this gap in knowledge when it undertook its review of the financial consequences of divorce.[5] Our research has been an attempt to begin to fill it.

In an attempt to acquire some of the information needed to obtain a clearer picture of the longer-term financial consequences of divorce, in September, 1981 we interviewed a nationally representative sample of people who had been divorced since 1971. The latter date was chosen because, on 1 January of that year, the divorce law as reformed by the Divorce Act 1969 came into effect and brought with it the extended powers currently in use by the courts to make orders concerning the financial and property affairs of divorcing parties. The details of the sample and the methodology have been fully set out elsewhere[6] and will not be repeated here. We will only state that, although in some matters, when broken down into specific categories, our sample yielded smaller numbers than we would have liked, we are nevertheless satisfied that it does provide a genuinely representative picture of the divorced population and not some selected sub-group within it.

The three kinds of divorce

In a letter to the journal, *Family Law*,[7] a solicitor recently complained:

'In justice there are only two types of divorce law that one can have. One can have divorce based upon substantial misconduct with maintenance, or divorce virtually at will and no maintenance. One cannot in justice or equity have a situation where women are free to break up their marriages on trivial grounds and then claim financial relief.'

This view is essentially the same as that put forward by Kevin Gray when he wrote that 'the abrogation of personal responsibility for the success of the marital relationship necessarily entails the socialisation of the maintenance obligation after divorce' (Gray 1977: 327). This perception of the relationship between divorce and financial provision sees divorce as essentially a unitary phenomenon. To be sure, there may be differences in detail between individual cases, but the assumption is that a single policy should in principle be applicable to 'the' problem of financial provision on divorce. Criticizing the current statutory requirement that courts are to seek to place divorcing parties in the position they would be if the marriage had not broken down, Gray stated that 'the task given to the courts should, if anything, be that of reinstating not the position which would have resulted if the marriage had continued, but the position which would have occurred if the marriage had never taken place at all' (Gray 1977: 320). In a recent penetrating article, Deech (1982: 621) has argued that the reported cases can be divided into three categories related to the wealth of the parties. For the poorest, whose commitments entirely absorb their income, only a token order can be made, and this is represented as 'meeting basic needs'. Slightly better-off couples will have a house that can be allocated, and little else, and an order will be made about that so the husband will lose all his assets in the short to mid term. The second category covers the middle and upper classes, where income support based on the one-third rule appears to operate. For the final category, the 'really wealthy' cases, there is no limit, and adjustment can take into account a wide range of factors.

We would not dispute that an analysis of the cases reveals such an ordering among them. The financial circumstances of the parties and their available assets are clearly of crucial significance in determining the kinds of orders, if any, courts make. But the analysis of our data suggests that a still more fundamental distinction should be drawn between types of divorces reflecting the radically different social consequences divorce has for different couples. Furthermore, the distinction is significantly relevant to the financial arrangements made by the parties themselves and by the courts. We refer on the one hand to divorces where one or both of the former spouses continues the care of a dependent child or children and, on the other, to divorces where there are no children. The latter category breaks down into a further division between couples who never have had children during their marriage and those whose children are no longer dependent on them at the time of divorce.

We will demonstrate that there are important variations in the way financial and property adjustments are made between these categories. But we will also argue that the recognition of these three distinct types of divorce should form the basis of our approach to financial provision and that we must abandon the quest for a single underlying philosophy governing financial provision between all classes of divorced couples. How, we may ask, is it possible, once children are born, for courts or anyone else to re-instate the position that would have occurred if the marriage had not taken place, as Gray seeks? Do we really mean to apply a principle of 'divorce virtually at will *and no maintenance*' to the 60 per cent of divorces (Haskey 1983) that currently involve at least one dependent child? We will also argue that it is no answer to say that the current debate about the proper basis for financial relief is not about maintenance to children but solely about maintenance between former spouses. The Law Commission took this line in its 1980 Discussion Paper on the principles of financial relief. Having conceded that, where children are left with the former wife, 'there may well be some difficulty in distinguishing her financial position as a former wife from that as custodian of the children' they add that, as the principle that questions involving the custody or upbringing of the children should be resolved according to the children's best interests was not seriously in question, they decided to discuss no further the basis for assessing maintenance for children of the family.[8]

We consider this to be a serious error, for it perpetuates the fallacy that maintenance of children is relatively unproblematic and merely ancillary to the issue of maintenance between former spouses, around which the truly difficult issues revolve. We believe that the reverse is the true position. Cases where there are children are almost entirely concerned with the question as to what is a fair provision to be made for the family unit comprising the children and an adult. It is by no means clear whether, or how, the best interests of those children are implemented under the present practice, or even on what principles a balance is struck between their interests and those of the absent adult. To ignore the presence of children renders much of the complex argument on the proper approach to support a former spouse irrelevant. On the other hand, where there are no children, it is our view that, while no doubt important for a small number of cases, much of the debate has little relevance to the way couples usually settle their affairs.

Continuing support: orders made and income transferred

In the analysis that follows, we compare 'childless' with 'children' divorces. We include in the latter category all cases where, at the time of separation, there was one or more child under eighteen residing with the parties as a child of their family. Cases involving children over those ages at the time of separation fall within neither of the two present categories, and are treated separately. Our 'childless' divorces are those who never had children in their marriage. Of the 229 interview respondents in our sample, forty-six (20 per cent), of whom 29 per cent were men and 16 per cent were women, reported divorces that were 'childless' according to these criteria. These proportions are considerably lower than the proportion of divorces treated as 'childless' to children divorces in the national statistics, which, during the 1970s, was at a ratio of around 4:6 (Haskey 1982: table 2).[9] However, as we have seen, our definition of 'childless' is narrower than in the national data, which define childless divorces as those where there were no dependent children of the marriage at the time of filing the petition. But they could include instances where the divorce took place after the children were adult. Furthermore, 'dependent' is defined as being under sixteen. Many cases treated as 'childless' by those criteria would in fact fall within our category of 'children' divorces. We include children who are over sixteen but under eighteen in our definition of children because a child support order on divorce may extend up to eighteen (or beyond, if the child is in receipt of full-time education and training).[10] Furthermore, we have taken the time of separation rather than filing the divorce petition as the reference point for determining the presence of children. Chester (1971: 172) calculated the median interval from separation to 'final divorce'[11] to be 2.9 years. Even taking into account the changes in substantive and procedural law since Chester's findings, it seems possible that many cases where the youngest child is only fourteen or fifteen at separation will appear as 'childless' by the official definitions although we of course treat them as 'children' divorces. We calculate that if we had used the *official* definition our 'childless' cases would constitute 33 per cent of our sample.[12]

It seems right to choose separation as the point in determining whether the divorce is 'childless' or not, for at that moment some arrangements for their support need to be (and often are) made. It also seems to us unrealistic, especially at a time of high levels of teenage unemployment, to assume that dependency ceases at sixteen. We suspect that the 4:6 ratio under-represents the proportion of divorces where problems relating to child support in fact arise.

Using these definitions, the outstanding distinction between childless divorces and children divorces was that in only 5 (10·8 per cent) of the former was a court order made for continuing support and in only one (2 per cent) did we find a voluntary arrangement for this. By contrast, continuing support orders were made in ninety-seven (55 per cent) and voluntary arrangements in a further twenty-eight (10·2 per cent) of the latter cases. Even more strikingly, if we look at the position at time of interview, in *none* of the childless cases was any income transfer taking place at that time. Three of the orders had never been kept and one had expired. In the children divorces, on the other hand, income transfers were still taking place in 36 per cent of cases. If we narrow this down and look only at those children divorces where a dependent child was still living with the mother at time of interview, and she had not remarried or begun cohabiting with another man, income transfers were being made in 54 per cent of these cases.[13]

These findings are not merely a function of the length of the marriage. It is true that the childless divorces tended to end shorter marriages. 68 per cent of the childless marriages had lasted under five years compared to 32 per cent of the marriages that had produced children. But the few occasions where support was ordered or agreed between the childless bore no relation to the length of the marriage. In the nineteen cases where no arrangements were made for transfer of income to the custodial parents of children or children under eighteen at divorce, the reasons appeared to be related to ability to pay rather than to family circumstances. Ten of the nineteen men were not earning, two had left the country, two wives claimed to earn more than their ex-husbands, one case was not yet settled, and four were unclear.

Other research has confirmed the stark contrast between childless and children divorces in this respect. In Scotland, Doig (1982) reports that *claims* for periodical allowance were made in only 18 per cent of cases where there were no children (defined as children present *under sixteen*) and states that in 46 per cent of cases involving claims for periodical allowance, the judge awarded nothing (Doig 1982: paras 3.4, 6.15). On the other hand, claims for periodical allowance were made in 42 per cent of children cases, and more significantly, claims for aliment (child support) were made in 65 per cent of them. Awards were made in 95 per cent of the aliment claims (Doig 1982: paras 3.4, 5.1, 6.13). Gibson's survey[14] of divorce decrees granted in England and Wales in 1971 showed that less than 18 per cent of childless wives had a maintenance order at the time of divorce, whereas a maintenance order of some kind existed in 72 per cent of cases where the wives had dependent children at the time of the divorce.

We will return later to the distinction made, both in law and in the research findings, between orders made in favour of a former wife and orders in favour of children. The point we wish to make at this stage is only that, whether in the form of maintenance for the wife or child support, the problem of *continuing support* after divorce is almost entirely confined to children divorces.

The home and other assets (see Table 15)

Where the parties were living in local authority housing at the time of separation, the subsequent arrangements regarding accommodation were straightforward. The childless invariably left (nine out of the eleven interview respondents; but two of the five men had stayed). But where there were children, 79 per cent of the women interview respondents in this group (n = 52) and 30 per cent of the men (n = 21) stayed, all but one of the men having custody of the children. Of the few women who left, three returned (with their children) to their own families, four moved in with a new partner and in one case both parents left and were re-housed by the authority.

But, since accommodation in those cases comes from the public stock, their relevance to private maintenance law is limited. When we look at the housing outcome with respect to owner-occupiers, a more complex picture emerges. *Table 15* shows that childless and children divorces share one feature regarding the home. In almost half of each category, the owner-occupied home was sold on divorce. In the case of the childless, the reason for the sale seems to have been to allow the wife to realize her half-share in the house, for half the homes of such couples in their joint names were sold. If the house was not sold, it was much more likely that the husband would stay on in the home than the wife, but in that event the wife would invariably leave with a lump payment; the husband had bought her out. The three cases (13 per cent) where she left without a share, she went straight into a home provided by another man. Interestingly, if the house was in the husband's name alone, he was overwhelmingly likely to remain in it and the wife to leave without any lump payment. Possibly in some of those cases the wife went uncompensated for any beneficial interest she may have acquired in the home by reason of direct or indirect monetary contributions to its acquisition.[15] The advantage, from a wife's point of view, of joint legal ownership is clear, and the message of these data seems to be that, for childless marriages, not only is there rarely any continuing maintenance provision, but that a lump payment made to the wife is likely to be in the form of strict compensation for the transfer to the husband of a property interest.

Table 15 Housing position of owner-occupiers on divorce

(a) childless divorces

	total		house sold		husband stayed		wife stayed		husband left with share		wife left with share		husband left without share		wife left without share	
	col. %	no.	row %	no.	row %	no.	row %	no.	row %	no.	row %	no.	row %	no.	row %	no.
house in joint names	81	22	50	11	45	10[a]	4	1	50	11	77	17	0	0	13	3
house in husband's name	19	5	20	1	80	4	0	0	20	1	20	1	0	0	80	4
total	100	27	44	12	52	14	3	1	44	12	66	18	0	0	26	7

(b) children divorces

	total		house sold		husband stayed		wife stayed		husband left with share		wife left with share		husband left without share		wife left without share	
	col. %	no.	row %	no.	row %	no.	row %	no.	row %	no.	row %	no.	row %	no.	row %	no.
house in joint names	72	48	52	25[b,c]	25	12[c]	23	11[d]	38	27[c]	62	30	10	7[d]	10	5[e]
house in husband's name	18	12	33	4[f]	33	4	25	3	17	3	33	4	17	3	25	3
house in wife's name	6	4	50	2	0	0	50	2	33	2	50	2	33	2	0	0
don't know	4	2	0	0	0	0	50	1[g]	0	0	0	0	25	1[g]	0	0
total	100	66	46	31	24	16	26	17	48	32	54	36	20	13	12	8

a This may be an underestimate; more women reporters said the house was sold than men reporters. The latter reported a higher rate of men staying. It is possible the women assumed the house was sold (for they received a lump sum) whereas in fact the men stayed on.
b Includes two cases of foreclosure.
c Includes one custodial father.
d Includes three 'Mesher' arrangements (one by court order).
e Includes one case where husband kept custody of one child and one where a non-custodial mother left his share 'on trust' for the children.
f Includes one foreclosure.
g This was a 'Mesher' order.

It is striking that owner-occupied homes are just as likely to be sold in the case of children divorces as where the marriage was childless. Yet it is a frequently proclaimed policy of the courts that one of the primary goals of divorce settlement is to secure accommodation for the children (Eekelaar 1979: 253, 257-58; Deech 1982: 632-35). Is this policy failing? Are children divorces treated in the same way as regards the home as childless divorces? In considering these questions, it must be realized, first, that in a number of cases it might be unnecessary to keep the home for the children because they and the wife will be moving into accommodation provided by another man. Four (28 per cent) of the cases where the house was sold the woman moved in with a new partner. So in over a quarter of the cases where the home was sold, no accommodation problem for the children arose. What of the other cases? It seems that the sales in these cases might either have been desired by the custodial parent (wanting to move from the area) or forced on her by the financial situation. This can be deduced from the fact that the courts do appear to be adopting a different policy regarding housing where the divorce involves children from where it does not. In our findings, the wife stayed on in the house only once (3 per cent) in the childless case, but in *a quarter* of the children cases, irrespective as to whether the house was in joint names or in the husband's name alone. Put another way, the wife stayed in half the cases where the home was not sold. The reason for this is indubitably to provide accommodation for the children, and there is no reason to believe that this policy would not have been applied in those cases where the house was sold were it not for the fact that the wife desired the sale or had it forced on her. Indeed, a small number of the sales (10 per cent) were in fact the result of foreclosure by the mortgagee. Others may well have taken place to prevent this eventuality.

That the children should have been moved so frequently from the home in the divorces of owner-occupiers illustrates the extent to which such children suffer residential disruption. Yet we should recall the findings reported in *Children*[2] that about three-quarters of the divorced mothers still single and with dependent children who had been in owner-occupation at the time of their separation were still living in *the private sector* at the time of interview. The lump sum acquired by the sale, or support from the former husband, or payments from the supplementary benefits authorities cushioned the *extent* of the deterioration in their housing circumstances, or, at least, the degree to which they needed to throw themselves on to the public housing authorities for assistance. It is plausible to suppose that a move from the private to the public sector will frequently have greater socially disruptive effect, especially as regards the children's school environment, than moves within a sector. Our data showed that, of the women who moved, half (seven) were able to buy in the private sector (three of them later remarried). Only three (21 per cent) moved into public housing.

As regards the circumstances of divorcing men, neither our findings reported here nor in *Children* support claims of disturbing degrees of hardship visited upon them. In the childless cases, the man either keeps the house or sells it, taking his share. Even where there are children, he is likely to stay on in the house in one-quarter of the cases. Where the wife stays, we find no evidence that she was joined by a cohabitee or a new husband. The pattern seems clearly to be that, where a new partner enters the scene, it is to a home provided by him that the wife and children will go.[16] Where, in the children divorces, the home is sold, the husband will invariably take his share. There were, however, a few cases (13 (22 per cent) of those where either the house was sold or the wife remained in it) where the husband left without any apparent immediate compensation for his capital loss. However, four involved a 'Mesher' arrangement, whereby the house is settled on trust for sale for both parents but sale is postponed until the youngest child reaches a certain age (usually eighteen or on completion of full-time education) or until court order.[17] Thus the husband is not deprived of his capital; his enjoyment of it is simply postponed. Of the seven cases where the husband left without taking any share of the asset, three forewent their share in discharge of their support obligation, one went to a new partner with a house, and we have no information on the others. It should be remembered, of course, that when it is the man who leaves, it will usually be very difficult for the wife to raise sufficient capital to pay him a lump sum. Her inferior earning power and commitments to the children effectively preclude such a course.

Little need be said about other assets. As we explained in *Children*,[18] our respondents reported very little of any substance as regards capital assets other than the home. Twenty-three (50 per cent) of the childless divorces and ninety-two (52 per cent) of those who had dependent children made reference to the disposition of such property in the interview. Seventeen (74 per cent) of the childless indicated that they had come to satisfactory arrangements regarding sharing this property out. A small group (17 per cent), comprising men and women equally, seemed dissatisfied with the distribution, thinking the other party had effectively taken everything. One said the only problem concerned debts. But when we look at the children divorces, only 56 per cent referred to a satisfactory distribution. A rather smaller group than the childless (9 per cent) seemed unhappy about the asset division. The reason for this was that as much as *one-third* said the problem was sorting out debts, not assets. Nothing could make more clear the marginality of rules of asset sharing to the problems of children divorces. The commitments of family living throw many couples into debt. How these commitments are to be met over the longer term is the real issue they face on divorce.

Use of legal services and other processual matters

There is a marked difference between childless and children divorces with regard to the cause of breakdown alleged in the divorce petition.[19] Half of the former petitioners chose the two-year separation with consent condition in contrast to only a little over a quarter of the latter. Only 11 per cent of the childless chose the behaviour condition, whereas it was used in one-third of the children divorces. However, there was little difference in the use of adultery (35 per cent by the childless, 39 per cent by those with children). Variations in the use of these conditions are little understood (Eekelaar and Clive 1977) and we can only speculate on the reasons for these differences. The most plausible explanation seems to be that, where there are no children, the urgency of dealing with ancillary matters (support, occupation of the house) is not so compelling. Where there are children there may be a more immediate need to activate the divorce jurisdiction so that these issues can be dealt with.

This explanation receives some support by considering the use of legal services. Of the childless 61 per cent had seen a lawyer, compared to 87 per cent of those with children. Almost all the women with children had done this. The childless seldom received legal aid (only 9 per cent) whereas 63 per cent of those with children did so. The result of the operation of legal aid was, however, that, although using legal services more than the childless, those with children were more likely to end up without having to pay any legal bills (70 per cent were in this happy position) than the childless were (of whom only 55 per cent escaped all legal costs). On the other hand, a very small number (4 per cent) of those with children eventually paid very heavy legal bills (over £500), whereas none of the childless was in that position. For those of them who had to pay legal fees at all (just under one-half), the amount was usually less than £200 (three-quarters of the cases).

The picture which emerges is of the relative simplicity of the childless cases. Urgent financial questions requiring immediate legal advice or the intervention of the judicial system will rarely arise. The parties will tend to use the simplest means of establishing irretrievable breakdown of the marriage and rarely concern themselves with the complexities of setting up arrangements for continuing support or the provision of accommodation. The only significant legal transaction for the childless will be the sale of the house or the purchase by one (usually the husband) of the joint legal interest of the other. In a very small number of cases (6 per cent) a solicitor was consulted about the disposition of other assets. Children cases are quite different. Since continuing provision is so often made in these cases, it is reasonable to suppose that it is on such matters that legal advice is usually sought. As we have seen, court orders for such provision were made in 55 per cent of these cases. In the 10 per cent where the arrangement was voluntary, legal advice had in fact been taken in half of them. We do not, of course, suggest that serious legal disputes do not occur on the termination of childless marriages. Some of these find their way into the law reports. But when the divorcing population as a whole is observed, it seems that childless couples are generally able to rearrange their affairs on divorce between themselves with relatively little need for external intervention. Once again, the major calls on the legal system are generated by the problems of supporting and accommodating children after divorce.

Present status and economic position

As may be expected, the most significant difference between the childless and children divorces with respect to the present status of the adult parties (at interview) is how much more likely the former group are to remarry (63 per cent as against 46 per cent). No significant difference emerged in this respect as between men and women. Couples from children divorces (especially the men) were rather more likely to be cohabiting now. The higher remarriage rate of the childless may, of course, be partly a function of the age of the parties. But the importance from our point of view of the data lies in its economic implications. As we showed in *Children*, the single most significant event that improved the economic position of the divorced mother with children is her remarriage.[20] This (usually) introduces a second income earner into the household and simultaneously solves the problem of accommodation.

Table 16 describes the present economic position of men and women with and without dependent children at separation.

Table 16 **The household net disposable income of the divorced population with and without children at separation* as a percentage of their national supplementary benefit entitlement**

Divorced men and women without children:
% with present incomes above 140 per cent supplementary benefit entitlement

		now alone	*now reconstituted*
men	70%	20% (n5)	80% (n15)
women	73%	43% (n7)	74% (n19)

Divorced men and women with children under eighteen at separation
% with present incomes above 140 per cent supplementary benefit entitlement

		now alone	*now reconstituted*
men	47%	44% (n16)	48% (n29)
women	40%	18% (n60)	59% (n71)

*This table excludes those with adult children only at separation. The national figure for the percentage of the general population with incomes above 140 per cent supplementary benefit entitlement is 71 per cent (see *Social Trends 1982,* p. 72, referring to 1980 data).

It appears that men and women who divorced without having had children resemble the proportion of the general population having incomes above the poverty line. Although within this group those with new partners fare better.

But both men and women divorcing with dependent children, remarried or not, are unlikely to reach the national proportion of the population living above the poverty line. Clearly the remarried, particularly the remarried women, do a little better, and the non-remarried women are clearly the worst-off group. But the group as a whole, as indicated in *Children,* are unlikely to achieve fully the national average standard of living.

The small group of three men and four women with only adult children at separation present an interesting picture. The men vary. But the women, all with incomes below the poverty line, and half moving into local authority housing, resemble the position of the single mother at its most difficult, compounded with career chances foregone, membership of the older age group, and little likelihood of remarriage.

Conclusions

It is our submission that the source of many of the difficulties into which modern maintenance law has fallen lies in its failure overtly to recognize the distinction between divorces where there are children and other divorces. It is not enough to admit half-heartedly, as the Law Commission did, that 'there may well be some difficulty in distinguishing [a custodial mother's] financial position as a former wife from that as custodian of the children'[21] and then to proceed as if the basis for assessing child maintenance is straightforward and the presence of children only one of many possible variables in determining an issue primarily deemed to be between the independent adults. In truth, the financial position of a former spouse as wife and as mother are for practical purposes identical. It is nonsense to imagine that the economic position of the children is settled by the 'additional' sums usually added on as 'child maintenance.' They will take their standard of living from that of their mother. This fact is conceded by the practice of the courts regarding the matrimonial home. It is invariably the presence of children that determines whether the former wife is allowed to continue in occupation of the home, or sometimes even be given its title absolutely. Although ostensibly an order in favour of the woman as former wife, it is in fact an award in favour of that family unit.

It is for this reason, too, that the much-vaunted 'principle' of the clean break, or its attenuated relation, the 'rehabilitative' order, make no sense in cases where there are children.[22] For if, as is always conceded, the support obligation to the children remains, it is not possible to apply entirely different principles to the provision for the former wife. Decisions about that matter will inevitably have an impact on the children. Hence any reduction in 'her' maintenance due to considerations of 'conduct' inevitably lower the children's standard of living also. If we see the custodial mother and her children as a single economic unit, much of the discussion about the method of determining 'her' continuing maintenance, in particular the one-third rule, appears misplaced. The point of the one-third rule is that, *assuming the father is making provision for the children* (a

221

matter usually considered unproblematic), the wife should, on her own account, receive no more than an amount equal to one-third of her and her former husband's joint incomes. The result would be that, together with the 'child' maintenance, her family unit would receive more than one-third of that sum, and indeed this would seem only proper for it would be very difficult to argue that she *and the children* should be limited to one-third of the joint income. But in deciding what is 'fair' to order by way of continuing support, it is the total income of the mother and children that should be measured against the income and commitments of the father. Clearly, the one-third criterion can have no relevance to that exercise.

Some cases, especially of lower income families, show the courts working on this basis. In *Scott* v. *Scott*[23] Cumming-Bruce LJ expressly stated that the one-third rule was of no assistance to him because 'on these family finances the dominant feature is the necessity of providing for three young children and the requirement of providing a home for them by means of mortgage payments'. The court had to look at the incomes of both the father and the mother (who cared for the children) and decide whether the order produced the result that the two families had a 'comparable' standard of living. In *Shallow* v. *Shallow*,[24] Ormrod LJ made essentially the same comparison. But in so doing he referred to the one-third rule in determining the maintenance payable to the wife. But this was really irrelevant since it was the combined total of her maintenance and the sums ordered for the children that was weighed against the former husband's income. If that had revealed a significant disparity, either the wife's maintenance or the children's maintenance would have been adjusted accordingly.[25]

In cases where the parties are wealthier, there is less readiness to compare the total incomes of the families. *Wachtel* v. *Wachtel*,[26] which is the leading modern authority for the one-third rule, illustrates this. The Court of Appeal upheld an award of £1,500 per annum to the wife on the basis that this would leave her with one-third of the parties' joint income. But the trial judge had also ordered the husband to pay £500 per annum for the child for whom the mother was caring. As to this, Lord Denning MR simply stated that 'we think the figure . . . is considerably too high' and reduced it to £300. No indication is given as to the basis on which this was done, and this is indicative of the cavalier attitude often shown to the 'child' element of the award. If the amount was deemed too high as a result of comparing the former wife's net position with that of the husband, this might equally indicate that the figure reached for the wife's 'own' maintenance by way of the one-third rule was wrong. In *Slater* v. *Slater*,[27] a case where £2,000 per annum was ordered on the former wife's account and nearly £3,000 per annum for the three children, Sir John Arnold P spoke of examining the net effect of 'the' order (in favour of the former wife) 'against the one-third guideline', apparently ignoring the effect of the award in favour of the children. *Sibley* v. *Sibley*[28] underlines an even more bizarre result of separating the former wife's and the child's award and applying the one-third rule to the former. It was here decided that the sum which the husband was paying towards the child's education should be deducted before dividing his earnings by three in order to reach the sum to be ordered for the former wife. This was because it was thought that the wife, too, should contribute to the child's education. But the result is, of course, to depress 'her' award and, in consequence, the child's standard of living.

In our view the only rational way of calculating the maintenance to be awarded to a man's former family is on the basis of a comparison between his present income and the total income of the former family. If he has formed a new family, the whole income of that family should normally be taken as the figure for comparison.[29] In many cases, then, we are comparing the standard of living of two families. In *Children*,[30] where we consider in detail the financial position of families with children after divorce, we suggested that this would best be done by expressing the income of a family in terms of its relationship to the notional supplementary benefit entitlement of that family. This takes into account the demands on resources generated by family size. We can, then, compare the standard of living of the two families not only against one another, but also against an objective criterion, which we propose should be the average national income of a two-adult, two-child family, also expressed as a proportion of such a family's notional supplementary benefit entitlement. We would argue, then, that the *prima facie* legal duty of the former husband would be to transfer to his former family sufficient income to keep them at the standard of the notional average family. We are doubtful whether he should have a *legal* duty to maintain them above that standard. However, if he does not have the means to achieve this result without bringing his own family (or himself) below the notional national average, it would be necessary to decide whether, as a matter of policy, his new family should be favoured over his earlier family and be permitted to rest at that level to the detriment of the former family or whether he should be required to bring it below that level and that the families attained comparability in income.[31]

We do not think that techniques and principles such as these would appropriately be applied to cases of divorce where there were no dependent children to be cared for afterwards, whether because it was a childless marriage or because the children had already become independent. That the settlement of financial matters on such divorces should be covered by principles we do not doubt, but they are of a different order from the children cases. Their nature, however, falls outside the scope of this discussion.

Notes

1 If present trends continue, about 1 in 3 marriages will end in divorce in England and Wales and 1 in 5 children experience their parents' divorce by the age of sixteen (Haskey (1982, 1983)).
2 We discussed the question of the effects of divorce on children in Maclean and Eekelaar (1983), *Children and Divorce: Economic Factors*, hereafter referred to as *Children*.
3 This is reviewed in *Children*, pp. 18-23.
4 This criticism instigated investigation by the Law Commission (*Family Law: The Financial Consequences of Divorce: The Basic Policy*, Law Com. No. 103 (1980) Cmnd 8041, p. 1) and culminated in the presentation of a Private Member's Bill in the House of Commons in December, 1982. The Bill fell on the dissolution of Parliament in 1983. It was re-introduced as a Government measure and was passed in July 1984.
5 Law Commission, *Family Law: The Financial Consequence of Divorce*. Law Com. No. 112 (1981), paras 8-12.
6 *Children*, pp. 13-18. We interviewed 229 men and women, screened out nationally from 180 sampling points, with a response rate of 85 per cent at in scope addresses.
7 Letter from Adrian J.G. Perelman (1983) *Family Law* 13: 60.
8 Law Com. No. 103, p. 4.
9 Law Com. No. 103, p. 3.
10 Matrimonial Causes Act 1973, s.29.
11 This seems to be taken as the time of decree nisi rather than decree absolute. He found the median interval from filing the petition to 'granting of the decree' to be less than seven months. It is almost certainly less than this under the reformed procedure.
12 There might have been some under-reporting of divorces involving short, childless marriages taking place many years before our screening interviews.

13 See *Children*, p. 31.
14 Private communication.
15 A wife can acquire such an interest under the line of cases represented by the House of Lords' decision in *Gissing* v. *Gissing* [1971] AC 886.
16 See also *Children*, p. 24.
17 See *Mesher* v. *Mesher* [1980] 1 All ER 126n.
18 *Children*, p. 23.
19 Matrimonial Causes Act 1973, s. 1(2).
20 *Children*, p. 40.
21 See note 8 above.
22 See *Dipper* v. *Dipper* [1981] Fam. 81.
23 [1978] 3 All ER 65.
24 [1979] Fam. 1.
25 See also *Wright* v. *Bye* (1975) 5 *Family Law:* 44; *Stockford* v. *Stockford* (1978) 8 *Family Law:* 53. In *Dipper* v. *Dipper* [1981] Fam. 81, the trial judge had ordered maintenance for the children only, dismissing the wife's application. The Court of Appeal held he was wrong to do so, apparently because of the disparity between the incomes of the father and the mother and the children. It is, however, not at all clear on what principle the award for the mother (£9 per week) was reached. It certainly bears no relation to the one-third rule.
26 [1973] Fam. 72.
27 (1982) 12 *Family Law:* 153.
28 (1981) 11 *Family Law:* 121.
29 See Sir John Arnold P in *Slater* v. *Slater*, above.
30 See *Children*, p. 16.
31 In *Children* we also discuss the interaction of the maintenance obligation with state benefits and suggest the introduction of a limited disregard of maintenance payments when assessing supplementary benefit entitlement of the recipient family.

References

Chester, R. (1971) The Duration of Marriage to Divorce. *British Journal of Sociology* 22: 172.

Deech, R. (1982) Financial Relief: The Retreat from Precedent and Principle. *LQR* 98: 621, 632-35.

Doig, B. (1982) The Nature and Scale of Aliment and Financial

Provision on Divorce in Scotland. Central Research Unit, Scottish Office.

Eekelaar, J.M. (1979) Some Principles of Financial Provision on Divorce. *LQR* 95: 253, 257-58.

Eekelaar, J.M. and Clive, E. (1977) *Custody After Divorce*. Oxford: SSRC Centre for Socio-Legal Studies.

Gray, K.J. (1977) *Reallocation of Property on Divorce*. Abingdon: Professional Books.

Haskey, J. (1982) The Proportion of Marriages Ending in Divorce. *Population Trends* 27: 4.

——(1983) Children of Divorcing Couples. *Population Trends* 31: 20.

Leete, R. and Anthony, S. (1979) Divorce and Remarriage: A Record Linkage Study. *Population Trends* 16: 5.

Maclean, M. and Eekelaar, J.M. (1983) *Children and Divorce: Economic Factors*. Oxford: SSRC Centre for Socio-Legal Studies.

CHAPTER 14

Old families into new: a status for step-parents

Judith Masson

The research which provides the background for this paper was undertaken by the author with Daphne Norbury and Sandie Chatterton between 1978 and 1981 (Masson 1982: 7; Masson, Norbury, and Chatterton 1983) as part of the DHSS monitor for Parliament of the Children Act 1975. The project was designed to provide information about the families who sought to adopt their step-children and their motives; the processes of step-parent adoption both in the courts and social services agencies and the effects of the introduction of the new law of adoption and joint custody. It involved a number of interrelated studies each undertaken in three geographical areas. Information about the applicants, the children, and the non-custodial parents came chiefly from application forms and guardian *ad litem* reports in a sample of 1,733 cases.[1] In addition, the researchers received letters from some step-families and a small but unrepresentative sample of families were interviewed. Details of the court process were obtained from the records of all step-parent adoption applications lodged in the three areas between 1 January, 1975 and 31 December, 1978 and interviews with a sample of court staff. The information about social work practices was obtained by long interview and postal questionnaire from a sample of those who had acted as guardian *ad litem*. Samples of management staff in both social services and probation departments were also interviewed. Details of the use of advice services by step-parents came from a postal questionnaire to all solicitors who were known to have acted in a step-parent adoption case within the sample; a survey of CAB and other advice agencies; interviews with social services duty officers and finally contact with the editors of women's magazine 'problem pages'. All this material enabled the researchers to provide the most comprehensive picture of current practices in step-parent adoption.

Three alternative strategies for providing a status for step-parents were considered in the conclusion of the report to the DHSS: return to law and practices operating before 1976 by the abolition of subs. 10(3); retention of subs. 10(3) but with changes in practice which could ensure the use of more experienced personnel; the abolition of both adoption and joint custody for step-parents and their replacement with a single status which could be obtained without court proceedings. This paper concentrates on this last strategy – the abolition of adoption and the provision of a new status for step-parents. The material from the study is used to help describe the needs and wishes of step-families and to explain why adoption, joint custody (or custodianship) are not appropriate ways of giving step-parents a legal status. The survey also provided information about the ways would-be applicants became aware of subs. 10(3), the use step-families made of advice services, and the steps they took before deciding to seek adoption. This information is important because it recognizes that there may be difficulties in ensuring that step-families become aware of changes that will affect them and it helps show how these could be minimized.

Step-families are created when a parent marries someone who is not their child's natural parent. The parent may not have been married previously; alternatively his/her marriage may have been ended by divorce or death. Little information is available about the size and composition of the step-family population.[2] However, it is clear that the number of divorcing couples with minor children has increased markedly over the last fifteen years (OPCS FM2) while death-rates for young adults have remained low and comparatively stable (OPCS DH1; OPCS 1978: 16-22). It has been estimated that half the divorced women under forty-five years remarry and that the chance of remarriage is not reduced for women with two or less children (Leete and Anthony 1979: 5). The pattern of illegitimate births is changing but it has been suggested that more children are being born to stable unions, and are thus less likely to become part of a step-family than before (Lambert and Streather 1980: 56; Leete 1978: 9). It is probable that the majority of children now living in step-families have lost a parent through divorce. Many of them have lived with their mothers in one-parent families and acquired a step-father when she remarried. Thus the step-family is not the only family these children have known; some still have important relationships with their non-custodial parents.[3] Since the step-family encompasses only part of the network of relationships for the children and adults, this has implications for the manner of providing a legal status to step-parents.

When a person marries and becomes a step-parent, in law she/he acquires neither rights nor duties in relation to the step-children (*Tubb* v. *Harrison* 1790). However, if she/he and her/his spouse treat the children as members of their family the step-parent may, in court proceedings, be required to maintain them and may also obtain custody or access rights.[4] (Domestic Proceedings and Magistrates' Courts Act 1978, ss.8, 20, 88(1); Matrimonial Causes Act 1973, ss.21, 42(1), 53(1)). Fathers are not always expected to play a large and active role in the upbringing of their children; it is not surprising then that the test for treatment is not a severe one. It appears that few step-parents who have their school-aged step-children living at home will be found not to have treated them as members of their family (*Snow* v. *Snow* 1971). There appears to be some general expectation that step-fathers will financially support their step-children (and that step-mothers will care for them) but there is no public law obligation on them to do so.[5] This general expectation may be reinforced by the practice of the supplementary benefit authorities of withdrawing benefit to a mother for herself and her children when she cohabits and by the difficulties of enforcing maintenance payments from the natural father. It is clear that support from a step-parent is the most important way of improving the financial position of children of divorce. Consequently it has been suggested by Maclean and Eekelaar that remarriage should actively be promoted (Maclean and Eekelaar 1983: 84).

Although a parent and step-parent may agree between themselves how the children should be brought up (perhaps so that step-children and children born to the marriage are treated alike) the step-parent has no right to make decisions about her/his step-children. Therefore, for example, she/he is not entitled to receive school reports or to sign consent forms for medical treatment. Nor may she/he refer disputes about the children to court under the Guardianship of Minors Act 1971-78. Instead she/he must rely on the Domestic Proceedings and Magistrates' Courts Act 1978, the Matrimonial Causes Act 1973, or wardship. Any dispute which concerned the children rather than a general breakdown of the relationship would apparently have to be dealt with by the High Court. Despite living with the children the step-parent is in a weaker position than either the divorced non-custodial parent who retains residual rights in major decision-taking (*Dipper* v. *Dipper* 1980), or, if the Law Commission's proposals are enacted, the putative father who will be able to apply for an order that will give him some rights in such matters (Law Commission 1982).

On the death of her/his spouse, the child's parent, the step-parent acquires no rights in respect of the step-child unless she/he has been formally named by deed or will as a guardian. Even if she/he has been so named she/he must act jointly with the surviving (non-custodial) parent, either party being able to refer disputes to courts. If the deceased parent did not name a guardian the court may appoint the step-parent as a guardian to act jointly with the surviving parent but is not likely to do so unless the parent and guardian will be able to agree (Guardianship of Minors Act 1971, s.6; Hoggett 1981: 140). Step-children and step-parents have no rights to inherit from each other on intestacy but a step-child may claim as a 'child of the family' under the Inheritance (Provision for Family and Dependants) Act 1975. Thus, it seems that, apart from the law relating to 'children of the family'[6] the law has done little to recognize, support, or encourage relationships between step-parent and step-children.

The parents and step-parents whose adoption applications were read for the DHSS research were not generally aware of their legal position, nor were they clear what legal changes adoption would make. A few applicants were concerned about their legal position, particularly the need to safeguard the step-parent and children in case the custodial parent died. Frequently step-fathers described themselves on application forms as 'father by marriage' and stated to the guardian *ad litem* adoption was being sought 'to make the family like a proper family'. They were concerned that all the children in the family should have the same status (in 30 per cent of families a child had been born of the relationship; in another 10 per cent the female applicant was pregnant). Apart from the lack of legal status of one of the adult members, step-families differ from families of first marriage because there is often no common surname. This was clearly important to the majority of those who sought adoption;[7] it may also explain why very few step-mothers apply to adopt their step-children (only 3 per cent of applications in the DHSS study were by step-mothers). Other aspects of being a 'proper family' were freedom from inter-ference and security against threats from the non-custodial parent. Parents and step-parents resented the need to give explanation of the family's history and composition to public authorities such as hospitals and schools. Some genuinely (though unrealistically) feared that, because custody orders were reviewable, they could easily lose children who would be returned to the former spouse.

Reform of the law relating to step-families must take account of the needs the families perceive. Further research with non-adopting step-families would provide information about their wishes and needs. However, for both adults and children living in a step-family 'a proper family' cannot be defined only in terms of a family of first marriage. Rights given to step-parents which thus recognize the step-family as a unit must also take account of the interests of the non-custodial parent, of her/his family and of the children in retaining some relationship with them.[8] Security for the step-family cannot therefore be provided by ending access rights or making custody orders final following remarriage. The issue of names is likely to continue to cause disputes and ill-feeling whether the custodial parent obtains the right to change the name without consent or not.[9] A solution to the name issue may more easily be found in society's acceptance of different family patterns than new legal rules. It is, however, suggested that step-parents should be able to obtain a status that gives them decision-making rights in respect of their step-children, the right to refer disputes to the court, and makes them a guardian of their step-children on the death of their spouse.

Adoption, which was comparatively easily obtained before the introduction of subs. 10(3) of the Children Act 1975[10] gave step-parents all these rights, permitted name change, and excluded the non-custodial parent. It might therefore be argued that the needs of step-families could be best met by abolishing the subsection rather than by attempting to construct a new status. However, the contrary arguments are very strong. Even before 1976 only a minority of parents and step-parents, probably fewer than 20 per cent of those who had remarried following divorce, ever used adoption (Masson 1981: 93). The majority of step-families had no recognized status. There are a number of explanations for this. For some people ignorance of or an inability to deal with the law was a factor.[11] Others did not want to use adoption because of the effect it had on the natural parents' relationships with the children. Mothers did not want to become adopters of their own children[12] or end the natural father's legal relationship to the children.[13] The need to obtain or have the court dispense with the other natural parent's agreement discouraged or prevented some applicants who were unwilling to approach her/him for fear of unsettling the present arrangements. Even among those who made applications there were some who objected to the procedure[14] – the requirement for a guardian *ad litem's* investigation of the family – a few actually withdrew their applications because of this. Those who had chosen adoption did not do so because they wanted or felt a need to be *adopters*. Most were unaware of many of the differences it made to their legal status. They had applied for adoption because they felt it was the only way to make their family like 'a proper family'; they had not considered making wills, applying for permission to change the children's name, or (after 1977) joint custody. For a step-father adoption could be a positive demonstration he was taking responsibility for his wife's children, one which he felt he could not make in other ways possibly because they did not clearly put him in the position of father.[15]

In 1969 the Association of Child Care Officers published *Adoption: The Way Ahead*. They were strongly opposed to the use of adoption by step-parents and suggested that the motivation for such arrangements was often poor and that the children's welfare was not best served. The Houghton Committee, both in its working paper and final report, adopted these views (Houghton Committee 1970: 28; 1972: 29). It recommended initially that this type of adoption be abolished for legitimate children and replaced by a form of guardianship. Following overwhelming opposition to this new distinction between legitimate and illegitimate children it recommended that adoption and guardianship should be alternatives. Neither the ACCO nor the Houghton Committee based their conclusions on research; rather they relied on anecdotal evidence which recounted cases where adoption had been used to exclude relatives, to conceal the truth from the children, or had failed because of poor relationships in the family. The reasoning behind the recommendations of the Houghton Committee was defective. The Committee was concerned about the inappropriate use of adoption evidenced by the large and growing number of orders being made each year. The proportion of step-families adopting was probably already declining.[16] It was also concerned that adoption itself cut links beween the child and his natural family. Evidence from the DHSS research does not support this. Only seventy-six (14 per cent) of the children of divorce had any contact with their non-custodial parent at the time of the adoption application and just twelve of these were visited more than once a month. For the majority of children the links with their other natural parent had already been destroyed and for the 24 per cent who had never had access they had possibly never existed.[17]

The Houghton Committee was, however, correct to assert that adoption was an inappropriate way of providing step-parents with a legal status. Adoption had reinforced the idea that the nuclear family was the norm and it could not therefore provide a framework suitable for a more open family structure. Although families did not necessarily use adoption either to conceal the past or to end relationships, the adoption order effectively did that by replacing the birth certificate with an adoption certificate and destroying the legal position of the non-custodial parent. Even if the non-custodial parent continued to play a part in the child's life she/he was at law a stranger to them.

The Houghton proposal for two alternatives, adoption and guardianship, was based on beliefs that it would be possible for courts (and guardians *ad litem*) to determine in every case which was more appropriate. Also that guardianship would be attractive because it retained the natural relationship with the custodial parent. Neither of these presumptions appears to have been true.

The proposal became law as subs. 10(3) of the Children Act 1975[18] which requires the court to determine on a welfare basis whether adoption or joint custody is more suitable for each child (Priest 1982: 295; Rawlings 1982: 637). In the majority of cases in the study judges were faced with an unopposed application where both applicants and the child presented a united front requesting adoption, stating that it would help them be a better family, and also with a report from a guardian *ad litem* supporting the application. In addition, the non-custodial parent was usually not actively involved with the child and either favoured adoption or was content that it should happen. The applicants had been told of the alternatives but still wanted to adopt. Nevertheless, success rates for applications in comparable cases were 96 per cent, 64 per cent and 9 per cent in the three areas studied. The research showed without doubt that there were no agreed criteria for the decision required by subs. 10(:3).

In general, guardians *ad litem* continued to recommend that orders be made[19] unless circumstances were clearly adverse (for example the marriage was unstable). Some judges made orders while others did not.[20] When they refused adoption they did so because they thought a reviewable order, like joint custody, was intrinsically better or because they, unlike the family and the guardian *ad litem*, thought the prognosis for family relationships would be improved if an adoption order were not made. Since almost nothing is known about the development of children in adopting and non-adopting step-families such a conclusion is hard to support.

A joint custody order gives the step-parent the status as a joint guardian of her/his step-children during the marriage and therefore permits her/him to make decisions about the child. Although it does not permit name change it goes a considerable way to satisfy the legal needs of the step-parent without fundamentally affecting the balance between her/his interests and those of the non-custodial parent. It is not clear what effect the death of the custodial parent has on the order (Hoggett 1981: 152). Joint custody has not apparently[21] been widely used. Its availability is not generally known and even when explained it is not easily understood by those who could benefit from it. Perhaps the term guardianship, which was used by the Houghton Committee, would have been better.[22] Joint custody applications are simpler than those for adoption[23] but the process, which is like that for any variation of a custody order, is still likely to be daunting. Another defect is linked with this; joint custody is available only to those who have been divorced. It does not therefore create a status for all step-parents but marks out one section of the community for this special order. Consequently, it is unlikely to appeal to those who want a status in order to be like other parents. In particular, while procedures differ according to the circumstances of the original breakdown, families reconstituted by the marriage of divorced and widowed parents cannot have the same status in relation to all the step-children.[24]

Does joint custody need to involve a judicial rather than an administrative process? If not, then the application procedure could be simplified and separated from the divorce jurisdiction thus allowing its use for other types of step-family. Theoretically, the decision whether a custody order should be varied to joint custody in favour of parent and step-parent must be based on the welfare principle, that is, the order should only be made if it is in the child's best interests. However, this raises the problem of choice for the decision-maker; there are no bases on which judges may rely in order to determine whether or not to grant joint custody. The parent and step-parent will presumably share their home with the child whether or not the order is granted. They will probably even arrange the child's care in the same way. In most cases the only difference the order will make is that it will allow the step-parent to behave as the child's guardian in dealings with outsiders – schools, hospitals, etc. With or without the order the couple will still treat the child as a member of their family and thus give rise to the possibility of maintenance payments by (and custody or access orders in favour of) the step-parent if the marriage breaks down. The reality is that the effect on the child's welfare of making or refusing the order probably cannot be assessed or even discerned. This suggests that an administrative procedure would be adequate, but without a judicial hearing there would probably be less consideration of the views of the non-custodial parent or the children. This must be a matter of concern but it is far from clear that even under the present system the courts would accept their objections as determining the issue of joint custody.

The custodianship provisions (Children Act 1975, part II) (recently implemented) provide, *inter alia,* rights (similar to those granted by a joint custody order) for step-parents who have married widow(er)s or unmarried parents. The order is granted to the step-parent alone; the custodial parent retains her/his natural rights. The procedure for custodianship appears to be more like that for adoption than for joint custody; applicants will have to notify the local authority of the application and the authority will then arrange for a report to be made to the court about the child, the applicant, and their family (Children Act, s.40). If the applicants seek adoption the court will be able to grant custodianship instead (Children Act 1975, s.37). In any event, the court appears again to be forced into the impossible choice between no order, custodianship, or adoption. Moreover the procedure, like that for an adoption, appears to have been designed to handle applications by those who are not related to the child rather than developed for step-families. Nor are the distinctions between the procedure for joint custody and custodianship justifiable. It seems unlikely that custodianship will be attractive to step-families who found the adoption process too complex or too intrusive.

If a process of obtaining rights is to be provided for step-families more needs to be known about how best to bring new law to their attention. One of the reasons joint custody has not been widely used is that step-families only found out about it after they had started adoption proceedings. By this stage they were already committed to adoption and were thus resistant to suggestions that the alternative might be more suitable. In the research project a number of attempts were made to find out how and when step-parents had first heard about adoption and what made them decide to apply. No clear patterns emerged but it seemed that there was greater reliance on informal systems of information, family, friends, and acquaintances, than on advice agencies or professional sources. Some parents had discussed remarriage with their solicitor at the time of their divorce but most, particularly those who had not been divorced, were unlikely to see remarriage as a legal matter. Adoption, which existed long before the legal rules were introduced fifty years ago, is well known in the community as a method for creating binding ties between parents and children. Considerable efforts will have to be made if any other system of rights for step-parents is to become commonly understood.

Where there is heavy reliance on informal sources of information, offering a fairly subtle choice between statuses this is unlikely to lead to rational decisions. Applicants often do not get enough unbiased information on which they can rely. Moreover, where the choice is not between equals – adoption gives more rights than joint custody – the desire for the more important status may encourage applications that are later thought to be inappropriate by the courts. The DHSS was aware that such a refusal could cause bitterness and ill-feeling and its circular LAC 76(22) stressed the need for good advice to would-be applicants. This could not prevent problems arising where advice was only sought *after* the decision to apply had been made.

If adoption were not available for step-families the problem of choice could be eliminated; it should be easier to disseminate information about one type of status than two. The proposal to abolish adoption and to leave only a status like joint custody might be thought unsatisfactory because of its failure to take account of different step-family patterns. However, the status itself could provide for this; allowing the step-parent to be a guardian and share rights with her/his spouse would permit flexibility and thus be adaptable to different family arrangements. There would, of course, be losses if adoption were abolished – both legitimacy and nationality can be changed by an adoption order. These concern only a minority of step-families; and it would be better if amendments were made to these laws rather than reliance put on adoption to solve such problems

The type or extent of rights granted and the method used to provide them must be considered together. The question whether a judicial or an administrative process is more suitable has already been discussed briefly in relation to joint custody. If the law is to put the step-parent in the position of a parent to the exclusion of the non-custodial parent there must be more investigation of the situation and consultation than if it merely recognizes the position she/he has as a member of the household involved in the day-to-day care of the children. Also, if the law offers to step-families few rights as it does by joint custody (and custodianship) it is unreasonable to expect them to be willing to submit to long, complex, or intrusive processes in order to obtain them. Simplicity and ease of understanding are key factors both for the status given and the way it is to be acquired.

What is the appropriate balance of rights between the non-custodial parent and the step-parent? An acceptable answer for today's social climate might be the one that best promotes the child's welfare. While a child lives with a parent and step-parent this other natural parent should not be able to undermine their decisions about his care but nor should they have the right to exclude her/him at least if she/he has an access order. After all, many step-parents are themselves also non-custodial parents. The law should not be seen as encouraging adults to make fresh starts with new families at a time when continuity is considered vital to children.

What rights then should step-parents be granted and how should this be done? The balance considered above must be preserved but account also has to be taken of the needs felt by step-parents and the realities of daily family life within different reconstituted families.

The solution suggested here is that a person married to a parent should be able to share whatever parental rights her/his spouse has. Thus a step-parent married to a parent who had been awarded custody in divorce proceedings would share the rights of both a natural guardian and a custodian of the child. She/he would be able to make decisions relating to the child's upbringing, consent to medical treatment by signing as 'parent or guardian' and refer disputes (with either the parent-spouse or the non-custodial parent) to the court. She/he would not be permitted to change the child's name or to remove him from the jurisdiction. Her/his share in the parent's rights would be equivalent to the joint guardianship held by married natural parents in that either of them could act alone without the other's consent. It would not therefore be necessary to obtain the signatures of both the parent and step-parent for an operation but this would still be required for adoption. On the parent's death the step-parent would retain rights of custody and guardianship but the parent would be empowered to name a different person to act as testamentary guardian. The step-parent would also have this right.[25] Disputes between the testamentary guardians would be referred to the court.[26] A step-parent married to a widowed parent or to a previously unmarried parent would similarly obtain a share in the spouse's rights of guardianship. A person married to a non-custodial parent would also be able to share whatever residual rights she/he had. On break-down of the marriage the court would be empowered to make orders removing or restricting the step-parent's rights.[27] Although such a scheme could also give inheritance rights between step-parent and step-child it is not proposed that this should be done initially. A similar approach was taken with regard to inheritance and adoption in the Adoption of Children Act 1926.

Under this proposal how decisions are reached, who is consulted, what discussion takes place, and whether certain powers are exercised (for example, the power to discipline the child) are all matters left for the parent and step-parent to determine between them as they are in families of first marriage. Intractable disputes about the children's upbringing would have to be referred to the courts as they are between parents and guardians today. Litigation concerning matters other than custody or access is rare. Legal recognition of the step-parent's position should not encourage or inflame disagreement within reconstituted families. Rather it should provide some framework for its resolution. The law does not limit disputes merely by failing to recognize one party's interests and hear her or his case. The availability of rights for step-parents will perhaps serve to make discussions about the children more important before marriage. It is unlikely to effect fundamentally intra-family arrangements though it may have considerable effect on dealings with outside bodies.

A law that provides for the sharing of rights by a remarried parent potentially dilutes her/his legal position and may therefore be opposed because it further undermines existing rights. More particularly, it may be thought to disturb the balance of power relations within step-families where the dependence of the woman (usually the parent) already makes her weaker than the man (step-parent). Such criticism fails to consider problems where the woman is doubly disadvantaged by being financially dependent and the step-parent. It presumes that financial dependence makes the woman weak in the family but does not consider that lack of any clear role other than breadwinner for the step-father makes his position weak there too. Nor does it provide any justification for the preferred solution of imposing duties on step-parents without legal recognition. Since the 'rights' concerned are parental rights account must also be taken of the fact that they may always be overridden by a court order granted to promote the child's welfare (Hall 1972: 248). They cannot thus be seen as the exclusive property of the parent but rather as privileges attaching to those responsible for children.

The change suggested above is comparable with that introduced when grandparents were given the right to apply (in certain circumstances) for access to their grandchildren. Applications could always be made by those who could afford wardship proceedings but the

Domestic Proceedings and Magistrates' Courts Act 1978, ss. 14 and 40 provided a procedure that was more accessible. Thus the dilution of parental rights was small and was acceptable partly as an extension of the circumstances when the child's interests could be considered.

Non-custodial parents may also feel that their position is undermined by a law giving their former spouse's new partner rights. This is not so. The modern law of parental rights has never allowed decisions to be made on the basis of head counting – that more people favour a particular outcome than dissent from it. Moreover, if adoption for step-parents were abolished, as is recommended, the non-custodial parent's position would be strengthened since she/he will not be able to have her/his rights permanently and absolutely terminated.

Under adoption (and custodianship) law there is a requirement that the social worker's report includes information about the child's wishes and feelings. Under Scots law the agreement of a child over twelve years is required for adoption. Should a new law providing rights for step-parents include such a provision? The children's views are likely to be crucial to the success of any arrangement the parent and step-parent make; parental rights can really only be exercised with the consent at least of adolescents (*Hewer* v. *Bryant* 1970). On the other hand to require the children's agreement in order for the step-parent to share her/his spouse's rights (not just for their exercise) would give children far more control over a parent's decision to remarry than any other decision, such as that to move house, separate, or divorce, which might equally affect them. It would consequently mark out the provision of rights to step-parents as something extraordinary and be out of keeping with the general tenor of the change; it is intended to provide rights alongside the existing duties and thus match the legal situation with the practical one.

The question remains in what circumstances step-parents should acquire rights. Should they be granted automatically on marriage to the parent; on condition that the step-parent satisfies an appropriate test, for example that the couple have treated the child as a child of their family; or only on application of the step-parent and the parent. A status imposed automatically on marriage would apply to all step-parents; there would be no need for a new procedure and the operation of the law would therefore be simple to explain. On the other hand, the status would be imposed on some people who had no interest in their spouse's children and who did not want and would not in practice share parental rights. The requirement of sharing might also discourage single parents from marrying because of a desire to retain control of the lives of children they had brought up alone.[28]

Provision of rights to only those step-parents who, with their spouses, treated their step-children as members of their family would clearly provide rights where the law already imposes duties and also equalize the position over custody and access during and after the marriage. However, it would require a formal application and provision for an appeal to a judicial body so that disputes about whether the condition was satisfied could be heard. If a formal application were required it is unlikely that many would take the steps to obtain the rights but those who did so would probably be interested in their step-children. An application that did not require proof of any condition other than legal marriage could be made a simple administrative matter. The process could then be straightforward and might also be used to mark as an important event the taking on of rights and responsibilities for the children. On balance, if it is thought more important for step-parents to have rights and for there not to be different classes of step-parents, a status provided automatically will have to be introduced. A compromise of rights granted automatically with a provision for contracting out by the couple might be a more acceptable way forward. This would, of course, preclude the step-parent obtaining the rights where the parent/spouse opposed this but these most difficult cases would still come within the jurisdiction of the High Court.

The case for changing the law is based on a need to recognize step-families as legal family units where both adults have rights and duties. The method to provide these rights is chosen to ensure that every step-family is recognized. Although the claim for privacy in reconstituted families is, I believe, as great as that in families of first marriage, the law is not intended to minimize welfare intervention in family life but rather to channel it to those cases where there are disputes or standards of child care which justify concern (Dickens 1981: 463). Step-families may possibly have more difficulties than families of first marriage but these are not solved by requiring investigation before rights can be provided. Indeed, it has been cogently argued that the guardian *ad litem* in adoption should not take on case-work with the families on whom report is prepared (Rowe 1968: 264). Moreover, the research among a sample of step-families where rights were requested suggested that it is not possible at present to distinguish between those where the child's welfare will be better protected by granting the step-parent rights and those where it will not be.

The notion of parental rights is already quite weak in English law. This proposed change, broadening the categories of people who have those rights, might be seen as a further weakening. If this ran contrary to other trends that sought to strengthen the position of parents and the bonds in families of first marriage it would be a matter of concern. This is not the case. It is accepted that children may lose parents through divorce as well as death and that parents may lose children after placing them with strangers or in local authority care. What is important is that the people who care for children are able to take responsibility for them and get disputes to court. The proposed reform will do this by enlarging notions of family rather than by shattering them.

Notes

1 This was a 100 per cent sample of step-parent adoption cases in the courts studied; 1,629 of the cases included a guardian *ad litem*'s report.
2 OPCS does not collect data on the number of step-families (Dunnell 1979: 5).
3 Compliance with both access and maintenance orders is low but the view that access improves children's adjustment following divorce has received increased support (Wallerstein and Kelly 1980).
4 Custody and access orders can be made in relation to any child under eighteen but there are restrictions for maintenance to children over the age of sixteen (Domestic Proceedings and Magistrates' Courts Act 1978, s.5). Supplementary benefit is payable to unemployed children over school age who are not in full-time education; these children may be paying for their keep and could be living in the family as lodgers not being treated as family members.
5 Step-parents are not liable relatives – Supplementary Benefits Act 1976, s.17. Between the introduction of the Poor Law (Amendment) Act 1834 and the abolition of the Household Means Test in 1948 they were.
6 A 'child of the family' need not be related to either adult. She/he is not necessarily a step-child.
7 Almost all applicants stated (para. 14 of the adoption application

form) that they intended to change the child's name. Eleven per cent had already done so informally. Court proceedings would only be required for name change when the parents had been divorced and the non-custodial parent objected.

8 Maddox stresses the need to recognize step-families as particular types of families with special needs and qualities arising from the step-relationship (Maddox 1980: 201).

9 Some natural fathers refused their consent to the adoption telling the guardian *ad litem* that they wanted their children to retain their name.

10 The Home Office study in 1966 found that 94 per cent of applicants resulted in orders (Grey and Blunden 1971: 59). The figure for the Step-parent Adoption Study was 92.6 per cent for 1975.

11 Members of social class V were under-represented amongst adopters in the Step-parent Adoption Study.

12 This was also reported to the Houghton Committee; consideration was given to a change that would permit step-parents to adopt alone but preserve the natural custodial parent's rights. This was found impractical (Evidence of Registrar General).

13 Suggested *inter alia* by the very low level of access where adoption was sought.

14 Applicants were often not aware of the processes they would have to go through (nor were their solicitors (Platt 1979: 46)).

15 It is perhaps easier for mothers to show they are taking on the child by daily care which is expected of them (Newson and Newson 1972: 30).

16 That is, the number of divorces and remarriages creating step-families was increasing faster than the number of step-families seeking adoption orders.

17 Ten per cent of the children were unborn when their now-divorced parents separated, another 30 per cent were under the age of two years (Step-parent Adoption Study).

18 Subs. 10(3) was implemented on 26 November, 1976. The Matrimonial Causes Rules were amended to allow for joint custody orders to be made from 17 January, 1977 (MCR 1977 r.92(3)).

19 Only 34 recommendations were made *against* adoption out of 648 applications after the introduction of subs. 10(3) (Step-parent Adoption Study).

20 Differences of opinion were clear in the discussions at the Judges' Conference held on 27 October, 1978.

21 There are practical problems researching these orders, which are

not filed separately from other custody orders. A request to the staff of two divorce county courts to notify the researchers of any applications made during one month of 1980 revealed no applications.

22 The need to clarify terminology in the area of parental rights has long been recognized (Eekelaar 1973: 210; Hall 1972: 261).

23 It is not a concept that is easy to understand. One step-father interviewed for the DHSS study who had obtained joint custody remained perplexed by it and described it as 'being like something mixed up in a bowl'.

24 Sixty children in the study lived in families formed in this way.

25 There is no reason to prevent the step-parent naming a guardian whilst a non-custodial parent may do so.

26 Some amendments would be necessary to the Guardianship of Minors Act 1971 to ensure that courts have the power to grant access to a guardian who is not a natural parent.

27 A case could be made for a similar provision to apply to parents' rights but there is considerable danger that it would be used inappropriately to inflame further custody disputes.

28 The need felt by single parents to keep control was instrumental in the changes the Law Commission made following its working paper on illegitimacy (Law Commission 1979, 1982).

References

Association of Child Care Officers (1969) *Adoption: the Way Ahead.* London: ACCO.

Dickens, B. (1981) The Modern Function and Limits of Parental Rights. *Law Quarterly Review* 97: 463.

Dunnell, K. (1979) *Family Formation 1976.* London: OPCS Social Survey Division.

Eekelaar, J. (1973) What Are Parental Rights? *Law Quarterly Review* 89: 210.

Grey, E. and Blunden, R. (1971) *A Survey of Adoption in Great Britain.* London: HMSO.

Hall, J. (1972) The Waning of Parental Rights. *Cambridge Law Journal*, B: 261.

Hoggett, B. (1981) *Parents and Children.* London: Sweet & Maxwell.

Houghton Committee (1970) *The Adoption of Children.* London: HMSO.

Houghton Committee (1972) *Report of the Departmental Committee on Adoption.* Cmnd 5107. London: HMSO.

Lambert, L. and Streather, J. (1980) *Children in Changing Families.* London: Macmillan.

Law Commission (1979) *Illegitimacy, Working Paper No. 74.* London: HMSO.

——(1982) *Illegitimacy, Report No. 118.* London: HMSO.

Leete, R. (1978) Adoption Trends and Illegitimate Births 1951-1977. *OPCS Population Trends* 14: 9.

Leete, R. and Anthony, S. (1979) Divorce and Remarriage: A Record Linkage Study. *OPCS Population Trends* 16: 5.

Maclean, M. and Eekalaar, J. (1983) *Children and Divorce: Economic Factors*, Oxford: SSRC Centre for Socio-Legal Studies.

Maddox, B. (1980) *Step-parenting.* London: Allen & Unwin.

Masson, J. (1981) Step-parent Adoption: A Socio-legal Study. Unpublished PhD thesis, Leicester University.

——(1982) Step-parent Adoption. *Adoption and Fostering* 6(1): 7.

Masson, J., Norbury, D., and Chatterton, S. (1983) *Mine, Yours or Ours: A Study of Step-parent Adoption.* London: HMSO.

Newson, J. and Newson, E. (1972) *Infant Care in an Urban Community.* Harmondsworth: Penguin.

OPCS FM2 *Marriage and Divorce Statistics* (published annually). London: HMSO.

——DH1 *Mortality Statistics* (published annually). London: HMSO.

——(1978) *Demographic Review 1977.* London: HMSO.

Platt, F. (1979) The Guardian *Ad Litem* in Step-parent Adoptions. *Adoption and Fostering* 96:45.

Priest, J. (1982) Step-parent Adoptions: What is the law? *Journal of Social Welfare Law,* p. 295.

Rawlings, R. (1982) Law Reform with Tears. *Modern Law Review* 45: 637.

Rowe, J. (1968) *Parents, Children and Adoption.* London: Routledge & Kegan Paul.

Wallerstein, J. and Kelly, J. (1980) *Surviving the Breakup.* London: Grant McIntyre.

Cases

Dipper v. *Dipper* [1980] 2 All ER 722
Hewer v. *Bryant* [1970] 1 QB 357
Snow v. *Snow* [1971] 3 All ER 833
Tubb v. *Harrison* 4 TR 118

CHAPTER 15

Matrimonial property and divorce: a century of progress?

Ruth Deech

It would be wrong to allow the centenary of the Married Women's Property Act 1882, the Act that laid the foundation of a major portion of family law, to pass unnoticed and uncelebrated. The century since its enactment has undoubtedly seen major changes in family law, ownership, and in the perception of the rights of wives, changes that are qualitatively and quantitatively greater than those prompting reform in the century preceding the Married Women's Property Act. The question is now raised whether the Act needs replacement or retention in order accurately to reflect the realities and aspirations of modern family property holding. Proposals for reform are ranged on a spectrum of statutory co-ownership at one end and greater individualism within the family at the other, and attitudes are likewise divided: women's property or citizen's property, special regimes or no regimes? One element is beyond doubt and controversy and that is that property rights in marriage, on divorce, and protection of occupation are so confused that the requirements of one aim spill over or are anomalously attached to another and this is epitomized in the very phrase 'matrimonial property'. Complaints about the efficacy of the laws in one area tend to be attributed to the workings of another and, above all, the tension between the alleged demands of an efficient property law, especially conveyancing, and of family law bedevil the attainment of justice in either area.

The enactment of the Married Women's Property Act

Taken in isolation from later needs and factors the Act was, and is, an instrument of equality and non-discrimination and represented a milestone in the progress towards the modern conception of the rule of law, or civil liberties. Separate identities for husband and wife have become the norm in other fields since 1882. There is no dissent from the proposition that tort actions between spouses should be allowed.[1] There are no more special rules concerning larceny.[2] The wife has full power to make contracts.[3] As recently as 1981 it was confirmed that a husband and wife could conspire together for the purposes of the law of tort[4] and the medieval fiction of unity was declared obsolete except in so far as retained by statute. Parents are now separate and equal.[5] The same attitude was taken in *Williams and Glyn's Bank* v. *Boland*.[6] Where unity is still maintained, in revenue and social security, it is increasingly under attack.

Before the mid-nineteenth century, as is well known, on marriage a woman's personal property and income became her husband's. Over her real property the husband exercised the right of control and disposition for his lifetime and on his death her property was available for eventual inheritance by her family. It is interesting to note that, even then, outright disposition of the fee simple of a wife's property could be achieved during marriage only by joint consent. It is also worth remarking that family inheritance was a major consideration and that the wife's family retained their rights, by and large. This issue is overlooked, or regarded as unimportant today, in the re-allocation of property on divorce or in the proposals for co-ownership for, by operation of either scheme, a parent's property may be diverted from his children or family to 'complete strangers' *via* the former spouse.[7]

The first legislative attempt to achieve separate property was an unsuccessful bill, introduced in 1856 and again in 1857. This was the date, of course, of the establishment of modern divorce law and it is no coincidence that the attempt to give married women separate property was abandoned on passage of the Matrimonial Causes Act 1857. The 1857 Act was designed in part to allay disquiet about property because it contained provisions for independent control on separation and divorce, then, as now, the obvious occasions for dispute. The 1857 Act perhaps also accustomed public opinion to the contractual view of marriage, although the real pressure for separate property came from the facts that more women were earning an independent living and that primary education was established for all by the Education Act of 1870. The 1882 Act was the culmination of a series of Acts dealing with property (Holcombe 1983).

Some of the social background of the time is relevant. According to

246

the 1861 Census, there were 3,488,952 married women in the population, of whom 838,856 were at work.[8] There was also a disproportionate number of (involuntarily) single women in the population, many of whom needed to earn a living. The most interesting feature of the time was the paucity of owner-occupation taken in conjunction with the low rate of divorce. It has been estimated that in the late nineteenth century only about 10 per cent of households lived in property that they owned (Murphy and Clark 1983: ch.1). A housing shortage for all types and conditions of persons, married or not, was the dominant theme up to 1945, and the great expansion of owner-occupation, building societies, and accessible mortgages came after the first world war. In the four-year period 1881-85 there were a mere 1,678 decrees absolute of divorce and annulment. Separate property and divorce had no bearing on each other at all; allocation of housing on divorce was not an issue except in so far as there was a housing shortage for everybody and these issues emerged and coincided much later, as will be seen.

Criticism of the principles of the 1882 Act came from two directions. One was the internal or subjective, that is, stemming from a certain view of women as creatures in need of protection who would lose their attractiveness if endowed with property rights.[9] Modern expressions of equivalent sentiments are readily to be found.[10] Two hundred years ago this pretty image of woman was used to justify the husband's acquisition of his wife's property. It is tempting to use it now to justify co–ownership and transfer of property on divorce. Thus does the popular stereotype of the wife come to be used to justify the scheme of the moment, whether it is a giving or a taking away.

The other, external criticism of the 1882 Act was that it achieved too little. It was not until the Sex Disqualification (Removal) Act 1919 that all legal obstacles in the way of women's jobs were removed and so it is said that, despite the 1882 Act, men continued to control the property of women, even if only in the capacity of advisers, because women could not earn or qualify sufficiently to make use of the Act. Wage earning women were enabled to keep their wages by the Act; wealthy women still had settlements, but nothing was achieved for the middle-class housewife. It is true that she remains the main object of concern even today but this criticism is misdirected. In 1882 her husband probably owned no freehold and her vulnerability was the product less of law than of social and economic fetters. The attitude taken at that time was that non-legal constraints should be tackled, in preference to adapting the law to cushion the inequalities. The 1882 Act has also been attacked for being consistent with the social and legal attitudes of the period which emphasized the equality of the parties before the law, without regard for their differing material circumstances. Whether this is a genuine ground for critical comment remains a moot point today.

Development of the Married Women's Property Act in the twentieth century

How has the jurisprudence of the Act developed in this century? Detailed consideration of the use made of implied, resulting, and constructive trusts is omitted here as too well known but mention of the complexities inherent in concurrent ownership draws attention to a coincidence of no mean significance. 1882 was also the year in which the Settled Land Act was passed. The year that saw the introduction of separate property for married women also saw the establishment of property doctrines that would end attempts to keep land in the family and that still today mean that a forcibly shared house is a dissipated asset. The Settled Land Act gave the tenant for life under the settlement wide powers of dealing with land without the consent of the other beneficiaries and provided for overreaching: the conversion doctrine was well established in trusts for sale, which were in fact dealt with in the Settled Land Act in the same fashion. These doctrines mean that no practical housing benefits can ever be achieved by giving a wife a share in a husband's property – subject only to *Boland*. The only device the law has been able to provide for sharing, whether in 1882 or in the Law Commission's co–ownership plans, is overreaching, and the conversion of real property into cash. Modern solutions to this dilemma are control rights, to prevent liquidation of the asset and, from this point of view, those who want protection of the fruits of the endeavours of a non-titled spouse/owner should welcome the House of Lords' decision in *Boland*. Nevertheless in general terms the requirement of registration of a land charge is today seen as the solution to any social problems caused by 1882 and 1925 property devices. The mere grant of ownership other than express joint tenancy is now clearly an irrelevancy, for it gives no benefit if the usual property and conveyancing principles are adhered to.

Where a wife acquires a tenancy in common by contributing to the acquisition of property in the name of her husband or, in the alternative, were she to be deemed a co-owner under the Law

Commission's scheme, the property is held on trust for sale. Apart from the *Boland* decision, the situation is that the title holder can almost certainly dispose of the property without his wife's consent and, in case of conflict, her claim is reduced to one for a share in the proceeds, proceeds on which there are prior claims for mortgage debt and legal aid repayment. The only alternative currently under consideration requires the non-title holder to register her claim as a land charge, an act which is admittedly unlikely to occur. There is now no way in which one piece of property can benefit in equal fashion two owners who do not wish to live together other than by division of the proceeds. The result of the Settled Land Act 1882 and the Law of Property Act 1925 and the legal aid regulations is that any manipulation of title is destructive of the asset in costs, or grossly unfair.[11]

After a century of operation of the Married Women's Property Act the stage has been reached when the house has ceased to be a source of productivity or wealth (if it ever was) and when to share its title by manipulation of law is largely meaningless. Security of occupation is regarded as the more desirable objective, without reliance on the state of ownership of the property in question. The solution to the problems of the Married Women's Property Act has been found in ignoring it in real property questions. Unfortunately it has also been ignored in the very area to which it was originally directed, namely, that of earnings and allowances. Economic disparity between spouses might better be reduced by laws enabling women to receive a greater share of cash resources, presently directed towards the husband, than by attribution of beneficial shares in real property.

S. 17 of the Married Women's Property Act and the law that grew from it are scarcely ever used nowadays because later statutes have provided different remedies, because it is more common for property to be in joint names, and because disputes almost invariably occur on breakdown of the marriage. Couples disputing property rights are directed away from the Chancery Division to the Family Division.[12] During marriage the ownership of the home is of legal interest only to creditors and third parties. The result, at a superficial glance, is that separate property is buried. During marriage there are control rights, to be examined below, and on dissolution there is discretion.

Mitigation of the separate property principle

The main twentieth-century social changes affecting property relations are the growth in owner-occupation and inflation of house values; a housing policy of eliminating homelessness, preserving occupation, and controlling rent; an increase in the proportion of women earning wages, and a high divorce rate coupled with a divorce law based on irretrievable breakdown. How have these been reflected in the mitigation of separate property in the twentieth century?

Security of occupation laws apply to the public as a whole and tend to filter down to a wife through her husband. His occupation and rent are protected by Rent Acts, Housing Acts, the Administration of Justice Act 1970, and the Protection from Eviction Act 1977; hers, largely derivatively, in the same Acts and additionally by the Matrimonial Homes Act and the decision in *Boland*. The protection is fairly complete and whenever a weakness appears in the statutory remedies, the legislature has not been loth to amend the law.[13] Where gaps remain in the wife's protection, they reflect the limits set to any member of the public's right to occupy, that is, her right can be no greater than his at its limits. Where the husband is bankrupt the court will usually order the sale of the house.[14] It has been presciently commented that property has ceased to be a right to exclude others and has become more concerned with the right not to be excluded from the use or enjoyment of something (Reich 1964). The attitude of the courts towards title as a key to security has undergone a metamorphosis from *Tarr* v. *Tarr*[15] to *Richards* v. *Richards*[16] and the cases concerning eviction of husbands and of cohabitants under the provisions of the various statutes show most clearly the demise of separate property.

The risk of disinheritance has been described as an unsatisfactory feature of separate property. Inherent in this criticism is the assumption that the widow should inherit most of the property of her late husband (and not the home alone) and that her claim is stronger than that of his children, questionable assertions. In so far as there was an explicit inheritance policy before 1882 it favoured the heirs as much as, if not more, than the widow. The Administration of Estates Act 1925 shifted the balance decisively towards the widow. This Act, together with the Intestates' Estates Act 1952 and the Family Provision Act 1966 had the effect of passing the whole estate of most men to their widows. The 1952 Act contains special provisions designed to preserve security of occupation of the matrimonial home for the widow. Children and other relatives get short shrift but of course claims can be made to alter the basic distribution under the Inheritance (Provision for Family and Dependants) Act 1975. Taken overall, the rules give effect to a concept of inheritance dominated by dependency, not by kinship and certainly not by title or free disposition.

The feeling that a wife should have some control and occupation rights over her husband's property, rights that were wrongly confused with the issue of title, has been converted by legislation and judicial decision into rights assertable against third parties: the Matrimonial Homes Act, *Boland,* the Housing Act and s.24 orders. This adds up to a considerable amount of matrimonial property law and counters the specific criticisms that have been made of separate property.

So the main argument against the separate property principle remains the psychological one: a woman has no property of her own during marriage. This argument assumes that all women have no property and lack the means to buy it. It also assumes that the only asset in which they are interested is the home. The Royal Commission of 1956[17] pointed out that a woman might feel that she was entitled to furniture and the profits of a husband's business where she had worked in it unpaid. Neither of these is available for sharing today except on divorce. The Morton Commission also commented that economic dependence contributed to the stress of married life. If this is true, it is debatable whether it is best removed by separation of property, co-ownership, or access to increased wealth outside the confines of family law.

Property and dissolution

The most direct attack on the ills of separate property is the power of the court to transfer property on dissolution, now found in s.24 of the Matrimonial Causes Act. The connection of separate property with the risk of a wife's homelessness on divorce stems from 1937, when desertion became a ground for divorce along with cruelty and insanity,[18] desertion being the ground that has the most bearing on the property question under discussion. Separate property in this context ceased to be a problem when the forerunner to s.24 came into effect in 1971.[19] 1937 to 1971 accordingly saw the dramatic interpretations of s.17 of the Married Women's Property Act that have led to the present position of implied, resulting, and constructive trusts coupled with a wide view of a wife's contribution to the acquisition of the home, a development that terminated and culminated in the Court of Appeal cases of the early 1970s. This was avowedly undertaken to ensure that a divorced or divorcing wife could get a share of the family assets, for there was no provision other than for maintenance until 1963, when s.5 of the Matrimonial Causes Act of that year gave the courts the power to order payment of a lump sum on divorce.

Why was separate property not a problem in divorce before 1937? It was and perhaps is still the common law duty of the husband to provide for the reasonable needs of the wife. The obligation remained even when they were living apart unless she had committed adultery or was in desertion. She had authority to pledge his credit in respect of necessaries, if she could obtain credit, until s.41 of the Matrimonial Proceedings and Property Act 1970 ended this and acknowledged the superior efficiency of social security in this area. The husband, after 1882, could not evict his wife from the house lawfully as he could not sue her in tort.[20] The unavailability of detinue, conversion, trespass to land, ejectment, and nuisance mitigated separate property. The husband could not sue his wife even after desertion or separation.[21] He could only use s.17 of the 1882 Act for that purpose and under the doctrines developed in that connection the court would not order her out unless he provided suitable alternative accommodation. Because the husband had to use s.17 the strict law of property during marriage was tempered and replaced by the discretion of a judge.[22] The wife could apply for an order restraining him from selling the house under s.17.[23] Her rights were not enforceable against third parties but in practice she would often have had time to obtain a *Lee*-type injunction. Then, as now, the husband might have sold the house suddenly while the wife was absent. If the house belonged to the wife, she could, unlike the husband, sue in tort to evict him by permission of s.12 of the Married Women's Property Act. She was then, still is and will be under the co-ownership plan, vulnerable to bankruptcy and mortgage debts.

So before 1937 if a husband owned a house in his name alone, and the rarity of this owner-occupation has already been alluded to, and deserted his wife, she was reasonably secure if there was no resort to divorce. In 1936 there were a mere 5,575 petitions for divorce and in that era house ownership had not assumed the tremendous social and economic importance that it has today; nor would it have been the case that the home was the major asset of most families. This is a modern phenomenon: the deprivation of the divorced wife would have been a real hardship only from roughly 1949, when the passing of the Legal Aid and Advice Act made divorce a possible option for many more, to 1971. The opening up of divorce to wives in 1937 by the addition of three grounds, especially desertion, likely to be used by wife-petitioners, would have been a mixed blessing because divorce would have ended her security of occupation. The wife's inability to divorce the husband for desertion before 1937 did at least preserve the matrimonial remedies for her, *via* s.17 of the Married Women's Property Act.

S. 24 of the Matrimonial Causes Act 1973

S. 24 gives greater advantage to a wife today than reliance on her strict property rights. The earliest cases on s.24 were dominated by the demand for lump sums and a division of the proceeds that would give both parties some capital, the house being sold.[24] Then the courts developed the so-called *Mesher* order: the disadvantages of such orders led eventually to the disavowal of the device by the Court of Appeal.[25] Now outright transfer to the wife is frequently made, this being the ultimate answer to criticism of the 1882 principles. Compensation to the husband may take the form of a charge for a fixed amount or a percentage, postponed until the wife's death or remarriage.[26] Sometimes the husband is not compensated at all.[27] The latest device to receive attention is the payment of rent to the ousted spouse to compensate for loss of capital.[28]

There are social, legal, and economic drawbacks to each of the methods of forced reallocation of title developed under s.24. The section is a convenient tool for the redistribution of property and the minimizing of reliance on public support (Gray 1982). But, as has been argued in relation to maintenance, there is no clear reason, apart from that one, why one adult should be made to give his house to another simply because of need. There remains a conflict between the expectation that the wife will continue to care for the children and the risk of divorce that is not soluble by property allocation in the middle classes.

In application of s.24 two types of fetter bind the wife/beneficiary and appear to deny her the advantages of separate property and the rights of a feme sole granted to the divorced wife by the Matrimonial Causes Act 1857. The first are the conditions imposed by the court if the property is directed to be held on trust for sale. It may be a charge in favour of the husband, the existence of which will make it hard for the wife to raise money by way of second mortgage and diminishes the proceeds when the house is eventually sold. Then there are the conditions on which sale is postponed, commonly children remaining in education and the wife not remarrying, cohabiting, or wishing to move. The stipulations echo the *dum sola et casta* clauses once found in maintenance orders of another age. They put the children's needs second and they prevent the wife moving, for no matter how good a reason, because sale will activate the husband's right to his share of the proceeds. The second fetter is legislatively imposed and that is the need to repay legal aid. Since 1976 only the first £2,500 of legal aid is exempt from repayment,[29] with the result that litigation eats up the house. The impoverished divorced wife who has successfully claimed outright transfer of the house still has to pay off the mortgage, and supplementary benefits can be relied on only for interest discharge, leaving an even greater than normal capital debt to be discharged on sale together with the legal aid debt. The advantages of the ruling in *Hanlon* v. *The Law Society*[30] are the saving to the taxpayer and the incentive to litigants to settle but it nevertheless cripples legally aided wives and not the litigant who pays her own costs or whose husband pays them.

The general costs of s.24 jurisdiction are very high. As much as 60 per cent of civil legal aid is taken up in matrimonial causes and it is a fair estimate that much of this relates to disputes over the home. The s.24 discretion makes divorce long and expensive and encourages hostility and interaction for years after the decree, especially when the division of property is unpredictable. Whatever the rationale behind the orders that usually emerge from s.24 applications they will be seen as deprivation by husbands, despite the theory that guilt and deterrence are no longer to influence divorce. Moreover, custody of children and claims to the house are inextricably linked; are claims to children and the seeking of ouster injunctions free of ulterior motives or are they key moves in the struggle for the house? The plea that the children's interests are to be protected is less convincing when one considers that the average family moves house voluntarily every five years and that the allocation of property on divorce has the effect of taking it away from the children's ultimate reach in favour of the other spouse.[31]

Reform

The radical reform called for is equal division of matrimonial assets, not just the house, in order that the non-property-owning population be not further disadvantaged (Scottish Law Commission 1981). The division must logically be limited to the property acquired by the spouses, other than by gift or inheritance, in the period between marriage and separation. It makes no sense to include, as at present, premarital property and property unconnected with the marital partnership. Many marriages are of short duration and should not be allowed to become opportunities for 'gold-digging'; others take place later in life or as second marriages, likely to be of even shorter duration than first ones, and to redistribute all of a man's property not only further deprives the children of his first marriage but leads to the expensive, painful investigation of possibly hidden assets that is the most unpleasant feature of modern English divorce procedure. The Scottish Law Commission considered the problem that the home might form the greatest part of a couple's property and is not susceptible to equal division but the Commission nevertheless expressed the opinion[32] that any departure from the principle of equal sharing should be kept to the minimum and cast doubt on the principle of English jurisprudence that children should never move house. Their argument implies a norm of sale and division and this could iron out the differences in result that exist in English law between owners and non-owners on divorce.

The disillusioned comparative lawyer might say that imitation of the legal institutions of other countries with very different economic, housing, social, and educational practices, for all that they speak English, is not useful or an end in itself, simply a source of ideas. (Scotland should be exempted from these strictures on comparison!) In that spirit, there should be renewed consideration of deferred community systems, combining, as they do, separate property during marriage with equal division of assets on dissolution. These systems differ in their definition of matrimonial property but it is never limited to the house; nor does it extend to property unconnected with the existence or date of the marriage.[33] The partnership view of marriage, said to prevail today, can hardly lead to any other approach and it contrasts markedly with the concentration in English divorce law on the totality of assets of the husband, all of which must be revealed before negotiations can begin (Scottish Law Commission 1983: 5.3).

Deferred community differs from community of acquests because the former preserves separate ownership until the breakdown of the marriage, although there tend to be restraints on disposition by one spouse, while the latter provides for shared ownership from the date of marriage. Both systems feature guaranteed sharing and definition of rights *at marriage*, not *on dispute*. Taking into account all the laws that affect the property of husband and wife in England it could well be said that there is already in operation here a system of deferred community, lacking only its allegedly greatest advantage, the equal division on dissolution. The scheme could be perfected by substituting for s.24 of the Matrimonial Causes Act a procedure for division of property as proposed for Scotland or an accounting and equalization procedure as operated in West Germany.

Related to this but beyond the scope of this article are reforms that could be made to the social security and taxation system to achieve separation and independence. Joint taxation goes back at least to the Property Tax Act of 1806, which provided for income tax purposes that 'the profits of any married woman living with her husband shall be deemed the profits of her husband'.[34] The tax laws continue as if separation of property and the right granted to the wife to keep her own wages in the 1870 Act had never taken place. Separate treatment in national insurance, pensions and all state benefits would be nothing other than beneficial.

Co-ownership

What function remains to be carried out by the scheme of co-ownership proposed by the Law Commission in 1978, once the shadow of title is separated from the substance of security of occupation and resolution of disputes on divorce?

The arguments against the scheme have been fully explored elsewhere (Deech 1980; Scottish Law Commission 1983: 5.22–5.31; Zuckerman 1978). The scheme was never a desired aim in itself but a compromise reached, at a time when the full effects of s.24 could not have been foreseen, between doing nothing and instituting full community. Public opinion on the matter is unclear. Naturally people questioned in a survey will respond affirmatively to the suggestion that they see themselves as sharing. This does not mean that they would accept with equal pleasure the losses and restraints that might affect them, as sharers, on disposition or indebtedness (Todd and Jones 1972: 39). No doubt also the impression formed by the public would be that equal sharing would be the norm on divorce if co-ownership were instituted in marriage; yet the retention of the s.24 discretion would render co-ownership irrelevant at the very time that it should be most relevant.

If women were asked how best to rectify the economic inequalities between them and their husbands co-ownership is unlikely to be the answer. All the matrimonial property regimes ever invented rest on certain assumptions about the spouses' duties, especially the wife's, and co-ownership is no exception. It is assumed that the wives are not working and have never had any income. This view is in contrast to another, equally tenable, that all young people are in an equally strong (or weak) position to earn in the usual gap between finishing education and having the first child.[35] Under separate property laws the fact that a wife is able to make even a minimal contribution to the acquisition of the first house will give her an interest, and there is no reason today why she should not be able to make such a contribution. These views about women and their need for protection and compensation are ultimately subjective: it is so easy to forget that Sir Jocelyn Simon's alleged dictum that 'the cock can feather the nest because he does not have to spend most of his time sitting on it'[36] was no more than his opinion, a nice turn of phrase in a speech, its colourfulness blinding us to the need to seek the unvarnished truth.

If the wife does need compensation co-ownership is certainly not the way to do it as long as the trust rules deny her real benefits; moreover it seems wrong to reward and console a woman for remaining primarily a housewife and child rearer, thus further cementing her into position, rather than widening her choices outside the home. To accept co-ownership rather than make individual choices is to become yet more economically dependent on a family arrangement that is vulnerable and only deceptively protective. Co-ownership accords well with that other facet of the Victorian age, the values returning to fashion today, and it also accords well with rising rates of unemployment.

Conclusions

Attention has been drawn here to the nineteenth-century background to our present law and this has been done in order to establish that there is a risk of recreating the same difficulties today by amalgamating the fortunes of husband and wife in the name of protection of the wife as currently pictured in certain quarters. In several respects we are in danger of reverting to the situation that prompted the 1882 reform.

Although the wife's income no longer belongs to him, the husband is responsible for her tax and must discover all her sources of income, while she has no comparable rights and duties in relation to his income.

The Class G registration requirement in the co-ownership scheme could become the modern equivalent of the marriage settlement of the rich wife in the 1860s, giving her separate property rights if she was well advised.

The exercise of the jurisdiction to oust from the matrimonial home before divorce and of the powers of s.24 may lead one to conclude that on breakdown of marriage the husband's property becomes the wife's for life, just as hers used to become his on marriage.

The effect of *Mesher* orders, their variants and conditions, is to reimpose something akin to the restraint upon anticipation and the *dum casta* clauses.

A century after the Married Women's Property Act came into force, its advantages should not be overlooked. There is a case for saying that it should continue to be the basic principle of family law and property reforms and that it should be reactivated in the sphere of incomes, lest we return to the conditions that prompted the reform.

Notes

1 Married Women's Property Act 1882, s.12; Law Reform (Husband and Wife) Act 1962.
2 Larceny Act 1916, s.36.
3 Law Reform (Married Women and Tortfeasors) Act 1935.
4 *Midland Bank* v. *Green (No. 3)* [1982] Ch. 529.
5 Guardianship Act 1973, s.1.
6 [1981] AC 487 at 505 *per* Lord Wilberforce.
7 Law Commission, *Third Report on Family Property: The Matrimonial Home (Co-ownership and Occupation Rights) and Household Goods* (1978), L.C. No. 86, Recommendation (3), p.109.
8 Census of 1861, Parl. Papers (1863) 53 (Part 1) 33.
9 'The relations of husband and wife were founded upon a condition of things which had existed without exception in all times and in all parts of the earth – the husband being the protector and support of the wife and the latter subordinate to and reliant upon him . . . and . . . the law obviously ought to follow in the same track' (Lord Penzance (1869) 198 HL Debs. 982).
10 Lord Denning, for example, in the section devoted to his achievements in family law in (1980) *The Due Process of Law* (London: Butterworth), prefaces the cases by these words:
    'No matter how you may dispute and argue, you cannot alter the fact that women are different from men. The principal task in life of women is to bear and rear children: and it is a task which occupies the best years of their lives. The man's part in bringing up the children is no doubt as important as hers, but of necessity he cannot devote so much time to it. He is physically

the stronger and she the weaker. He is temperamentally the more aggressive and she the more submissive. It is he who takes the initiative and she who responds. These diversities of function and temperament lead to differences of outlook which cannot be ignored. But they are, none of them, any reason for putting women under the subjection of men. A woman feels as keenly, thinks as clearly, as a man. She in her sphere does work as useful as man does in his. She has as much right to her freedom – to develop her personality to the full – as a man.'

(p. 194)

'This freedom, which women have achieved, carries with it equal responsibilities. If they live up to their responsibilities, their equality is not only a matter of absolute justice but is also capable of great benefits to the human race: and of all their responsibilities, the chief is to maintain a sound and healthy family life in the land. To this chief responsibility all other interests must be subordinated.'

(p. 201)

This train of thought leads him on first to an extract from *Gurasz* v. *Gurasz* [1970] P. 11, a case of joint tenancy:

'Some features of family life are elemental in our society. One is that it is the husband's duty to provide his wife with a roof over her head: and the children too. So long as the wife behaves herself, she is entitled to remain in the matrimonial home.'

and then it leads inexorably on to approval of the co-ownership plans (p. 146).

11 In *Hanlon* v. *The Law Society* [1981] AC 124, it was revealed that the equity in the former matrimonial home was worth £10,000 and the wife's legal costs amounted to £8,025, of which £5,950 related to the property adjustment order. Mrs Gissing claimed a half share in the matrimonial home by virtue of £220 spent on it. In the Court of Appeal (*Gissing* v. *Gissing* [1969] 2 Ch. 105) Lord Denning ordered the husband to pay the wife's costs from his half-share of the home, the total equity of which was worth approximately £6,000, and gave him leave to appeal subject to not disturbing the order for costs. The House of Lords nevertheless

awarded costs to the husband, the sum not disclosed, but clearly considerable by then ([1971] AC 886). In Cooke v. *Head (No.2)* [1974] 1 WLR 972 the proceeds of sale of the bungalow in question were £2,456 and the plaintiff's party and party costs of £1,200 were ordered to be deducted from the defendant's share with the result that he would receive £98 from the sale.

12 *Williams (J.W.)* v. *Williams (M.A.)* [1976] Ch. 278; *Fielding* v. *Fielding* [1978] All ER 267.

13 E.g. Matrimonial Homes and Property Act 1981.

14 *Re Bailey* [1977] 1 WLR 278; Matrimonial Homes Act 1983, s.2(7).

15 [1973] AC 254.

16 [1983] 2 All ER 807 (HL). The reversal of the Court of Appeal decision ([1983] 1 All ER 1017) was unconnected with rights of ownership.

17 The Morton Report, Cmd 9678.

18 Matrimonial Causes Act 1937, ss.2, 3.

19 Matrimonial Proceedings and Property Act 1970, s.4.

20 This was not possible until the Law Reform (Husband and Wife) Act 1962.

21 *Hutchinson* v. *Hutchinson* [1947] 2 All ER 792; *Pargeter* v. *Pargeter* [1946] 1 All ER 570; compare the wife's ability: *Shipman* v. *Shipman* [1924] 2 Ch. 140.

22 *Stewart* v. *Stewart* [1948] 1 KB 507.

23 *Lee* v. *Lee* [1952] 2 QB 489.

24 *Coleman* v. *Coleman* [1973] Fam. 10; *Bigg* v. *Bigg* (1976) 6 *Family Law*: 56; *Goodfield* v. *Goodfield* (1975) 5 *Family Law:* 197. The judgment of Scarman LJ in *Goodfield* is a striking contrast to more recent judgments, e.g. *Harvey* v. *Harvey* [1982] Fam. 83, in its attitude to the wife's rehousing.

25 Deech, R. (1982).

26 *Hector* v. *Hector* [1973] 1 WLR 1122; *Dunford* v. *Dunford* [1980] 1 All ER 122; *Carter* v. *Carter* [1980] 1 All ER 827; *McDonnell* v. *McDonnell* (1976) 6 *Family Law:* 220 and [1977] 1 WLR 34.

27 *Hanlon* v. *Hanlon* [1978] 1 WLR 592; *S.* v. *S.* [1976] Fam. 18.

28 *Harvey* v. *Harvey* [1982] Fam. 83; *Brown* v. *Brown* (1981) 3 FLR 161; *Flatt* v. *Flatt* (1973) 4 *Family Law:* 20.

29 Legal Aid (General) (Amendment No. 2) Regulations 1976, SI 1976, No. 628, r.2.

30 [1981] AC 124.

31 *Preston* v. *Preston* [1982] Fam. 17 at 25 *per* Ormrod LJ and at 40

Matrimonial property and divorce

per Hollings J; *Draskovic* v. *Draskovic* (1980) 11 *Family Law*: 87.
32 Para. 3.83.
33 In Ontario the property to be shared on dissolution is called
'family assets', defined as 'a matrimonial home . . . and property
owned by one spouse or both spouses and ordinarily used or
enjoyed by both spouses or one or more of their children while
the spouses are residing together for shelter or transportation or
for household, educational, recreational, social or aesthetic purposes' (Family Law Reform Act (Ont.) 1978, s.3). In Newfoundland
it is the house plus other assets acquired during marriage (Matrimonial Property Act 1979, s.16). In New Zealand it is post-
maritally acquired property plus the house, whenever acquired
(Matrimonial Property Act 1976, s.8(d)).
34 46 Geo. 3, c.65, s.56.
35 The median age for marriage by a woman is 22 and the interval
between marriage and the first child is 28 months (*Social Trends*
(London HMSO 1983) p. 30).
36 *Pettitt* v. *Pettitt* [1970] AC 777 at 811 *per* Lord Hodson.

References

Deech, R. (1980) *Williams and Glyn's* and Family Law. *New Law
Journal* 130: 896.
——(1982) Financial Relief: The Retreat from Precedent and
Principle. *Law Quarterly Review* 98: 621.
Gray, K. (1982) The Family Home on Divorce. *Cambridge Law
Journal* 41: 228.
Holcombe, L. (1983) *Wives and Property*. Oxford: Martin Robertson.
Murphy, W. and Clark, H. (1983) *The Family Home*. London: Sweet
& Maxwell.
Reich, C. (1964) The New Property. *Yale Law Journal* 73: 733.
Scottish Law Commission (1981) *Report on Aliment and Financial
Provision*. Scot. Law Com. No. 67.
——(1983) *Matrimonial Property*. Consultative Memo. No. 57.
Todd, J. and Jones, L. (1972) *Matrimonial Property*. London: HMSO.
Zuckerman, A. (1978) Ownership of the Matrimonial Home –
Common Sense and Reformist Nonsense. *Law Quarterly Review*
94: 26.

PART FOUR

FUTURE PROSPECTS

CHAPTER 16

The family court

Elizabeth Szwed

'Today was an anguished day in which I was part of a case conference where the decision of the conference – police, health visitor, general practitioner, area social services officer and two team leaders – was that we had no ground for a place of safety order.'

This statement forms the opening sentence of a letter that was given a prominent position in the *Times* letters page on 3 December, 1981. The author, who describes himself as a co-ordinator of a family centre, writes that his job is to prevent the reception of children into care, where appropriate and possible, by providing support for families and children at home. In the author's words he 'provides resources and manages risks'. The letter lists the various concerns that those present at the case conference felt about the two children and their mother, and then continues, 'We could institute care proceedings in the future but run the risk that the mother may overdose them (the children) rather than lose them. There is a slight fear that children may die even though we provide support for the family'. The author then comments that when things in 'risk management' go well the press does not know, but when they go wrong 'uncovering failures of communication is commonplace' and 'reporting of such cases (with some exceptions) now looks to apportion blame'. In conclusion the author states, 'It is now seven years since the Finer Committee recommended the establishment of family courts. Which political party will establish them this century?'

Clearly, this letter publicizes the very real dilemmas and difficult decisions that professionals concerned with the welfare of children, at times, have to face and make. It illustrates the frustrations and anxieties that they may consequently feel. However, my purpose in quoting from this letter lies not with the problems that it identifies but with the particular response or solutions which the author implies – family courts.

Such expectations of the role and purpose of the family court concept are by no means uncommon. Much literature both of legal and social work orientation, as well as the popular press, have urged the ever elusive family court both as a remedy that would improve or rectify defects in the administration of family law and as a panacea for certain critical family crises and problems. Such is the appeal of a family court that political pressures have been fairly unrelenting in England and Wales. In the mid 1970s the Select Committee on Violence in the Family received submissions urging the creation of family courts, and, in 1983, so did the Select Committee on Children in Care. In 1977 the Labour Government felt unable to accept the recommendation of the Select Committee on Violence in the Family that a Green Paper on a family court system in England and Wales be prepared, giving as major reasons expenditure and lack of resources. Nevertheless in 1984, in times of greater financial stringency, the Select Committee on Children in Care has recommended a system of family courts for England and Wales (although there was no consensus about the form it should take) (Clode 1983: 2; Crine 1983: 14 House of Commons 1984: para.85).

Whereas the idea of a family court seems to attract general support there would, however, appear to be little consensus on such matters as ideology or structures beyond vague generalizations. The family court tends to be perceived as some utopian tribunal capable of dealing with a whole array of family problems as well as meeting some of the deficiencies of the welfare agencies.

This is a self-deception which, I believe, has obscured many serious issues which the family court concept raises, such as matters of ideology and form, the procedures the family court should employ, and the law it should administer. These in turn raise questions about the extent to which a family court could or should facilitate or circumscribe an interventionist approach towards families and in personal relationships. So the very serious implications that a family court system could have on questions about the allocation of power and responsibility in many aspects of family life can sometimes be forgotten when discussions focus too much on the more fashionable concepts that tend to be ascribed to the family court ideal, such as informality and conciliation.

By and large, family court models and proposals also tend to focus more on the problems of separating couples, whereas litigation concerning children is both increasing and highlights just how anomalous, fragmented, and confusing areas of the law relating to children can be. Moreover, society's vested interest in ensuring the proper nurturing of its future adult members also means that this branch of family law provides the greatest potential for state interference and control of family life and so merits prominence in any debate about family courts.

With the above points in mind I propose to examine certain key issues such as unity of law and procedures, informality, inquisitorial procedures, specialist tribunals, and conciliation, which are often advocated as advantageous to the proper administration of family law and are common to certain existing and proposed family courts.

Courts or Panels

Distinct characteristics that are generally associated with family courts and account for their popularity are: their accessibility and flexible approach, their informal atmosphere and procedures, and their specialist tribunals complemented by a range of professions who are said to be sympathetic and experienced in family matters. The traditional notion of a family court as described in broad outline in the Report of the Finer Committee (1974) and the Law Society's (1979) proposal, and as can be seen in some American, Canadian, and Australian models, embraces the idea of an institution that is judicial, but by use of such techniques as specialist judges, professional staff, modifications in rules, and physical designs is more adapted to the needs of family law adjudication. Needless to say, the various family court proposals and models differ in the extent to which they embrace some or all of these features. But they tend to share certain features not generally associated with traditional courts and litigation. To most lawyers it may seem obvious and essential that an institution that is described as a 'court' should be judicial, but it cannot be assumed that this is a universally accepted requirement. Nor can the views of those who also argue against a court as being the proper forum for determining family disputes and problems be that easily dismissed.

There is little doubt that matrimonial, domestic, and juvenile courts deal with problems where the issues are not exclusively legal, especially in children's cases. As Professors Kay and Mnookin have separately written: custody and child protection cases involve 'complex questions of analysis and prediction of human behaviour that cannot be resolved by simple application of legal formula' (Kay 1968:1207; see also Mnookin 1975). Such cases tend to attract a greater involvement by behavioural scientists and other experts, who claim to be more impartial, than is found in other areas of litigation. In turn, the very presence and contribution of this expertise raises issues of who indeed makes the decisions – the courts or the experts? We also find that litigants are increasingly being encouraged, and in some cases compelled, to turn to the experts in the behavioural sciences or to other counsellors in conciliation bureaux and schemes for assistance in reaching decisions in family disputes, particularly where children are concerned. Meanwhile those components that are a strong feature of traditional litigation, such as consideration of individual cases according to legal rules and sanctions to ensure obedience, seem at times inept and ill-suited to family matters where a court is dealing with personalities and emotions.

So, as the more traditional functions assume less importance, or become redundant or ill-suited, and courts become more willing to abdicate their functions to the experts, it seems hardly surprising that the idea of 'panels of experts' or some other kind of non-judicial tribunal gains in attraction and importance, particularly to those who are either uncomfortable in court or stand to gain greater control in a non-judicial process. As Charlotte Lodge, the chairman of the British Association of Social Workers project group on family courts, is reported to have, perhaps unwittingly, claimed,

> 'as long as the social worker has expertise and knows the law, care proceedings can be dealt with equitably in the juvenile court. . . . the major advantages of a family court would be in employing a panel, using inquisitorial procedures, and in having a welfare and conciliation services attached, "to help disentangle children's interests from those of parents".'

(Crine 1983: 15)

As well as presuming that children's and parents' interests never coincide, this seems to imply that courts are acceptable so long as the social work expert feels comfortable and confident, and, dare one even suggest, in control of the proceedings. Other recent support for a family court panel came from some members of the Select Committee on Children in Care, who were reported as arguing strongly for a family court model based on the Scottish system of Children's hearings (Clode 1983: 2; see also House of Commons 1984 paras.87-91).

My own preference however is for a court, and I share Foster's (1978:55) view that 'just as the declaration of war is too important a matter to be left to the generals so custody decisions cannot be abdicated to the experts, the rule of law rather than the postulates of behavioural science must determine and control'.

My view is that the attractions of the non-judicial process mask many real dangers to the individual which the history of the American juvenile courts demonstrates only too well. There the pre-occupation with state paternalism prompted a complete disregard of due process for the protection of the individual as required by the American Constitution. This was not tackled until the Supreme Court decisions of the mid and late 1960s, notably in *re Gault* (387 US (1967)) which drew attention to the iniquities that can arise when in the name of welfare and state benevolence traditional safeguards are abrogated.

The advantage of retaining the judicial process is that it provides a system of well-established and recognizable procedures which provide the individual with legal safeguards, accountability, and review. However, the present lack of accountability and review of certain powers that are vested in local authorities, such as their complete discretion over children in care, is a matter of considerable concern and disquiet.

Family law does provide some system for the regulation of rights and obligations within the family and between the family and society as a whole. Since these rules are determined by law, their interpretation and application should remain the prerogative of the courts.

Unity

Most advocates of the family court in England and Wales, as elsewhere, have been in part inspired by the need to unify and rationalize the various procedures, remedies, and jurisdictions in the field of family law. The various anomalies and problems that stem from a fragmented jurisdiction and unco-ordinated substantive laws have already been well catalogued elsewhere (Neville Turner, 1974), especially in various family court proposals for England and Wales published in the 1970s and early 1980s, particularly in the Finer proposals (1974) in which the importance of unity is stressed as essential to all aspects of the family court and its operations. I believe that unification and uniformity of law and procedures should be a fundamental aim of any family court system if the intention is to provide a service that is comprehensible and consistent, efficient, accessible, and fair.

In England and Wales it is children's cases that seem to reflect best the confusions and inconsistencies and injustices that stem from our fragmented jurisdiction and plurality of both law and procedures. Freeman (1982) has identified some eleven legal routes for children to come into care, and the legal criteria applicable are even more numerous. Though all three jurisdictions, the High, county, and magistrates' courts, have the power to commit children to care, the majority of those children whose retention or removal to care is of a compulsory nature are regrettably dealt with by the juvenile court, whose procedures are ill-suited to these responsibilities, and tends to be regarded as a court of inferior status.

Although in the 1970s we have witnessed a number of judicial and legislative attempts designed to improve and clarify care proceedings in juvenile courts, nevertheless the unco-ordinated approach has made these developments somewhat amorphous and unsound, as for instance the implementation in May 1984 of those sections of the Children and Young Persons Act 1969 (as amended by the Children Act 1975) and the Child Care Act 1980 that provide for the appointment of guardian *ad litems* for the children in civil proceedings in the juvenile court. New juvenile court rules governing the guardian *ad litem*'s duties now require the guardian to give first and paramount consideration to the child's welfare throughout, whereas the 1969 and the 1980 legislation directs courts and parties to concentrate only on proof of specific legal criteria. We may thus witness in these proceedings a head-on collision of two dissimilar approaches.

There is little doubt that the law regulating the delicate balance of rights and responsibilities has been long overdue for radical re-thinking and re-organization. But any re-assessment of substantive law needs to be complemented by its integration into a single system, if it is to be successful. Unity is more likely to encourage uniformity and fairness, which in my view are essential if this very important area of law is to command the confidence and respect it deserves. Otherwise continual tinkering with the different procedures and proceedings in children's and other areas of family law, no matter how well intentioned, will perpetuate the 'double standard' Finer refers to, as well as exposing the administration of family law to disorder, confusion, and disrespect.

Although in this country we do not face the problems presented by a federal system of government, the road towards unity is nevertheless problematic. As can be seen from various family court proposals there is no general agreement about the sort of business the court should deal with or the jurisdictions it should absorb. In this respect the future of the juvenile court with its dual civil and criminal jurisdiction is in itself likely to provoke polarized debate. Although its civil business could be sensibly transferred to a family court, there is nevertheless little ideological agreement on how to approach the problems of juvenile delinquency, and consequently as to which is the best forum for it – the criminal juvenile court or the family court with its therapeutic overtones. My own view is that the unhappy marriage of juvenile delinquency and child protection in the juvenile court has been partly responsible for the many procedural anomalies and injustices that plague both sets of proceedings and therefore they are better kept quite distinct.

Formal or informal

Informality is often said to be an important feature of a family court. The benefits of a relaxed atmosphere, informal and flexible procedures, are stressed in almost every family court proposal where the intention is to create a court that is uninhibiting, therapeutic, and conciliatory. Protagonists of the family court movement advocate that a system which operates informally and flexibly, simply, and speedily combines the best in terms of fairness, efficiency, accessibility, and economy. Consequently the procedures of traditional courts, with the legal ritual they engender, tend to be rejected from the family court arena as counter-productive, intimidating, and cumbersome.

However for all the enthusiasm it inspires the idea of an informal court has little agreed definition and there are differing opinions about the types of procedures and the degree of form appropriate to a family court. Wade (1978) reminds us that there is very little comprehensive research on how 'family courts' discharge their functions or how they compare with other courts, and so he argues that proposals which include recommendations as to the desired degree of formality or the 'family court ideal' are therefore necessarily subjective. In his view, they are suggesting that applying their value judgments to the perceived fact situations leads to the conclusion that the traditional court system has undesirable features' (Wade 1978: 821). These, so the argument goes, can be removed without creating an excess of counterbalancing undesirable side-effects.

I believe that there is a real possibility that enthusiasm for the therapeutic and conciliatory, or the reassuring and accessible, atmosphere could produce unfair and adverse consequences. Unbridled abrogation of the customary rules of court proceedings is probably more likely to result in sloppiness and disrespect rather than reassurance. But, more importantly, as the history of the American juvenile courts illustrates, over-hasty abandonment of the essential features of the judicial process could seriously jeopardize those legal safeguards that ensure, and as I have already argued, justify, the existence of a court rather than a panel.

These risks are particularly high in children's cases and particularly in the area of child protection where state intrusion into family life is already a considerable force to deal with. The breadth of discretion inherent in existing standards that govern such intervention is such that without adequate judicial procedures there is a risk that decisions would be made in an arbitrary and bureaucratic manner. As Mnookin (1975) has argued, the tests commonly applied in children's cases are usually vague, elusive of objective definition, and provide enormous scope for subjectivity and prejudice. Such concepts as the welfare and 'best interests' test, as well as other loose tests found in child protection cases, easily permit, as King (1983) has argued, the influence of dubious 'expertise' in these proceedings. A family court with its army of professionals could soon seek to control family life and personal relationships unduly unless properly restrained by an identifiable system of procedures that allow for accountability and review.

More observable features such as courtroom buildings, mode of dress, and language are also seen as affecting the atmosphere and degree of form present in a court. So the case for modifications and improvements in these areas tends to find favour with those who desire a family court that is therapeutic, informal, and conciliatory. For instance, in British Columbia and Australia the introduction of family courts saw a radical change in courtroom design and facilities and the wearing of robes was abolished. Perhaps not surprisingly these changes have attracted varying comments from both lay and professional persons. My own observation of some English juvenile and domestic court buildings and the physical facilities they offer is that they vary enormously. Some are excellent, and no doubt the comfort, design, and luxury of some could make them prime candidates for family court requisition. Others are quite deplorable.

My impression is that physical features, no matter how pleasant, seem less influential in affecting atmosphere than do the attitudes and behaviour of court personnel – the judiciary, the magistracy, ushers, and even welfare officers – all of whom are quite capable of regulating or contributing to a particular ethos, be it one of pomposity or empathy. As Anderson (1978) discovered in his study of two English juvenile courts, one formal, the other therapeutic, the atmosphere in a court is primarily one of attitudes and particular approaches to the law and legislation. A court that is sympathetic, conciliatory, accessible, and therapeutic is likely to be reflecting the attitudes of its administrators and participants and can therefore exist irrespective of the multiplicity of its rules and regulations.

Any attempts at developing a new image and ethos for the family court should perhaps focus more on those administering and professionally participating in the family court, including the advocates, rather than on matters of form, procedure, and physical appearance. A streamlining and reduction of rules may well reap benefits by encouraging speed, accessibility, and flexibility. Changes in the physical appearance of the court and in modes of dress may make a court less intimidating, but without a change in attitudes of the administrators and participants, such as the judiciary, legal profession, and ordinary court staff, there is no guarantee that those characteristics of an informal atmosphere will emerge which identify a family court as a more appealing forum for family matters. It is difficult to see how any amount of legislative or other formal change could guarantee the Law Society's aspiration (1979) towards a family court with 'a reassuring and accessible atmosphere'.

Adversarial v. inquisitorial procedures

The inquisitorial process is claimed to have special advantages for family courts, particularly in children's cases. It is said that, unlike adversarial proceedings, the inquisitorial process is free from hostility and is also more likely to ensure that all relevant matters are before the court so that it can thus somehow arrive at a decision that is truly in the interests of the child and family concerned. (This is however to deny that the inquisitor in inquisitorial proceedings can ever be hostile or oppressive!) Such claims however also ignore the reality that in this country as elsewhere courts with responsibility for domestic and children's matters already do employ certain features of the inquisitorial process and allow a certain relaxation of the rules governing the admissibility of evidence.

It is also interesting to note that common law jurisdictions that have recently introduced family courts have nevertheless retained the adversarial process, preferring to rely on the attitude of the judiciary and more sympathetic and substantive laws to remove hostility from the proceedings. In this country the Booth Committee (1983) was set up in order to examine the procedure and practice of the High and county courts in respect of matrimonial proceedings and was specifically directed to recommend reforms that could be made to mitigate the intensity of disputes, encourage settlements, and provide further for the welfare of the family. The Committee therefore looked at the propriety of the adversarial process in matrimonial proceedings. In their interim report (1983) the Committee proposes an initial hearing that is to be inquisitorial in character, but its purpose is to define the areas of dispute and give directions as to the future progress of the matter, not to carry out any major adjudicatory function (although certain of the interim decisions the court would be empowered to make, such as interim custody, might well require a more detailed investigation). However, for subsequent hearings dealing with issues in dispute the Committee's view is that adjudication should nevertheless be of an adversarial nature, because, as the Committee argues, the adversarial process is 'appropriate for divorce suits and financial hearings'. An inquisitorial element, the Committee acknowledges, is already evident in custody hearings. However the Committee's expectations of the judge's attitude, and no doubt also that of the advocates and court welfare service ('the sensitive handling and understanding' so that 'the element of contest can be eliminated from the adversarial approach and minds can be concentrated on finding the best solution to meet the needs and interests of the children concerned' (1983, 8)) is an important admission by the Committee, primarily considering rules and procedures, of the importance of human attitudes and behaviour in creating an atmosphere appropriate to the proceedings.

Thus in family matters the adversarial process seems to work and is retained because it is applied flexibly. Further amelioration of the adversarial process is undesirable for it could well jeopardize the impartiality desirable for a family court tribunal as well as many of those legal safeguards that distinguish the court from a panel keeping at bay the concomitant dangers of arbitrariness.

Is there a need for specialist tribunals?

The importance of selecting tribunals suited to deal with family matters has been recognized by certain of the jurisdictions in which family courts were recently established, notably Canada, Australia, and Taiwan. Within these jurisdictions, certain criteria have been imposed on the family court judiciary, such as age and marriage, experience and personality. Qualities such as patience, sympathy, and an aptitude for family work may be generally considered desirable of a family court judge but there is less agreement on the need for and extent of legal expertise required by the family court judiciary/tribunal. In this respect an examination of the children's panels in British Columbia provides an interesting observation. The rationale for introducing lay persons to sit with the judge on the adjudication of child abuse and juvenile delinquency matters was 'to ensure that the wisdom of lay people' influenced judicial decision-making that directly 'affects the welfare of the children and families whose values, standards and cultural backgrounds differ from a judge' and to 'increase the level of citizen-awareness of problems related to the neglect and abuse of children, delinquency and family breakdown within the community' (Amren and Macleod 1979:220)

Here it is important to note that a deliberate attempt, apparently with some success, was made to recruit a genuine cross-section of the adult population in order to counteract the fear that panel members would be middle-aged and middle class. The main impact of the involvement of panel members who came from the same socio-economic background as the court's clients was seen by Amren and Macleod as providing an improvement in the court atmosphere, mainly in terms of clarification and demystification. They noted that social workers and judges became more aware of their tendency to speak in legal and social work jargon and that participation of the panels compelled them to make a conscious effort to ensure that the proceedings would be intelligible to the panels and consequently also to the court's consumers. Although by the time Amren and Macleod's evaluation of the Family Court Project in British Columbia was completed, the use of panels had not been extensive, and hence their assessments as to their value was based on limited information (i.e. nine cases in all). Nevertheless their findings do seem sensible.

Although in England and Wales the idea of lay magistrates partici-pating in a family court has received a mixed reception (and greatest encouragement from the Justices Clerks Society), those who recommend it do so for different reasons. Even magistrates would have different views about the types of contributions they could make to a family court. Where proposals have recommended participation by lay magistrates, none have directed much attention to the criteria for selection or the need that they be truly representative of the litigants before the court. Instead comments seem to be directed at ensuring that magistrates should be given interesting work in the family court. While lay participation can in theory have a great deal to offer, nevertheless there could be many administrative difficulties and disadvantages in organizing lay participation in a family court due to the volunteer or part-time service of lay magistrates, who at present generally tend to deal only with the shorter and less complex matters.

The idea of a specialist family court, with its specialist full-time judge, seems to imply that the family court judge should be resident and adjudicate exclusively in the family court. There are clear advantages to this but less apparent are the potential drawbacks of such exclusivity and specialism, such as introspectiveness and narrowness. There is also the danger that a diet of cases concerning only family breakdown could become too monotonous, emotionally wearing, and may in turn blunt the sensitivity, patience, and other attributes of a family court judge which are so crucial in influencing the character of the court. In British Columbia even judges with an 'interest in, and aptitude for family court work', expressed the need for a break from time to time, and preferred not to be restricted to only family cases (Amren and Macleod 1979).

Conciliation and the family court

Concomitant with the growth of the family court movement has been the growth in the conciliation movement to the extent that conciliation has become associated with the family court concept. Indeed, a number of family courts and proposals for family courts provide for a conciliation service as part of their structure.

The dangers of wholesale espousal of the idea of conciliation without greater clarification and control of the direction that the movement is going in have been well documented. Concern has been expressed about matters such as the conciliators' role, their influence and objectivity; the possible inequality of the parties' bargaining powers; the difference in the parties' intellectual, emotional, and material resources; incomplete disclosure of information and the parties' ignorance of their legal rights and the legal process.

Disillusionment with traditional litigation in family matters, has, as I have commented, prompted the search for alternatives such as 'expert panels' or other tribunals, and in the same vein conciliation has emerged as another such alternative. The protagonists of conciliation do not as a rule advocate the abolition of the court's role in family matters. Nevertheless, as conciliation takes root, gaining in popularity, so the judicial role is in danger of being diminished in its importance and influence, and risks being merged or submerged.

It is difficult to find fault with a concept as virtuous and admirable as conciliation, especially when practised in the arena of family strife and breakdown. However the introduction of compulsion into conciliation, as is evident in some in-court schemes and recommended in two recent reports – the interim report of the Booth Committee (1983) and the Report of the Inter-departmental Committee on Conciliation (1983) – is a matter of considerable concern.

Compulsion in conciliation, be it of a formal or informal kind, militates against that which has been said to be the first requirement of 'effective conciliation', 'the voluntary participation of both parties' (Parkinson 1982: 15). Second, it smacks of paternalism, so that which has been decreed beneficial must therefore be experienced irrespective of individual preference or feeling. Third, and perhaps more worryingly, it institutionalizes conciliation as a respectable quasi-legal process, but one that is clearly lacking the usual safeguards the individual can expect of the judicial process, and which, in family law, serve to restrain unwarranted intrusion and control of family life and personal relationships. As Bottomley and Olley (1983: 9) observed, in America, 'court officers heady with the success of establishing conciliation in custody cases . . . are now looking for other potential areas'.

'The skills involved in conciliation are not the prerogative of the social work profession', writes Davis (1983: 10) but human qualities that 'reflect a general approach to conflict as much as learned techniques'. Nevertheless, with court welfare officers (admittedly some times aided by registrars) tending to monopolize in-court schemes and the National Conciliation Council (to which out of court schemes affiliate) requiring that conciliators be social workers, probation officers, or marriage counsellors, the 'helping professions' already have a formidable grip that they show little sign of loosening. Unfortunately their training and experience leads them to be more authoritarian and interventionist if not judgemental than is perhaps appropriate to conciliation.

Somewhat remarkable, however, is the degree to which the courts, legal profession and establishment, who, by perhaps allowing themselves to be seduced by the prospect of less emotional and more compromising litigants and clients, have welcomed the rival activity of conciliation. Comments such as 'one of the objects is to change the way that lawyers think' (Davis 1983: 9) and 'it is essential that the values and strategies appropriate to mediation and conciliation be accommodated as part of the legal process' (Davis 1983: 12) seem to have met little opposition. Indeed the response of the legal profession seems to be enthusiastic with the Family Law Bar Association even being reported as having proposed their own form of non-judicial process for quick resolution of financial matters.

Thus with the seemingly tacit collusion of the legal establishment, conciliation of the compulsory kind may well be allowed to flourish in this country under the auspices of court respectability, but in the nature of things possibly developing its own 'professionalism', specialisms, and systems. Instead of the judicial process, with the application of legal rules and safeguards, we may see the emergence of the therapist emphasizing apparently acceptable personal agreements between the parties in dispute, which so far the courts show little inclination to interfere with, though the rights of one or other of the parties risk being severely diminished by the non-judicial approach.

Thus the status of family law within the English legal system or the merits of it remaining within the legal system are in danger of becoming suspect and untenable as the alternatives superseded litigation.

Conclusion

The idea of a family court, although seductive, is not unproblematic. There is little doubt that the administration of family law in this country and other jurisdictions has, with some justification, attracted criticism. Whether a system of family courts offers any solution will depend on several factors such as the philosophy behind them as well as their method of operation. Much also depends upon the expectations held of a family court, its aims, and of the role of family law in meeting legal and social needs.

Reference

Amren, B. and Macleod, F. (1979) *The British Columbia Family Court Pilot Project 1974, a Description and Evaluation: Victoria B.C.*

Anderson, R. (1978) *Representation in the Juvenile Court*. London: Routledge & Kegan Paul.

Booth Committee Interim Report (1983) *Matrimonial Causes Procedure Committee, Consultation Paper*. London: Lord Chancellor's Department.

Bottomley, A. and Olley, S. (1983) Conciliation in the U.S.A. *LAG Bulletin* (Features) January.

Clode, D. (1983) *Social Work Today* 14(34): 2.

Crine, A. (1983) Family Courts: On the Right Tracks? *Community Care*, 2 June, p.16.

Davis, G. (1983) Conciliation and the Professions. *Family Law* 13: 6-13.

Finer Report (1974) *Report of the Committee on One-Parent Families*. Vol. 1. Cmnd 5629. London: HMSO.

Foster, H.H. (1978) Trial of Custody Issues and Alternatives to the Adversary Process. In I.F.G. Baxter, and M.A. Eberts (eds) *The Child and the Courts*. Toronto: Caswell; London: Sweet & Maxwell.

Freeman, M.D.A. (1982) The Legal Battlefield of 'Care'. *Current Legal Problems* 35: 117–50. London: Stevens.

House of Commons (1984) Second Report from Social Services Committee: Children in Care, H.C.360. London: HMSO.

Interdepartmental Committee (1983) *Report of the Inter-Departmental Committee on Conciliation*. London: HMSO.

Kay, H.H. (1968) A Family Court: The Californian Proposal. *Californian Law Review* 56(5): 1205-248.

King, M. (1983) Experts in Whose Best Interests. *LAG Bulletin* (Features) June.

Law Society (1979) *A Better Way Out*. A discussion paper prepared by the family law sub-committee of the Law Society. London: Law Society.

Mnookin, R.M. (1975) Child Custody Adjudication: Judicial Functions in the Face of Indeterminacy. *Law and Contemporary Problems* 39: 266.

Neville Turner, J. (1974) University of Birmingham–Institute of Judicial Administration, Family Court: Comments on a paper prepared by the Family Court Working Party of the Law Commission. *Family Law* 4: 39-44.

Parkinson, L. (1982) Bristol Courts Family Conciliation Service. *Family Law* 12: 13-16.

Select Committee (1977) *First Report of the Select Committee on Violence in the Family. Vols I –III*. London: HMSO.

Wade, J. (1978) The Family Court of Australia and Informality in Court Procedure. *International and Comparative Law Quarterly* 27: 820-48.

Cases

Re, Gault 387: US I (1967).

Statutes

1969 The Children and Young Persons Act
1975 The Children Act
1980 The Child Care Act.

CHAPTER 17

Conciliation: present and future

Antonia Gerard

Introduction

The Finer Report (1974) saw conciliation as assistance to the parties of a marriage on breakdown in *every* area of difficulty that called for decisions on future arrangements. It was thus envisaged ten years ago that decision-making in two crucial areas, children and finance, could be facilitated by the introduction of conciliatory processes.

What has been achieved since then is both more, and less. More, in that the majority of schemes at present operating do not confine their assistance to married couples, but are prepared to deal with cohabitants as well. Less, and this is a serious matter, in that most of the existing schemes limit their assistance to problems relating to children. There are plausible reasons for this one-sided development; but I think that it is important, when patting ourselves on the back for the great progress made in the past few years, that we do not become complacent.

Emotional consequences of separation/divorce

Increasingly, the population expects not just instant coffee, but also the instant gratification of its wishes. 'Buy/Enjoy/Live Now, Pay Later' has become an acceptable motto. Coupled with easy, quick, and cheap divorce, the number of divorced and separated spouses and cohabitants, and the number of one-parent families, has increased considerably in the last decade. This is commonplace. I repeat it now because, as lawyers, we often fail to appreciate that separation may be an emotional trauma (quite apart from the financial problems involved), that in virtually every separation at least one of the parties feels rejected, unloved, inadequate, and that it may take years to

281

recover from these negative feelings. Add further that in the 1980s separating couples are beginning to include that generation who were the children involved in the first easy divorces of the early 1970s – the large numbers who have known only a succession of ersatz fathers and mothers, and are now well on the way to emulate their own parents' lack of a stable family life.

A society that provides for easy divorce is under a moral obligation to do what it can for the victims (or potential victims) of divorce, that is, the children; and to do that, it must render assistance to the adults in dealing with the consequences of separation and divorce. In this context, 'consequences' really means 'reorganization' of one's life. This is one of the most important aspects of conciliation: to assist adults to come to terms with their emotions so that they themselves can make rational decisions about their and their children's lives.

Changing attitude to courts

People seem to have been turning away from courts and lawyers in all walks of life. Arbitration in the shipping and commercial community has been with us for a long time; trade arbitrations, the several conciliation agencies in the industrial and labour fields are other examples. Litigation is no longer regarded as the only or necessarily the best method of settling disputes (see further Abel 1982; Eekelaar and Katz 1984).

The alternative solution in family matters does not seek to oust the court as the final tribunal; what it does seek to do is to replace expensive, time-consuming and acrimonious litigation by negotiation and concilation leading to consent orders. Contested cases will continue to require formal adjudication.

We now have two types of conciliation running parallel: in-court and out-of-court conciliation schemes.

Out-of-court conciliation

Out-of-court schemes which have been set up, and those which hope to be operational soon, number something like fifty at this moment. Some (like Bristol) are well established in terms of past experience, but face an uncertain future because of lack of funds; at the other extreme, some schemes are only just reaching the drawing board; some are in their first infancy.

It seems that the fifty schemes operate, or plan to operate, in about fifty different ways. Shortage of space prevents me from giving an exhaustive catalogue of the differences. They range from the type of premises and the number of conciliators attending any one session to the manner in which sessions are held and the type of problems dealt with. What they all have in common is enthusiasm on the part of staff, conciliators, and satisfied clients – and lack of funds. Local schemes may become affiliated to the National Family Conciliation Council, provided they meet the requisite criteria of uniformity of aims, of professionalism, and confidentiality. It is essential that the Council should obtain not only recognition from central Government, but also funding, so that it can effectively transform the fragmented small units of local schemes into a fully co-ordinated professional service. As a result of the Inter-Departmental Report on Divorce Conciliation (1983), such a prospect can only be seen as unlikely.

In-court conciliation

In-court conciliation also has many variations. In some schemes conciliation is done by the registrar, with or without the active participation of a welfare officer; in others, it is the circuit judge himself (not his registrar) who conducts conciliation.

The way in which the Bristol scheme works has been well publicized (see e.g. Davis and Bader 1983), and I will say no more about it. I propose to confine my remarks to the pilot scheme at Somerset House in London about which little is known yet. The Senior Registrar agreed to talk to me about the first six months' experience. I confess I went to the interview with a great many preconceived ideas, full of prejudice against the scheme. I came away with some of my ideas radically changed, and almost enthusiastic.

The waiting time for conciliation appointments is about three weeks. Two of the registrars do conciliation work every day during term time (one during vacation), each with his own welfare officer. Appointments are listed at forty-five minutes' interval. The procedure is very similar to the one adopted at Bristol except of course, for the formal setting, the presence of solicitors and sometimes counsel, presided over by a judicial officer with his welfare officer. If agreement cannot be reached, the parties may adjourn to a consultation room with the welfare officer and continue their discussions. If and when agreement is reached or is close, they go back and the registrar makes a consent order or helps to iron out the last few wrinkles. If no agreement can be reached, the registrar will order a welfare officer's report and adjourn the matter to the judge in the usual way.

Initially, I felt very uneasy about the requirement[1] that secondary school-age children are to attend. But the Senior Registrar assured me that the vast majority of children are only too delighted to make their own views known to a neutral welfare officer without having to show disloyalty to either parent. The registrars themselves do not normally see the children. A great deal depends on the character of the registrar concerned, and also on the relationship between the registrar and his welfare officer. So far, matters have worked well on both scores.

It is, of course, far too early for a full assessment of the pilot scheme's success rate. A systematic study will be prepared in due course. So far, I have only one set of figures available: in the first three months, 282 new cases of custody/access fell to be processed in the Principal Registry. Without the conciliation scheme, welfare officers' reports would have been ordered in about two-thirds of the cases (say about 188). With the pilot scheme in operation, only 45 reports were ordered, the balance of cases (about 237) having been disposed of by consent. On the basis that a welfare officer's report may cost approximately £700–£800 each, the saving in the first three months at Somerset House alone would amount to nearly £10,000!

Approval of agreed arrangements

A question frequently asked concerns the welfare of children. What happens if, following a conciliation session (whether in or out of court), the parties reach an agreement not in the best interests of the child? Personally, I find it difficult to envisage a situation in which parents could make such arrangements under the eyes of a conciliator or welfare officer. He/she would undoubtedly express views concerning the child's welfare in a way the parties can understand and accept. The situation may be different in the USA.

Financial arrangements

All the in-court and most of the out-of-court schemes deal with problems of children only. Yet, a potentially even greater stumbling block to an amicable parting of ways is the allocation and reallocation of capital and income. This is a much more difficult problem to solve without advice and adjudication properly so-called. The future of children – whether the father is to have access on Sunday or the mother is to have them for the Christmas period – are questions that may evoke deep emotional reactions, but their solution does not depend on facts and figures, and can therefore be resolved without documentation, and without legal advice. Details of contentious financial matters on the other hand cannot be resolved without pay-slips, tax returns, valuations, accounts, careful calculations of needs, liabilities and some knowledge of matrimonial property law, including revenue, social security, housing, company, insurance law, etc.

Some of the out-of-court schemes[2] do undertake conciliation in financial matters; but their activities in this sphere must, at this stage, be limited *either* to referring the parties to solicitors and suggesting the type of information they should have available, *or* to getting the parties to agree the principles on which they would wish to deal with their property and income ('I could not live with myself', a wife is reported to have told a conciliator in London, 'if I claimed the whole house as my solicitor has advised; I only want half – that is fair').[3]

The Family Law Bar Association set up a sub-committee in 1981 (of which I was a member) to work out a scheme which, like conciliation, would reduce confrontation, stress, and bitterness, and lead to consent orders in financial matters. We came up with two schemes: Recommendation and Arbitration, both of which are meant to cater for the married as well as the unmarried. However, neither is 'conciliation' properly so-called.

The *Recommendation Procedure* is destined for the majority of cases, particularly those where the family's finances are of a relatively simple nature: a house with a mortgage, perhaps some savings, earned income, and possibly some interest or dividends on savings. A recommending barrister would be either agreed by the parties or selected by the secretariat from a panel of barristers with substantial relevant expertise. The 'recommender' would be presented with the agreed facts and figures and would be instructed by the parties jointly to recommend appropriate solutions. It is anticipated that his recommendations, rather like a Joint Opinion, would be accepted by both parties and lead to a consent order. Apart from the modest fee payable to the recommender via the secretariat and the cost of the consent order, no further costs would be incurred. If the scheme meets with general approval and if money can be found to set it up, we would hope that legal aid would become available for the recommendation.

The *Arbitration Procedure* is intended to be more formal, more costly in both time and money, and not dissimilar to the usual court proceedings. The arbitrator would be a senior member of the Bar, either chosen jointly by the parties or selected by the FLBA secretariat. He is to have discretionary powers to apply such procedure as is necessary 'for the just, conciliatory, expeditious, economical and – so far as the law permits – final determination of the matters in issue'.[4] We envisage oral hearings, with or without legal representation. The parties themselves would have to provide for the cost of the arbitration. It is a procedure suitable only for particularly complex and substantial cases, where speedy resolution is of the essence.

Our proposals are now embodied in what we have called a First Working Paper. Having been given the green light by the president, it has been sent to the Lord Chancellor, to his Inter-Departmental Committee, to the Booth Committee and to various other bodies for comments.

Present procedural law and lawyers

Conciliation will spread. Not only because it will be encouraged as a money-saver, but (I believe) for two other reasons as well.

First and foremost, the adversarial character of the legal system. In the nature of things, 50 per cent of litigants come out as 'losers'. Yet, in an on-going relationship such as parenthood, there should never be either gloating winners or smarting losers. The adversarial character of the system shows its effect long before any hearing takes place in court. Affidavits in support of any application will dwell on the negative features of the other party; positive features (that the respondent was a good mother or that the petitioner had always been careful with money) are not mentioned. This attitude makes it very difficult for adults to resume a civilized relationship with an opponent in any event; and if they cannot get over the hurt and anger caused or aggravated by what they perceive as mud-slinging lawyers, parents' hostility to each other can cause serious damage to children.

Second, solicitors are, I believe, somewhat less popular than they used to be. The reason for that could be their lack of time and lack of compassion, sometimes real, always apparent. Legal aid is no longer available for undefended divorces (except for the very limited Green Form Scheme). Solicitors are thus no longer prepared to spend many hours, unpaid without legal aid, listening to matrimonial histories. It is partly, at any rate, the listening function which conciliators can and do take over from busy solicitors.

Current reform activities

That family law and procedure is in a state of flux (again or still?) is best illustrated by the fact that, apart from the Bills awaiting parliamentary time, there are a number of committees, all chaired by High Court judges, at present considering reforms. These do not include the Law Commission, the Family Law Bar Association or the newly formed Solicitors' Family Law Committee.

Reports or final reports are awaited from all the Committees. What is uppermost in everybody's mind is the urgent need to save money. Legal aid in civil cases is estimated to rise to some £110 million in 1982/83, of which about two-thirds will be for matrimonial proceedings. And this at a time when divorce is practically a DIY job!

The future

What, then, can we expect from all these activities? More particularly, what is the likely future of conciliation? It is bound to be a substantial money-saver, a fact that was very much in the Inter-departmental Committee's mind (1983).

The Committee under the chairmanship of Booth J. has recommended a number of procedural areas in which both bitterness and costs can be saved, and these include a positive recommendation in favour of in-court conciliation. Its Consultation Paper proposes that it should be the duty of the registrar or judge to consider at a preliminary hearing whether or not to refer the case to a welfare officer or other conciliation officer (1983, para.4.8). It is to be hoped that this will lead to more in-court concilation and the availability of more money to extend schemes more widely. The Legal Aid Advisory Committee as well as the Law Society advocated in-court conciliation as an integral part of early proceedings even before the publication of the Consultation Paper (see *The Times*, 6 July 1983).

I am much more pessimistic about the financial future of out-of-court conciliation, a pessimism borne out by the report of the Inter–Departmental Committee on Divorce Conciliation Services (1983). It recommended that the emphasis in conciliation should be on in-court conciliation. Out-of-court conciliation services, not being susceptible to control by the courts, are in effect characterized as unsatisfactory, even untrustworthy, and therefore something for which central Government should not be responsible. Instead, any local community that chooses to run a scheme should find its own resources to do so (see further Yates 1983). This narrow thinking compares very unfavourably with that found in an official New Zealand report (Beattie 1978). This enthusiastically embraced the goal of conciliation and led to the Family Proceedings Act 1980, including a series of provisions for facilitating counselling for the purpose of conciliation or reconciliation. Australian developments (see Family Law Act 1975, s.14(5)) are also more favourable to the concept of conciliation.

My proposals

My own view is that it would be quite wrong to put all the available money and effort into in-court schemes, leaving the National Council with its affiliated out-of-court bureaux out in the cold. The accumulated expertise is far too valuable to ignore. Instead, systematic research into the respective merits of the two parallel schemes should be undertaken as a matter of urgency.

Asked to do some crystal gazing, I would predict that the research will show that the two schemes complement each other, and the future lies in a fully integrated system. The two schemes' aim is the same, though they approach it along different routes, not unlike the GP and the hospital; thank Heaven, it has not yet been suggested that the NHS should only pay for one of them.

A number of problems will have to be solved; here are a few that spring to mind.

(a) Those in-court conciliation schemes that now operate successfully are fortunate in having the kind of registrars who are temperamentally well suited to do this type of work. But very great care will have to be taken before in-court conciliation is introduced throughout the country: there are too many registrars and deputy registrars who, though excellent lawyers, lack the necessary patience and understanding. Conciliation in their hands would soon become a mere formality.

(b) All in-court conciliation schemes suffer from a great drawback inherent in the scheme. Appointments listed at relatively short intervals (even if they are allowed to run on by registrars giving up their lunch time and sitting late) necessarily deprive the parties of that sense of time that is so very important to reach a meaningful agreement, genuinely hammered out rather than suggested by the registrar or the welfare officer and accepted under real or imaginary pressure. After all, we have had settlements under pressure outside the door of the court for a long time, and we aim at something better than that. This relaxed atmosphere *is* present at, and is of the essence of, out-of-court conciliation sessions.

(c) To achieve a fully integrated complementary system of concilation, there is a case for expanding the scope of all out-of-court schemes. Their work would be even more valuable and their influence far greater if they were all prepared to assist with *any* family problem instead of limiting themselves to children. How far, and how successfully, this can be done will require further research and wide discussion. My own view is that it is imperative that the distinction between 'advice' and 'conciliation' be maintained, and that the conciliator should always occupy, and be seen to occupy, a neutral non-partisan position.

Provided the problems can be solved, I would like to see couples attending an out-of-court bureau *before* they split up, knowing that they can discuss *all* their difficulties and their future with each other and one or two impartial persons in a neutral atmosphere. Conciliation at that early stage could achieve a great deal if parties could be assisted to make decisions on basic issues, including the occupation of the matrimonial home, custody and access and at least the principle by which their finances should be divided. (Conciliation at that stage may even in a few cases become *re*conciliation.) If they could make such decisions jointly at a very early stage of the breakdown, a vast number of ouster injunctions would never need to be applied for. Solicitors would continue to work out the details of ancillary matters and conduct court proceedings in court. Resort to the court would be limited to approving arrangements for the children and making orders by consent.

In this sort of procedure, in-court conciliation would only be resorted to in one of two situations:

1 if some or all the issues remained unresolved in the initial out-of-court conciliation. The authority of a judicial officer might be advantageous at that stage, leisurely discussions having already taken place, and it would not matter unduly that the registrar's time was limited;

2 in every case in which proceedings were commenced without prior out-of-court conciliation. If the appointment before the registrar failed to lead to agreed solutions he would not immediately order a welfare officer's report and adjourn the matter to a judge for a fully

contested hearing, save in exceptional circumstances. In the normal case, he would adjourn the conciliation appointment to an out-of-court bureau. This would enable the parties to continue their discussions on neutral ground with a conciliator, but at a leisurely pace. Only if that, too, failed would there be a contested hearing.

An integrated system of conciliation would also try to save parties from having to go back to court after an order relating to children has been made. At that stage, the out-of-court service could be useful in a number of ways:

1 The parties could refer themselves or be referred by their solicitors if they needed assistance over the implementation of the order.
2 If the initial order for, say, access was meant to run for a trial period only, the registrar might direct the parties to attend out-of-court conciliation at the end of the period to review the situation and agree a long-term solution.
3 If all conciliation attempts failed and the court order was made after a contested hearing, the order might well include what I would call an 'assistance order'. The idea is borrowed from s.64(5) of the Australian Family Law Act 1975, which enables the court to 'direct that compliance with the . . . order shall as far as practicable be supervised by a Court counsellor'. Supervision in this context has been held[5] to mean not 'policing' but 'assisting' the parties in various ways, such as

   – to accept the order,
   – to offer counselling to improve the relationship between the parties,
   – to encourage flexibility in the operation of the order relating to access,
   – to be available to the child concerned,
   – to help the parties to develop the capacity to work out problems among themselves without further contest before the court.

I think it is important that ideas and experiences should be shared. All who are involved in family disputes have contributions to make. Inter-disciplinary conferences should discuss basic issues, while lawyers and conciliators could well profit from each other's skill and experience by regular meetings.

Another suggestion I put forward is that whatever shape conciliation eventually takes, it will require a new attitude in new generations of lawyers generally, and family lawyers in particular. The fostering of this new attitude is primarily in the hands of law teachers. Law has been taught to students of other disciplines for years. Modern textbook writers, such as Eekelaar (1984) and Hoggett and Pearl (1983), accept that anthropology, sociology, history have a place in a course on family law. My plea is for the inclusion of at least the elements of social work (see also Freeman 1978) and of psychology in all family law courses. Merely teaching students, for example, that the welfare of the child is the first and paramount consideration, is in my submission not helpful. Law students need to appreciate what the elusive concept of 'the welfare of the child' means and that guidance on it may be sought not in legal precedents but in the evidence of modern psychology. Future generations of family lawyers might be better equipped to deal with clients, with litigation, and with conciliation.

Notes

1 See *Practice Direction*, 2 November, 1982.
2 E.g. Bristol and Divorce Conciliation and Advisory Service (DCAS).
3 Quoted from a client of DCAS.
4 Draft Rule 10.1.
5 *Bainrot and Bainrot* (1976) FLC 90-003.

References

Abel, R. (ed.) (1982) *The Politics of Informal Justice*. New York: Academic Press.

Beattie Report (1978) *Royal Commission on Courts*. Wellington, New Zealand.

Booth Report (1983) *Matrimonial Causes Procedure Committee – Consultation Paper*. London: Lord Chancellor's Department.

Davis, G. and Baker, K. (1983) In-court Mediation Observed. *New Law Journal* 133: 355-57, 403-05.

Eekelaar, J. (1984) *Family Law and Social Policy*. 2nd edn. London: Weidenfeld & Nicolson.

Eekelaar, J. and Katz, S. (1984) *The Resolution of Family Conflict: Comparative Legal Perspectives*. Toronto: Butterworth.

Finer Report (1974) *One-Parent Familes*. London: HMSO.

Freeman, M. (1978) Teaching Social Work to Lawyers. *Adoption and Fostering* 94: 36–40.

Hoggett, B. and Pearl, D. (1983) *The Family, Law and Society*. London: Butterworth.

Inter–departmental Committee Report (1983) *Divorce Conciliation Services*. London: HMSO.

Yates, C. (1983) Out of Court Conciliation Services: The Tolling Bell that Dropped a Clanger. *New Law Journal* 133: 993–94.

CHAPTER 18

Resolving family disputes: a critical view

Anne Bottomley

Conciliation is the word of the moment. For some it offers the excitement of new territory to be explored and colonized as an extension of their own professional practice and concerns. For others it seems a way to break with the too complex problems of the past and present. The word's mystical effect is akin to that produced by the term 'clean break'; it seems to cut through the Gordian knot and speak of a fresh start. In virtually every policy document, much contemporary academic work, and 'progressive' amendments to parliamentary bills its message reverberates and promises happier times ahead, a release from conflict and costs into a future of therapeutic understanding of common concerns. It has become the banner for those who distrust law and lawyers as well as the symbol of the concerned academic's recognition of the 'limits of the law'. Amongst the protagonists of conciliation we find a heady mixture of different political allegiances and interest groups all united on this one issue; that conciliation is the way out and the way forward. As with all spells this one must be broken. We must grapple with reality rather than marvel at the myth.

The images conjured up by the idea of conciliation are undoubtedly attractive. In the best of all possible worlds it would probably be the best of all possible ways. We are not in that world. Any seemingly new approach to dispute resolution has to be judged against both the immediate social context and the history of its origin and development.

Even the most fervent supporters of conciliation recognize, if only implicitly, that conciliation has not arisen in a vacuum and is not practised in one. The backcloth is the law and indeed, in that now famous phrase, conciliation and all bargaining is in 'the shadow of the law' (Mnookin and Kornhauser 1979: 950). It is indeed only the law that will finally determine the status and enforcement of agreements reached through conciliation. Further, the language of rights and due process are not the only jurisprudence that the law brings to dispute resolution; we have in this century seen the development of a much more flexible process of decision-making based on discretion and such elusive concepts as need and welfare, in particular the welfare of children. This more open-textured pattern is the background against which we must place the development of conciliation.

For many people it was the development of the Bristol Courts Family Conciliation Service in 1978 and the writings of Lisa Parkinson[1] that introduced the idea of conciliation. Much of the material was (as is necessarily the case with an initiative fighting for funding and survival) extremely self-laudatory and despite the fact that Bristol has now been joined by at least another fifty schemes, and that its particular characteristics are only shared by a minority of those schemes, it is still the most well-known and talked-of.[2] Although it is clearly wrong to conflate the writings of Parkinson with all that can be said about conciliation in this country, her writings do display much of the ideology, ambiguity, and contradictions that mark the practice of conciliation and give some clues as to why it is so appealing to particular groups of people.

It is often pointed out that the initiative taken in Bristol was as a consequence of a reference made in the Finer Report to the place of conciliation in a family court. Finer defined conciliation as: 'assisting the parties to deal with the consequences of the established breakdown of their marriage . . . by reaching agreement or giving consents or reducing the area of conflict' (Finer, 1974: 183). The objective is clear; to establish agreement and to reduce conflict.[3] It is this objective that unites all the conciliation schemes. Leaving aside for the moment the notion of agreement, we need to examine more closely the verb 'to assist'.

The idea of conciliation has an older pedigree than is often assumed. It is one of the basic models of dispute resolution identified in anthropological literature where it is more usually and more correctly named as 'mediation' (Roberts 1979, 1983). Other forms of dispute resolution share the objective of agreement rather than judgement; however in conciliation it is the parties who are deemed to be in control. The presence of a third party is simply to further face-to-face negotiations by 'assisting in' helping communication (the language here slips often into a quasi-therapeutic discourse) and, when necessary, to give technical assistance with the symbols of social recognition of an agreement having been reached, whether by eating and drinking or by the drafting of a document. The anthropological literature has long alerted us to the need to look behind the presentation of such a form of dispute resolution and ask two questions. First, is there equality of power in the relationship between the parties, and between the parties and the mediator? Such an 'open' process is open to manipulation. To be persuaded may be an invidious form of judgement and control. Second, despite the presentation of the mediator in terms of neutrality and objectivity the mediator may be the purveyor of a particular pattern of beliefs that would tend to favour a particular 'resolution' to which the parties give their formal agreement.

I have stressed the need to examine the model of conciliation for two reasons. First, there is too often a blur between 'conciliation' and what is essentially a process of arbitration, or indeed informal adjudication; in both cases the essential factor is the power of the 'conciliator' over the parties rather than the party control which is deemed the essence of conciliation. Second, it is to highlight a fundamental ambiguity in the role of the conciliator. In the literature the hall-marks of a conciliator are those of neutrality, objectivity, and 'assistance' rather than control. Whether such a role is actually achievable in the majority of cases, or indeed whether in some cases it is actually desirable, are moot points.

What does Parkinson say on the role of the conciliator?

'The conciliator's role is active and demanding; he or she needs to identify and clarify issues and assess priorities as well as being sensitive to clients' emotional states. The conciliator may perceive possibilities which had not occurred to either party or their legal advisors, and which may gradually emerge through joint discussion with both parties. The work calls for personal warmth, maturity, and objectivity, combined with professional training, knowledge and expertise. Further specialist training and experience can produce a particular blend of knowledge and skills which may not be readily available in other statutory and voluntary organizations.

(Parkinson 1983a: 23)

We have here an attractive blend of the common touch with professional expertise. The professional groups most immediately involved are social workers, and, in the in-court schemes, welfare officers (almost entirely probation officers). There are problems, of course, in conflating these two professional groups but they do share certain interests and concerns. Both are primarily involved in the family through a concern with child welfare, or, to use the term that Davis had used when writing on conciliation, 'child-saving' (Davis 1983a: 139). This comes out clearly in an article entitled 'Divorce and the Law and Order Lobby' (Francis 1981: 61) where the connection between divorce and delinquency is made, or rather, assumed.The author is a member of the Leicester in-court conciliation scheme; the purpose of the article is not only to introduce the scheme but also to present a rationale for the involvement of welfare officers. Lisa Parkinson, and many others who submitted evidence to the Inter-Departmental Committee on Conciliation make child welfare one of their central platforms. This is understandable given their professional concerns but dangerous if the implications are not fully explored. Davis, in one of the most penetrating of recent articles on the subject, examines the problems that arise when

> 'the common thread of an idea can be almost lost through the speed with which it is modified to suit the purposes of practitioners in different fields. The creation of a new role merely confuses the issue if the task is not clearly defined or if the mediator regards it as no more than a new name for dealing with an old problem'.
>
> (Davis 1983b: 11)

Apart from the possible covert use of conciliation to 'provide a cover for value-laden tampering with family life' (Roberts 1983: 139) or simply a slippage back into old ways in which guidance and support mean in reality direction and control by experts, too often there is also a conflation of dispute resolution with therapy. Parkinson increasingly alludes in her work to therapeutic techniques and in a recent article on conciliation refers to 'conflict resolution' rather than 'dispute resolution' (Parkinson 1983b). This is consistent with a welfare-orientated approach which would reject as false the abstraction of legal from emotional problems. Davis (1983a: 139) quotes the Finer Report as positing the legal system as one which 'treats people . . . in the last resort as the subject of rights, not as . . . patients for whom the legal process is just another kind of treatment'. However for two professional groups involved in the field of family law the emphasis would be on the latter and conciliation a further opportunity for penetration into the formal system of rights and due process.

Why is this a problem? First, because it attacks the credibility of the very idea of conciliation itself; the parties are transformed into clients. Second, because the conciliator is clearly not neutral but the purveyor of certain ideologies and practices. Psychology, therapy, or social policy are not neutral bodies of knowledge. However much the badly informed may attempt to treat the latest theory as revealed truth, each discipline has its methodological problems, theoretical disputes and clashes of, at root, ideologies. However, the theoretical paradigms which dominate the academic work, training, and practice of the worker in the field are those which tend to validate the existing social order and legitimate the role of the practitioner. Social workers and probation officers tend to share a common belief in the functionalism of the family, and a particular familial ideology in which roles are cast and those who do not fit are deemed not to be fit. They also share a concern with the increase in divorce and the need somehow to 'normalize' divorce so that it becomes less challenging to the images of stability and continuity that remain at the core of the family image. Much emphasis is placed on the fact that parents never divorce, only spouses: 'The court is asked in a divorce petition to dissolve the legal bonds of marriage, not the bonds of parenthood' (Parkinson 1983a: 24). Normalization is best achieved through images of continuity and consensus. Davis (1983a: 134–35) warns of the problems of a 'fabricated consensus'.

> 'An understandable human reaction to conflict is to pretend it does not exist, or at least, that it is not too serious or may be overcome. There are two reasons for this. First, conflict is painful. . . . Secondly, to pretend that conflict does not exist may be useful in getting one's own way.'

There are actually three forms of conflict that need to be addressed. First, there is the form I think is usually meant by many conciliators, that of general conflict between the parties. Second, there is the lawyers' perception of a conflict of interests; this is, I believe, far more specific and addressed to particular legal issues. The concern of lawyers to recognize conflicts of interest gives rise to the one-dimensional caricature of their approach as 'entirely adversarial'.[4] It may be true that some lawyers exacerbate general conflict but there is much evidence to suggest that family law practitioners spend time 'cooling out' clients. Nor should we forget that the reality of practice is that bilateral bargaining results in the vast majority of cases being settled out of court. The third aspect of conflict, one rarely recognized, is

297

that of a more structural character; it is the conflict between the interests and needs of men and women. To ignore such structural conflict is merely to reproduce an existing power relationship and not in any way to mitigate or challenge it. Women's needs, the consequence of their continuing position of disadvantage in society, their lack of bargaining power *vis-à-vis* individual men, and the conflation of their rights with their role as mothers, make them particularly vulnerable in conciliation procedures. Those of us who see the family as the site of women's oppression must necessarily be highly critical of any social policy that holds as its core familial ideology and uses the 'welfare' of children as its major access point (Wilson 1977).

The development of joint custody orders is very much part of the same thrust as the development of conciliation. Not surprisingly Parkinson (1983a: 24) is strongly in favour of joint custody. It presents an image of consensus and continuity. It also presents an ideal way for many men to continue to exert power over their ex-wives via the children. Joint custody is increasingly seen as a possible norm and the supporters of its growth are now gratified to have evidence in support of their claim that it is better for the children.[5] Undoubtedly there are occasions where joint custody is a preferable order but like 'clean break' it can become a meaningless catch phrase when indiscriminately applied to all situations. It says more of the ideology of those concerned to employ it, rather than of the actual situation of children and parents.

Having explored some of the problems of what is actually meant by 'assisting' the parties, we must now necessarily question the nature of an 'agreement'. Have the parties been persuaded as to what is best rather than having decided for themselves? In a role-play session led by a well-known probation officer–conciliator at North East London Polytechnic in 1983 we asked him if he would accept an agreed solution if he thought it was not in the best interests of the children. He unhesitatingly said no, and that he would continue the conciliation until 'the right solution' had been reached. How many 'conciliators' have the same approach, albeit perhaps less honestly recognized? The power of welfare officers in this situation is of particular concern: 'In Leicestershire the divorce court welfare officer's report, which was once a request for information, has now become an opportunity to mediate' (Francis 1981: 72). Given the other role of the welfare officer and the pressures of time and cost, this seeming mediation takes on the aspect of informal adjudication and should be recognized as such.[6]

After an exploration of the pervasiveness of 'welfarism' it becomes a little hard to swallow the presentation of conciliation as 'mutual responsibility' by Parkinson (1983a: 23): 'Conciliation does not take away responsibility. On the contrary, it encourages people, especially parents, to take control of their own affairs and to work out their own solutions.' Is this actually speaking out a classic therapy technique of 'empowering the client' or is it a genuine attempt to give control back?[7]

Certainly in the USA a major attraction of conciliation has been the image it offers to middle-class clients of 'control of their own affairs' as well as the seeming possibility of lower legal costs. The development of private conciliation services in the USA is now well advanced, sometimes as an extension to an existing therapy or legal practice and sometimes as a new agency. Numerous training establishments exist and there is now the question of licensing conciliators to practice. In 1982 I attended an American Bar Association conference on conciliation (Bottomley and Olley 1983) that covered both the private and 'public' (akin to our 'in-court' definition) systems. Although differences in professional practices and the market mean that we are not likely to see a similar boom in private conciliation in this country, it is interesting to note the concerns of lawyers engaged in conciliation. Two particularly contentious topics were the lawyers' concern with the enforcement of agreements, and 'legal ethics'. It was generally agreed that to satisfy both points conciliation should involve three stages: the drafting of a document outlining the areas to be discussed, including liability for costs and procedures in case of failure; then the mediation itself (as a general guide it was thought that at least four two-hour sessions were needed at a cost of c. $70–100 per hour); and finally the drafting of an agreement. For both the preliminary document and the final agreement separate legal advice was to be taken by the parties. If these guidelines were followed few clients would find conciliation financially advantageous. More importantly, the function of separate legal advice was to address the problems of unequal bargaining power, access to relevant information and knowledge of legal rights. These issues are clearly of relevance in any out-of-court bargaining process, whether bilateral or through conciliation. Our courts have already had to address this problem in relation to maintenance agreements.[8] As the pressure to settle increases and if courts become more reluctant to re-open issues the danger of inequitable or unconscionable bargains is increased.

In the USA, as in this country, when the argument about the

relative merits of conciliation becomes difficult someone always cuts across the doubts expressed with a reference to costs. We are told it is cheap. In fact more and more evidence throws doubt on this simplistic statement (Davis 1983b: 6). Conciliation is only cheap when no charge, or little charge, is made for the service and, if this is the case, funding must come from somewhere. So far much of the hidden cost of conciliation is covered by voluntary work and existing welfare officers taking on more work. If the conciliation is kept brief and an 'agreement' reached quickly, and not too much time or money is spent on training, then it may seem to be cost saving, but is it conciliation?

Why should the argument about cost be so attractive anyway? Family law has long been the Cinderella of the legal system. If there is a real commitment to justice in family law why should there not be a willingness to argue for adequate financial support for the right means of dispute resolution?

What we are experiencing at the moment is a pincer movement. On the one hand family law is being squeezed out of the formal legal system on arguments of cost and on the other hand it is being enticed out with promises of more fruitful pastures elsewhere. This shift towards de-legalization (Glendon 1977) must not be simply accepted but must be more closely examined. We need to recognize that the process of de-legalization is not one of de-regularization but is a shift from one form of social discipline to another. While the articulate middle classes will continue to buy the services of professional groups, others will become more and more the subjects of control by 'welfarism' (Donzelot 1980). Those who are most vulnerable will be caught between the unequal power relations of private ordering and a familial ideology rendered benign by welfarism in informal dispute resolution. Abel argues that the increase in informalism is in fact an extension in control:

'informal justice increases state power. Informal institutions allow state control to escape the walls of those highly visible centers of coercion . . . and permeate society. . . . But it is possible – and essential – to penetrate the comforting facade of informalism and reveal its political meaning.'

(Abel 1982: 6; see also Freeman 1984)

This paper has attempted to make some contribution to that project. It is to be hoped that legal academics will not join the cohorts celebrating conciliation but rather add to the recent literature giving more careful thought to its development and implications.

Although the task of de-constructing the discourse of conciliation is the immediate need, it is important to seize this opportunity to think more clearly and positively about the potential of law, lawyers, and courts. Conciliation must not be allowed to become a 'way out' or a diversion from the critical task of asking what the law has to, and should, offer in the resolution of domestic disputes. I am yet to be persuaded that articulating these disputes through a jurisprudence of rights, obligations, due process, and a recognition of conflict of interests is not more realistic, honest, and beneficial to those who are particularly vulnerable given social conditions and circumstances. While the law continues to define family, property, and individual rights and obligations these issues remain legal questions. To privatize or de-legalize these issues is merely to hide this fact. It is still the case that work produced by academic lawyers too infrequently addresses the basic questions of familial ideology, the relationship between the public and the private and fails to adopt a more positive approach to thinking in jurisprudential terms.[9] It is not a question of defence of the present system but rather a more rigorous examination of our own subject and a more critical view of what other disciplines and professional groups have to offer.

Notes

1 Lisa Parkinson has written extensively; only some of her articles are referred to in this paper. She is now training officer for the National Family Conciliation Council.
2 The nearest we have to a comprehensive review of existing schemes is the Report of the Inter-Departmental Committee on Conciliation (1983). Most schemes are based on 'in-court' services and it was these that were given support by the Committee. They also play an important part in the recommendations of the Matrimonial Causes Procedure Committee's Consultation Paper (Booth 1983). The development of in-court schemes pose even more sharply many of the points raised in this paper, e.g. the authority of the conciliator, particularly when registrars are involved. However, I have not had the space here to explore the implications of the Report and the Booth Report. They are addressed in a forthcoming paper: A. Bottomley, 'What Is Happening to Family Law?', in J. Brophy and C. Smart, *Women-in-Law* (working title), to be published in 1984 by Routledge & Kegan Paul.

3 For an interesting discussion on the vagueness of Finer on the actual role and practice of conciliation as part of a family court and an argument that it represents little more than 'an approach' see Roberts (1983: 538–39). It is of course the idea that is attractive; it presents an image of consensus that is so appealing to those with a welfare-based functionalist orientation.

4 The Inter-Departmental Committee on Conciliation (1983: 20) was usefully wary of such caricatures of the legal profession.

5 This evidence will be reviewed and the development of joint custody placed in relationship to the growth of conciliation, in which both are seen as part of a backlash against women, in an article by Julia Brophy in a forthcoming collection: J. Brophy and C. Smart, *Women-in-Law* (working title), to be published in 1984 by Routledge & Kegan Paul.

6 The blurring of the role of conciliator and welfare officer is particularly worrying in this context (see for instance Davis 1983b: 9), and Roberts (1983: 555). The problems are not, unfortunately, properly addressed in the Inter-Departmental Committee Report or the Booth Report.

7 Again the problem is particularly acute in in-court schemes and one must question the efficacy and ethicacy of any form of compulsory conciliation.

8 Contrast for example *Tommey* v. *Tommey* [1982] 3 All ER 385 with *Camm* v. *Camm* (1982) 4 FLR 577.

9 These arguments are developed in A. Bottomley, 'What is Happening to Family Law?' (see note 2 above). Many of my ideas have been formulated through work with the Rights of Women Family Law Group. The papers of the ROW 'beyond Marriage' Conference (1983) begin to address this issue. I also wish to thank Susan Olley, Belinda Meteyard, and Jeremy Roche for their comments on this paper.

References

Abel, R. (ed.) (1982) *The Politics of Informal Justice.* Vol. 1. New York: Academic Press.

Booth Report (1983) Consultation Paper of the Matrimonial Causes Procedure Committee. London: Lord Chancellor's Office.

Bottomley, A. and Olley, S. (1983) Conciliation in the USA. *Legal Action Group Bulletin,* January: 9.

Davis, G. (1983a) Mediation in Divorce: A Theoretical Perspective. *Journal of Social Welfare Law* 131.

——(1983b) Conciliation and the Professions. *Family Law* 13:6.

Donzelot, J. (1980) *The Policing of Families*. London: Hutchinson.

Finer Report (1974) Report of the Committee on One Parent Families Cmnd 5629. London: HMSO.

Francis, P. (1981) Divorce and the Law and Order Lobby. *Family Law* 11: 69.

Freeman, M.D.A. (1984) Questioning the De-Legalization Movement in Family Law: Do we Really Want a Family Court? In Eekelaar, J. and Katz, S. (eds) *The Resolution of Disputes In Family Law*. Toronto: Butterworth.

Glendon, M.A. (1977) *State, Law and Family*. London: North Holland.

Mnookin, R. and Kornhauser, L. (1979) Bargaining in the Shadow of the Law: The Case of Divorce. *Yale Law Journal* 88: 950.

Parkinson, L. (1983a) Conciliation: Pros and Cons (1). *Family Law* 13: 22.

——(1983b) Conciliation: A New Approach to Family Conflict Resolution. *British Journal of Social Work* 13: 19.

Report of the Inter-Departmental Committee on Conciliation (1983). London: HMSO.

Roberts, S. (1979) *Order and Dispute: An Introduction to Legal Anthropology*. Harmondsworth: Penguin.

——(1983) Mediation in Family Disputes. *Modern Law Review* 46: 537.

Wilson, E. (1977) *Women and the Welfare State*. London: Tavistock.

Table of cases

Table of statutes

Name index

Subject Index

secondary labour force, women as
53–4
secure accommodation 121
Select Committee on Children in
Care 263, 268
Select Committee on Social Services
118
Select Committee on Violence in
Marriage 71
Select Committee on Violence in the
Family 265
social breakdown 20–1, 52
social security 3–4, 13–14, 19, 20,
22–3, 25–33, 34, 36, 38, 43–4,
59–62, 185, 188, 190, 192, 216,
223, 241, 252, 256; family
allowance/child benefit 26–7;
pensions 201
social services 118, 142–44, 227; care
93, 102–11, 115–23, 139; care
orders 94, 95, 98–101, 102,
118–23, 140–44, 147, 153, 154–56;
v. family 93, 102–03, 104–11,
115–16; supervision orders 143,
150, 153, 154; voluntary care 94–5,
97–8, 116, 117, 122
solicitors, and attitudes to
maintenance 15–18, 20, 21–2
Somerset House, in-court
conciliation 283–84
Soviet Union 53
state, and children 93–4, 95–6, 101,
115–23, 124–38; and law of divorce
159–81; and women 7–90 *passim*,
295
state intervention 1, 3, 23, 25, 32–3,
66–9, 79–88, 112, 151, 156,
272; in child-rearing 1, 93–111,
115–23; in divorce 159–78;
taxation 38–9, 61; *see also*
maintenance; Netherlands; social
security; social services
step-parents 153, 192, 227–43;

abolition of adoption 228, 236–41;
and adoption 227, 230, 231–33,
236, 239; advice services 228;
custodianship 235, 236–37;
guardianship 232, 236–37; joint
custody 234–35, 236; legal status
228, 229–41
stereotyping 16, 17–18, 20–1, 32,
45–7, 52, 57–69, 247; alimony
drones 2, 10–12, 17, 20;
husbands 20–2
Supplementary Benefits Commission 58, 60
Switzerland 125

taxation 11, 38–9, 58, 61, 186, 189,
192, 256, 257
Trades Union Congress 84, 85
truancy 118–19

Victorian values 9

wardship 120, 139
welfare state 1, 3, 4, 9, 25–35; and
women 26–35, 57–62; *see also*
social security
welfarism 142, 297
women 10; and conciliation 297–98;
and domestic economy 65;
economic position 9–23, 25–33,
38–48, 57–9, 82–5, 89, 204,
219–21; employment 12, 19–20,
21, 25, 28–33, 47–8, 53–5, 67–9,
162, 188, 193, 197; equality 79–88;
legal protection 66–9, 79–88;
persons? 62–3; and property 11;
social position 52–5, 57, 59, 72;
status on divorce 162–63; and step-
fathers 238; violence against
66–72; wives or mothers? 17–18;
see also alimony drones; divorce;
maintenance; protection;
stereotyping